GETTYSBURG
DEATH AT THE ANGLE

STEWART COHEN, PH.D.

PUBLISHER'S INFORMATION

Author, Stewart Cohen
Richmond, Rhode Island
Paperback and EBook Design and Distribution by the EBook Bakery

ISBN: 978-1-938517-33-4

Copyright©2014 Stewart Cohen

ALL RIGHTS RESERVED

No part of this work covered by the copyright herein may be reproduced, transmitted, stored, or used in any form or by any means graphic, electronic, or mechanical, including but not limited to photocopying, scanning, digitizing, taping, Web distribution, information networks, or information storage and retrieval systems, except as permitted by Section 107 or 108 of the 1976 United States Copyright Act, without the prior written permission of the author.

The historical characters in this book are portrayed accurately in word and deed. John Scobell was a real person who worked as a Federal spy, initially for Alan Pinkerton during the Antietam campaign. His tales, as portrayed here, while encompassing the spirit of John Scobell's life, however, are fictional. Mathew Wilson, *New York Times* correspondent is an invented storyteller. His "grandfather," however, was a real participant of the Pennsylvania delegation to the Constitutional Convention, where, in the spirit of compromise, he proposed the 3/5 solution, AKA a pact with the devil awarding slave holders 3 votes for every 5 black people they held in bondage.

DEDICATION

To Joan C. Valade, my wife and partner for her inspiration and assistance in the creation of this work.

GETTYSBURG - DEATH AT THE ANGLE

In the Beginning vii
Prologue..xi
Forward... xv
Chapter 1 – The Beginning 1
Chapter 2 – Escapes 15
Chapter 3 – The Call to War 27
Chapter 4 – The Rescue Plan..41
Chapter 5 – The Killing Fields..53
Chapter 6 – Adversity and Friendship in War – Part I 63
Chapter 7 - Adversity and Friendship in War – Part II........73
Chapter 8 – The Blue and the Gray......................................79
Chapter 9 – The Listening Posts 93
Chapter 10 – The Colored Soldiers 109
Chapter 11 – Capture 123
Chapter 12 – Into the Woods...135
Chapter 13 – The Pursuit 147
Chapter 14 – June 1863: A Ticking Clock 159
Chapter 15 – Battle of Gettysburg – Day 1: 171
Chapter 16 - Battle of Gettysburg – Day 2: Part I 185
Chapter 17 - Battle of Gettysburg – Day 2: Part II 193
Chapter 18 - Battle of Gettysburg – Day 2: Part III...........201
Chapter 19 – July 3, 1863 – Day 3: Part I.........................209
Chapter 20 - July 3, 1863 – Day 3: Part II 219
Chapter 21 – Caught in the Draft Riots............................229
Chapter 22 – The Return 241
About the Author 229
Other Books by Stewart Cohen..251

IN THE BEGINNING

The First Sale

"The first object which saluted my eyes when I arrived on the coast was the sea, and a slave-ship, which was then riding at anchor, and waiting for its cargo. These filled me with astonishment, which was soon converted into terror, which I am yet at a loss to describe, nor the then feelings of my mind. When I was carried on board I was immediately handled, and tossed up, to see if I were sound, by some of the crew; and I was now persuaded that I was got into a world of bad spirits, and that they were going to kill me.

Their complexions too differing so much from ours, their long hair, and the language they spoke, which was very different from any I had ever heard, united to confirm me in this belief. Indeed, such were the horrors of my views and fears at the moment, that, if ten thousand worlds had been my own, I would have freely parted with them all to have exchanged my condition with that of the meanest slave in my own country. When I looked round the ship too, and saw a large furnace of copper boiling, and a multitude of black people of every description chained together, every one of their countenances expressing dejection and sorrow, I no longer doubted of my fate, and, quite overpowered with horror and anguish, I fell motionless on the deck and fainted. When I recovered a little, I found some black people about me, who I believed were some of those who brought me on board, and had been receiving their pay; they talked to me in order to cheer me, but all in vain.

I asked them if we were not to be eaten by those white men with horrible looks, red faces, and long hair? They told me I was not; and one of the crew brought me a small portion of spirituous liquor in a wine glass; but, being afraid of him, I would not take it out of his hand. One of the blacks therefore took it from him and gave it to me, and I took a little down my palate, which, instead of reviving me, as they thought it would, threw me into the greatest consternation at the strange feeling it produced, having never tasted any such liquor before. Soon after this, the blacks who brought me on board went off, and left me abandoned to despair. I now saw myself deprived of all chance of returning to my native country, or even the least glimpse of hope of gaining the shore, which I now considered as friendly: and I even wished for my former slavery in preference to my present situation, which was filled with horrors of every kind, still heightened by my ignorance of what I was to undergo. I was not long suffered to indulge my grief; I was soon put down under the decks, and there I received such a salutation in my nostrils as I had never experienced in my life; so that with the loathsomeness of the stench, and crying together, I became so sick and low that I was not able to eat, nor had I the least desire to taste any thing.

I now wished for the last friend, Death, to relieve me; but soon, to my grief, two of the white men offered me eatables; and, on refusing to eat, one of them held me fast by the hands, and laid me across, I think, the windlass, and tied my feet, while the other flogged me severely. I had never experienced any thing of this kind before; and although, not being used to the water, I naturally feared that element the first time I saw it; yet, nevertheless, could I have got over the nettings, I would have jumped over the side, but I could not; and, besides, the crew used to watch us very closely who were not chained down to the decks, lest we should leap into the water; and I have seen some of these poor African prisoners most severely cut for attempting to do so, and hourly whipped for not eating. This indeed was often the case with myself. In a little time after, amongst the poor chained men, I found some of my own nation, which in a small degree gave ease to my mind. I inquired of these what was to be done with us? they gave me to understand we were to be carried to these white people's country to work for them. I was then a little revived,

and thought, if it were no worse than working, my situation was not so desperate: but still I feared I should be put to death, the white people looked and acted, as I thought, in so savage a manner; for I had never seen among any people such instances of brutal cruelty; and this not only shewn towards us blacks, but also to some of the whites themselves. One white man in particular I saw, when we were permitted to be on deck, flogged so unmercifully with a large rope near the foremast, that he died in consequence of it; and they tossed him over the side as they would have done a brute. This made me fear these people the more; and I expected nothing less than to be treated in the same manner."
Olaudah Equiano

Author's Note: Olaudah Equiano was a slave of royal descent taken by slave hunters and send to England. Equiano's personal story and writings served to assist abolition ends.

CONSTITUTIONAL CONVENTION AND SLAVERY

PHILADELPHIA, JULY 1787

The Constitutional Convention held in Philadelphia in 1787 was a contentious affair. Some would argue that the founding fathers were faced with an insurmountable task in trying to mold a nation from an assortment of competing interests. Chief among the issues that had to be dealt with was slavery. In the vigorous discussion of proportional representation, as James Madison of Virginia, our fourth president, observed at the time, "It seems now to be pretty well understood that the real difference of interests lies not between the large and small but between the Northern and Southern states. The institution of slavery and its consequences form the line."

The conflicting views on slavery were manageable then. But as the nation looked west, and the economic value of slavery achieved prominence, the differences between the two sections of the country would strain relations between them and lead to the inevitability of war.

PROLOGUE

Gun at the Angle

May 5, 1861

"They do not know what they say. If it comes to a conflict of arms, the war will last at least four years. Northern politicians do not appreciate the determination and pluck of the South, and Southern politicians do not appreciate the numbers, resources, and patient perseverance of the North. Both sides forget that we are all Americans. I foresee that the country will have to pass through a terrible ordeal, a necessary expiation, perhaps, for our national sins."
Robert E. Lee, Commanding General, Army of Northern Virginia, CSA

"Let us not be deceived. Those who talk about peace in sixty days are shallow statesmen. The war will not end until the government shall more fully recognize the magnitude of the crisis; until they have discovered that this is an internecine war in which one party or the other must be reduced to hopeless feebleness and the power of further effort shall be utterly annihilated. It is a sad but true alternative. The South can never be reduced to that condition so long as the war is prosecuted on its present principles. The North with all its millions of people and its countless wealth can never conquer the South until a new mode of warfare is adopted. So long as these states are left the means of cultivating their fields through forced labor, you may expend the blood of thousands and billions of money year by year, without being any nearer the end, unless you reach it by your own submission and the ruin of the nation.

Slavery gives the South a great advantage in time of war. They need not, and do not, withdraw a single hand from the cultivation of the soil. Every able-bodied white man can be spared for the army. The black man, without lifting a weapon, is the mainstay of the war. How, then, can the war be carried on so as to save the Union and constitutional liberty? Prejudices may be shocked, weak minds startled, weak nerves may tremble, but they must hear and adopt it. Universal emancipation must be proclaimed to all. Those who now furnish the means of war, but who are the natural enemies of slaveholders, must be made our allies. If the slaves no longer raised cotton and rice, tobacco and grain for the rebels, this war would cease in six months, even though the liberated slaves would not raise a hand against their masters. They would no longer produce the means by which they sustain the war."
Representative Thaddeus Stevens, from a call for total war on January 22, 1862

Recent War Reports (Eastern Theatre)

"At Antietam Creek, near the town of Sharpsburg, Maryland on September 17, 1862, the Army of Northern Virginia, under the leadership of General Robert E. Lee experienced some 11,000 casualties, killed wounded or captured, in one day of fighting. The Federal Army, under the leadership of General George B. McClelland lost over 12,000 men. It was the bloodiest single day of battle ever fought on United States soil."
December 30, 1862

❖ ❖

"At Fredericksburg, in December of 1862, Major General Ambrose Burnside waited three weeks for pontoons to arrive in order that he and his men could cross the Rappahannock River in unison in order to attack the entrenched Army of Northern Virginia. By the time the pontoons arrived and the staging was set, enabling the Army of the Potomac to cross the river, it was too late. The Army of Northern Virginia was in place and the slaughter was about to begin."
April-May 1863

❖ ❖

"At Chancellorsville, Major General Joseph Hooker lead 120,000 Union troops into battle against Robert E. Lee and Thomas "Stonewall" Jackson who commanded 60,000 men. Before the battle, Hooker bragged, "May God have mercy on General Lee, for I will have none." However, despite his bravado, Hooker lost his nerve for battle by ordering a retreat and his troops were badly defeated.

While both sides suffered a significant number of casualties, Lee's ability to turn Hooker's army, through a series of brilliantly exercised maneuvers, provided the margin of victory. When Abraham Lincoln received news from the front, he exclaimed, "My God! My God! What will the country say?"

In the aftermath of Chancellorsville, General Lee convinced the Confederate President Jefferson Davis and his cabinet that he could inflict a crushing, decisive blow upon the Union by taking his army north into Pennsylvania. Lee believed that his army was invincible. He had said, "There never were such men in an army before. They will go anywhere and do anything if properly led."
April - May 1863

"At Gettysburg on July 1st, 2nd, and 3rd, 1863, within several months of its last confrontation with the Army of the Potomac, the Army of Northern Virginia led by General Robert E. Lee launched on offensive attack in which it lost approximately 28,000 men, killed, wounded or captured in three days of fierce battle; Union losses under newly appointed General George G. Meade accounted for 23,000 casualties of the Army of the Potomac and one civilian, a young woman from the town of Gettysburg by the name of Jennie Wade. Like many of those taken in the battle, she was a young person, just 20-years-of-age. July 15, 1863

FORWARD

THE SHADOWS OF WAR
THE AMERICAN CIVIL WAR
(1861-1865)

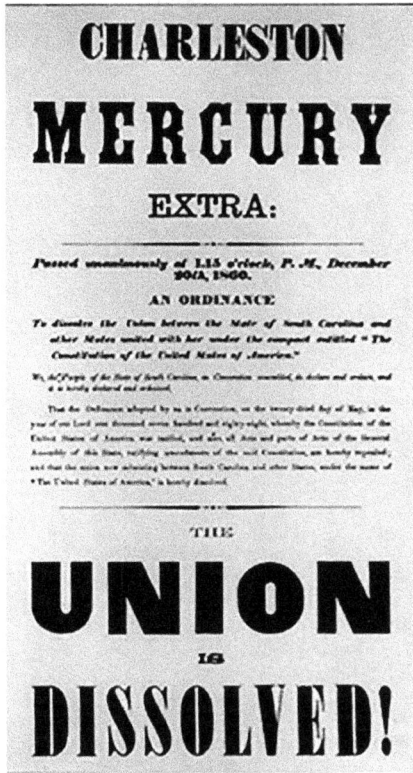

DECEMBER 1860

Separatist and regional tensions, among these, the issue of whether to permit the expansion versus the abolishment of slavery, were exacerbated with the election of President Abraham Lincoln in 1860. By February 1861, even before Lincoln had been formally inducted into office, seven states had seceded from the Union; six more would follow by the end of the year. On April 12, 1861, Confederate forces attacked Fort Sumter in Charlestown, South Carolina igniting an anticipated civil war among the conflicting parties.

More than 3.5 million Americans would fight in the Civil War; more than 2 million for the Union, some 1.5 million for the Confederate States of America. The Union Army would suffer more than 350,000 deaths, both battle and non-battle related. The Confederate forces would experience some 160,000 battle and non-battle related deaths. In total cost, approximately 750,000 soldiers would die; the Civil War would become the costliest war in American history.

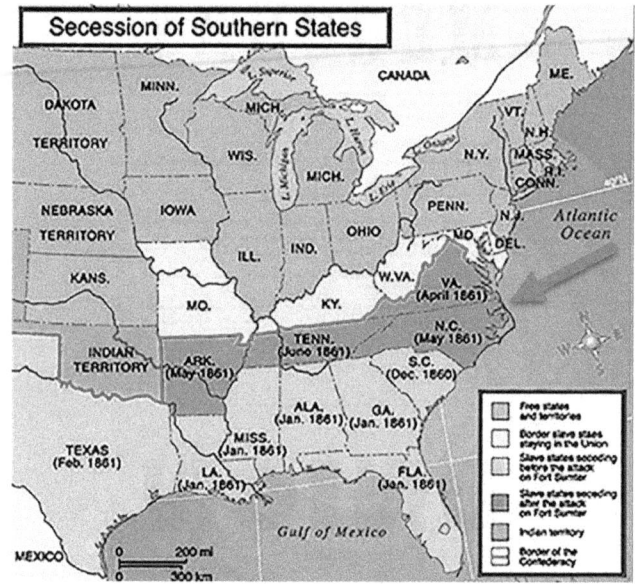

Division of the United States, Summer of 1861

June 19, 1879

> "War is at best barbarism…It's glory is all moonshine.
> It is only those who have neither fired a shot nor hear the
> shrieks and groans of the wounded who cry aloud for blood,
> more vengeance, more desolation.
> War is hell."

Major General William Tecumseh Sherman, June 19, 1879, Address to the graduating class of the Michigan Military Academy
April 1865

"As the Civil War grew in scale the theatres of combat and the number of combatants enlarged, as well. Moreover, the number and variety of players, including those who came to play critical, supportive roles, did too.

This chronicle is a journal of events that occurred during one of the critical battles of the war, the battle of Gettysburg, Pennsylvania, that took place on July 1st, 2nd, and 3rd of 1863. It is a tale of the real participants of that engagement, as well as those with other stories to tell. And it is a story of those, such as myself, who witnessed these events unfold.

The times were treacherous for the people of this era. Unbeknown to them, of course, their decisions and behavior created some of the most important historical events at that time and for future generations of Americans. Their stories are told within this context of events which surrounded the competing armies and those supporting the soldiers and the causes for which these men pledged their lives and fortunes."
Mathew Wilson, War Correspondent, *New York Times*

CHAPTER 1

The Beginning, Somewhere Outside Lancaster, PA January 1863

It is a desperate scene that we encounter as we enter this story. With knives drawn, and caustic talk embroidering their words, fueled by their frustration in the wake of recent events, Max "Mungo" Monroe and Smithy Larson confront each other in an abandoned, decrepit, wooden barn. These two competitors, former friends and now, enemies have run the gamut of business associations. They are now in the last phase of that ruinous cycle: desolation.

It might be argued that this last confrontation was predictable, if not inevitable. Nevertheless, over the last several months, the tenuous relationship of these two former allies has deteriorated to an explosive point, one sparked by anger and disappointment; and with it, their fury, while never well hidden from each other, has risen appreciably. And now, it has become aligned with a pallor of death that hangs, barely concealed, in the molted air that surrounds them.

The current state was well earned. As former allies, defeated in their joint economic enterprise as fugitive slave catchers, and equally, beaten in spirit, if truth be told, they had come to the end of their limited patience. They were defeated by a small band of blacks and two former confederate soldiers they sought to capture; furthermore, the fugitives whom they claimed as their prize were rescued by John Scobell, a Yankee spy and a black man, to boot, lending salt to the wound. As they confront each other at this juncture, they seek to quell an anger fueled by a nagging frustration that has been advanced over time and furthered in intensity through futile encounter.

Smithy Larson, a bully and a man conditioned by his own self-importance, is the more impulsive of the pair; he has learned to act first and think later, a combination of activity that has plagued him in the past. And as evident here, one that continues to do so.

As anticipated, he drew his knife first. Max "Mungo" Munroe, a more reluctant adversary and a more contemplative ally by nature, responds likewise by drawing his weapon. While he behaves in an uncharacteristic fashion, he knows, even at this stage, that he can not convince Smithy that there were still alternatives to their predicament. The present confrontation would be the termination of their relationship; their partnership ended some time ago.

As Smithy approaches his adversary snarling, he says, "I always said that you were too smart for your britches. You couldn't simply go along. You couldn't simply buy into a plan, other than your own, without question. No! You always had an alternative scheme, a better way, as you would insist, but one that failed, as often as mine. We lost the boy, our bargaining chip, and we lost Scobell, that black army scout too. Now we have nothing. Thanks to you," he spits.

Mungo, uncharacteristically angry, responds, "That's pig-headed. And you know it! And stupid, as well," he added.

"The loss of the boy was the luck of the draw. Our plan was good. His protectors, however, were better. And you always seem to forget that our adversaries have been smart and inventive. Also, you seem to discount the fact that they are often desperate, too, Clearly, they should be approached with caution."

"No one is to blame. Even you should be able to see that," responds Mungo in his exasperation.

But, as expected, his words are set upon a man who is deaf to his own limitations and to reason, a deadly combination. For Smithy, there is only one course of action.

"Well, let's see you talk yourself out of this mess," says Smithy, as he approaches Mungo, with the blade of his knife gleaming, reflecting the fading light.

But, as is often the case, especially for these two, fate intervenes. Just then the darkening sky burst into lumination as a streak of lightening appears striking the barn. Within moments the rotting structure is ablaze.

The Burning Barn

The decrepit timbers, while wet with precipitation, were not likely to be immediately consumed. However, a store of dry straw, highly flammable, was randomly struck by the bolt and burst into flames almost immediately.. There was no more time for quarrels. Both Smithy and Mungo recognized the present danger and each fled independently from each other, and the flaming barn, using opposing exits.

This postponed dispute would be settled later. These two would meet up again, but not for some time. The community of slave pursuers was a small one, usually organized by a number of leading families in each region. And that certainly was the case for Mungo's family, the Monroes. They had been in the business of trading black people and Indians a long time, primarily in Virginia. But, over time, as the business grew, they supplemented these with forays into Louisiana and Mississippi. Mungo's defeat, at the hands of a black man, would not go down well with them; it would require some redress relative to Mungo's tarnished reputation in the trade.

Smithy, hailed from the Carolinas. His family had been farmers, dealing in livestock, specifically, pigs. But trade in livestock held limited economic potential for their large brood. Moreover, the family did not take kindly to being known as "pig farmers." It was an unfair attribution, but nevertheless one that stuck. When the need for more labor increased in the South, particularly with the economic boom in cotton following the invention of the cotton gin, the family's elders saw a great opportunity for increasing their wealth by entering the slave trade and, from their perspective, "diversifying" their holdings. The slave trade in the Carolinas was a time-honored practice by this time and one that the Larsons embraced without misgivings.

While Max "Mungo" Monroe and Smithy Larson were competitors, and occasionally, partners, not withstanding the current environment, they faced a common enemy, John Scobell, the Union spy and scout. Scobell, was a black man, and a former slave, manumitted by his "owner". Since the beginning of the war John was employed by the Army of the Potomac, now under the direct command of Major General Winfield Scott Hancock, commander of the 2nd Corps. John was Hancock's unofficial informant and spy, serving as Hancock's principal conduit of information concerning the Army of Northern Virginia.

As a black man living in a society at war over slavery, John Scobell's status was frequently placed in jeopardy. He had encountered Mungo and Smithy as adversaries on several earlier occasions and had defeated them individually and in the their latest joint effort working together. Consequently, both Mungo and Smithy had subsequently sworn to avenge their "honor" against him and would attempt to do so in the future. A perceived affront by a black man to a white man was unthinkable and unforgiving at this time and regardless of the circumstances. And the circumstances surrounding their recent confrontation was a prime, and unforgivable insult.

Slavery

"If there is society on earth where there is the most perfect equality among white men, where labor is respected and the laborer honored, it is in the southern States; and the reason is obvious: There is an inferior race to do the menial service."

William Barksdale, antebellum Senator, State of Mississippi, and General, Confederate States of American

The rapid growth of agriculture in the south, especially the growing and processing of cotton, occasioned by the invention of the cotton gin, placed a premium on slave labor to perform the menial and retching tasks necessary to meet the increasing demands for the product in Europe and elsewhere. In the first half of the 19th century, land and slaves acquired immense economic value and subsequently changed the nature of southern society. The justification of the practice was orated by James Hammond of South Carolina. He argued in 1858:

"… in all social systems there must be a class to do the menial duties, to perform the drudgery of life…Its requisites are vigor, docility, fidelity. Such a class you must have, or you would not have that other class which leads progress, civilization, and refinement. It constitutes the very mud-sill of society and political government, and you might as well attempt to build a house in the air, as to build either the one or the other, except on this mud-sill."

James Henry Hammond, antebellum Senator, State of South Carolina in his *"Cotton is King"* speech to the US Senate

Priscilla's Story: A Slave Girl

Somewhere off the coast of Sierra Leone (1756)

"Where am I?" Why am I locked up in the bottom of this big boat? Who are these strange people locked up with me? Why are they in chains? They look like me, but they speak a different language? I tried speaking to them, but they turn away. Why is that woman carrying the dead child crying? Who is that man with the whip? Why are they here? Where are my parents? Can they hear me? Why am I alone?"

These and other bewildering thoughts must have occupied the racing mind and frantic occupations of this young 10-year-old black child, who found herself cramped aboard, and below in the hull of a living, constantly moving hell, the slave ship, *Hare*.

The child, later named Priscilla Polite by a strange white man who claimed to be her owner, was imprisoned and destined to a life of slavery. She had been playing near a river close to her village located in the heart of Africa. Without warning a group of black men (probably Fante slave traders from the coast) snuck up behind her and threw a bag over her head. Before she could cry out, she had been swept up and carried aboard a river barge, kidnapped, with no chance to alert others of her plight or to seek rescue from her parents or family.

She was taken by land and across unknown rivers with multiple stops along the way to the coast of Africa. She was not spoken to, cared for, nor properly feed for several weeks. She was weak and weary from her forced march, and she was afraid. Efforts to communicate with others also proved fruitless. Her captors managed to raid other villages on the journey to the coast. They kidnapped, probably according to plan, people who spoke different tongues, minimizing the possibility of a coordinated mass escape or any likely insurrection among those more able, and less traumatized captives in their midst.

Priscilla was taken to a slave center to be transported on the Hare to the colonies. She was alone, and despondent. There was little chance that she would ever see her native land, her village or her family again. And she never did.

The journey during the infamous "middle passage" was harsh and unforgiving. Many perished, some intentionally, others as a function of the brutal regimen practiced aboard the ship. But she survived. She was not especially cunning or skilled. She was simply ignored.

When the ship finally arrived on Sullivan Island, South Carolina, Priscilla and the other enslaved Africans in passage were quarantined in so-called "pest houses" before they were sold into slavery. There they recovered, under some care, from their arduous journey. It was believed (with some justification) that they needed to appear robust and presentable (obviously, a marketing strategy that operated in the sellers best interest) for the auction market.

When the Hare's "cargo" was ready for sale, Henry Laurens, one of the richest planters and slave dealers in Charleston and later an American patriot leader during the Revolutionary War, handled their sale. According to Laurens' records of the sale, Elias Ball, a wealthy rice planter, purchased

Priscilla and three other children from the Hare. South Carolina's staple crop at that period was rice, and Carolina planters were willing to pay high prices for Africans brought directly from the rice-growing regions of West Africa, including among them, Sierra Leone. Priscilla lived for many years on Ball family plantations. She bore 10 children in slavery, and died in 1811, at about 65 years of age.

Solomon Northup – A "Free" Slave

It was, in part, an example of being in the wrong place at the wrong time. But it was also part of the ongoing stigma attached to being black in a society that condoned and fostered slavery at every level.

"One morning, toward the latter part of the month of March,1841, having at that time no particular business to engage my attention, I was walking about the village of Saratoga Springs, thinking to myself where I might obtain some present employment, until the busy season should arrive...

"On the corner of Congress street and Broadway, near the tavern ...I was met by two gentlemen of respectable appearance, both of whom were entirely unknown to me. I have the impression that they were introduced to me by some one of my acquaintances, but who, I have in vain endeavored to recall, with the remark that I was an expert player on the violin.

"At any rate, they immediately entered conversation on that subject, making numerous inquiries touching my proficiency in that respect. My responses being to all appearances satisfactory, they proposed to engage my services for a short period, stating, at the same time, I was just such a person as their business required. Their names, as they afterwards gave them to me, were Merrill Brown and Abram Hamilton, though whether these were their true appellations, I have strong reasons to doubt. ... They were connected, as they informed me with a circus company, then in the city of Washington; that they were on their way thither to rejoin it... They also remarked that they had found much difficulty in procuring music for their entertainments...

So began the terrifying journey of Solomon Northup, in which the promise of employment led him to Washington, DC (a slave city at the time) and into captivity, sale and imprisonment for twelve long years, as a slave.

Solomon Northup denial of slavery, during every step of his decent into its maw, while courageous and expectant of a free man, simply lead to further abuse and inhuman treatment during his journey. As he was put into the slave pen, denying his free status, he experienced beatings (designed to produce compliance) that worsened in intensity, but miraculous, never defeated him.

As he writes of the experience, "… I was seized by both of them [his captors], and roughly divested of my clothing. My feet, as has been stated, were fastened to the floor. Drawing me over the bench, face downward, Radburn placed his heavy foot upon the fetters [chains], between my wrists, holding them painfully to the floor. With the paddle, Burch commenced beating me. Blow after blow was inflicted upon my naked body. When his unrelenting arm grew tired, he stopped and if I still insisted I was a free man, he continued the beatings. I did insist upon it, and the blows asked were renewed, faster and more energetically, if possible, than before. When again tired, he would repeat the same question, and receiving the same answer, continued his cruel labor. All this time, the incarnate devil was uttering most fiendish oaths. At length the paddle broke, leaving the useless handle in his hand. Still I would not yield. All his brutal blows could not force from my lips the foul lie that I was a slave."
Soloman Northup, *Twelve Years a Slave*

Thus began Solomon Northup's rapid descent into the bowels of hell. As others, Solomon Northup thought about his wrongful imprisonment and his plight of enforced slavery. His perspective, as a victim, of course, differed from that of privileged white practitioners and the owners of slaves. For them, slavery was supported by biblical practice and an ancient tradition and, as such, was morally justified.

"Slavery, in some form, has existed in all ages of the world, and it is sanctioned by Divine authority. We believe it to be right. It is interwoven with our whole social organization, with our very existence as a people; and we are determined at all hazards, to maintain it."
William Barksdale, antebellum, Senator, State of Mississippi

The Traders

The profits associated with the slave trade were enormous as the need for slave labor increased over time across the Americas. Coupled with this demand, the vast sums of money to be made were enough to compromise the principals and morals of citizens in all parts of the country, as well. From Bristol, Rhode Island and the huge slave empire built by the DeWitt's, to New Orleans, Louisiana entrepreneurs found that it was an easy path to wealth, involving little risk. This was especially true for those willing to commit the necessary resources, often underwritten by many, and those with the will to pursue the course. The path to riches was clear and without impediment. And there were many willing to take that route. Among them was Henry Laurens.

"The slaves from the river Gambia are preferr'd to all others with us [here in Carolina] save the Gold Coast ..., next to them the Windward Coast are preferr'd to Angloas."

Henry Laurens, Slave Trader

Henry Laurens, was a prosperous slave trader and leading member of the social-political upper class of his generation by the middle eighteenth century. Nevertheless, he started his quest for wealth and position from more humble origins. He came to the new world with his family, initially, in order to escape religious persecution. And at that time his family was of modest means. By 1747, however, he had established an import/export business in the Carolinas, and was a prosperous merchant, slave trader and planter with large estates. In Charleston he became an agent for the

London-based owners of Bronce Island, a British slave castle on the Sierra Leone River in West Africa. As their representative in America he was the chief receiver of "cargo" from their slave ships bound for Charleston harbor, where he posted advertisements in the newspapers for the sale of newly arriving slaves, managed auctions for their sale, and accounted for their disposition, as merchandise.

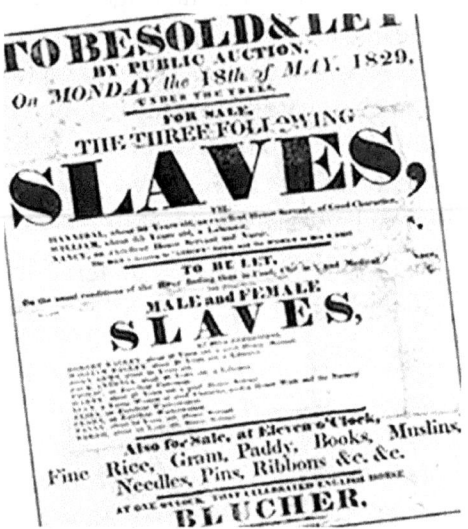
Advertisement of Slaves for Sale

For his participation in the trade he received a 10% commission on the sale of each slave, amassing a fortune for his efforts. He was also able, through his accumulation of enormous wealth, as acquired via the slave trade and correlated investments in land and slaves, to rise to the highest levels of social and political power both in his native state of South Carolina and within American society. In addition to becoming vice-president of the state of South Carolina, ironically, he also rose to become president of the Continental Congress in 1777. In 1779 Laurens became a diplomat for the new nation, by being appointed as a minister to the Netherlands. In this role, he was chosen in order to solicit Dutch financial support for the American revolution.

The Middlemen - Slave Pursuers

The slave pursuers would not end their activities; it was too lucrative an enterprise. For Smithy and Mungo, their destinies would likely take parallel paths converging at some point in the near future. For they were kindred spirits in both heart and soul, wherever each could be located. They both were purveyors of slaves, arbiters of other human beings, who bought and sold enslaved and often free, black men and women (when the opportunity presented itself and circumstances permitted) for profit. And that would not change at this time or in the future. Their certain paths would convene at some distant point in time.

1863, Philadelphia, PA.

Our players were gathered in the drawing room of Dr. James Wilson, army surgeon, in his home in Philadelphia. Among them was John Scobell, a free black man, army scout and spy for General Winfield Scott Hancock, and a friend of Dr. Wilson, with an entourage of people he bought with him. They included Aunt Amy, an older black woman from Virginia, seeking a new life as a free person, as well as Patrick O'Connor, a fugitive Confederate soldier and his ward, the boy Danny. Emma Pruett, the daughter of a prominent Philadelphia family was there too.

Two members of Scobell's party, Sean O'Connor, Patrick's cousin and Confederate comrade and William Tall Tree, a Cherokee Indian and friend of John were not present. They were wounded in a kidnapping encounter with Smithy and Mungo and their gang upon their journey to Lancaster, the group's intended destination. On that occasion, Captain Brady, an adjutant to Major General Hancock was killed, as well as two of Smithy's men, Big Red and Blue Ben.

Sean was recovering from a bullet wound to his leg, while William was recovering, and being cared for by Dr. Wilson, from a knife wound inflicted in a fatal hand to hand confrontation with Big Red. Both Sean and William were slowly healing under the watchful eye of Dr. Wilson and Emma Pruett, who served as their nurse, at his residence in the city.

Another participant at the gathering was Job Hunter, Dr. Wilson's butler. Job, a loyal member of the Wilson's household until recently, was uncovered by Scobell to be Mungo's puppet. In a newly discovered letter written to him by his wife Mae, Job was revealed as an abetting facilitator of Mungo's slave trading activities and as a reluctant informant of the Scobell group's activities.

The letter told of Hunter's family, that had been kidnapped and taken south earlier by Mungo, and how he held them as hostages over his informer. A recent confrontation between John and Dr. Wilson with Hunter that revealed this liaison with Mungo was obviously unpleasant and disheartening, but was now open to the entire household. Meanwhile, Hunter maintained an uneasy presence as a closely watched participant, as the group discussed its plans and his participation.

At this junction matters had been settled. John Scobell, would continue his mission. He and Aunt Amy, who would serve as a guardian over Hunter, as well as Patrick and the boy Danny and Big Jake, a free black man captured by Smithy and rescued by the Scobell party (and who had already left to rejoin his family in Lancaster) would establish four "listening posts" in southern parts of Pennsylvania. The plan, established with the aide of General Winfield Scott Hancock and Dr. Wilson, and with the concurrence of Major General John Reynolds, was based on the premise that now, as the North and South neared the beginning of the third year of the War, Lee would bring his army north to Pennsylvania to strike at the heart of the Union. For Lee, after defeating a variety of Union generals in 1862 with an incrementally diminishing army now was the time to strike. For Scobell the "listening posts" would help establish when and where this attack would occur, information that would be vital to the Army of the Potomac in the continuing war.

The year was 1863, about halfway into the bloodiest conflict to ever occur on the American continent. And with over two years of war remaining, a fact that none of its present participants could know at the time, the staggering costs of the war in terms of lives lost and property destroyed would go on. Next up in the Eastern theatre was Chancelorsville in May, and then three horrific, historical days in July at Gettysburg. It was that unknown, but anticipated occurrence in southern Pennsylvania that John Scobell and his colleagues were preparing to meet.

Mathew's Story

A letter from war correspondent Mathew Wilson, *New York Times*, Early Summer, 1863

"This country, this strange, magnificent Eden, this beautiful, this glorious country, this manifestation of God's benevolence and creativity... this paradox of freedom and servitude that we have spun, my country, yes, my dying, bleeding country... is once again at war. For the third time, since our founding, indeed, within the first hundred of years of our fragile republic, we are once again in battle. And now as earlier, we find ourselves in a monstrous, unyielding struggle."

"We started out just about 75 years ago, during the early 1770's, in search of a new kind of freedom, not freedom for women, blacks, or Indians, mind you, nor just about anybody else who was not a Protestant-Christian white man, however, but nevertheless, a new kind of freedom. This was a freedom where every man could face every other man without regard to his past or present status within an unwritten, but predetermined social or political order. And we espoused lofty goals, equality, fraternity, union. But, as it was not to be then, it is not to be now, as we are forced to take up arms, once again. And because of the unfinished work, both neglected and avoided, that we started earlier, we find ourselves in yet another, even bloodier fight than before. And make no mistake about it; it is a fight for our very lives. Yes, of course! It is another political battle. But this time the battle is one to which we have been warming up to since the beginning of our fragile, ill-defined republic, may God have mercy on its soul."

"This time, the fight is very different from those that have gone before; it is both more complex and more subtle. There is no foreign monarch as in the first two wars. And there is no evading army. There are no external threatening powers, no kings, no monarchs. In this particular fight, we are fighting against our very selves, often brother against brother, friend vs. friend, and in some cases old friends, many of whom fought together earlier. And it is a war between family, where kin are killing kin. Some have called it a war between the states, others, a civil war. I'm not quite sure what it is precisely. For those of us who have witnessed it directly, however, it is simply a war, a bloody destructive menace that has overtaken our land and has swept across, if not through, all of our lives. Moreover, it appears to be a war that will eternally damn this generation, staining all of us and, most likely, our children and their children for many generations to come."

"As you know, we have been at it a long time now, going on for over two years, since April of 1861. And by now it is any body's guess, including our President Lincoln, and probably Jefferson Davis, President of the Confederacy, as well, of where or when, or if, and even how, it will end. But I am getting ahead of the story. Let me introduce myself first since I seem to have drawn your attention."

"My name is Mathew Wilson. I am a special war correspondent for the *New York Times*, stationed in New York and Philadelphia. Some of you might know of my family, the Wilson's of Pennsylvania. We have been here a long time. Actually, we have been here since the beginning of our republic. Like others in our story we have a lot at stake. But I'll tell you more about us as we move along. For now, I am here to report to you, my old readers, and those of you that have just jumped aboard about this war, where it has been, a little about where I think it might be going, and, most importantly, since this is where our story begins, what is happening right now. Because at this juncture things seem to not only be heating up once again, but we may be heading in a different direction, as well."

CHAPTER 2

ESCAPE OF JOHN HENRY HILL FROM AUCTION, RICHMOND, VIRGINIA, JANUARY 1, 1853

"... John Henry at that time, was a little turned of twenty-five years of age, full six feet high, and remarkably well proportioned in every respect. He was rather of a brown color, with marked intellectual features. John was by trade, a carpenter, and was considered a competent workman. The year previous to his escape, he hired his time, for which he paid his owner $150. This amount John had fully settled up the last day of the year. As he was a young man of steady habits, a husband and father, and withal an ardent lover of Liberty; his owner, John Mitchell, evidently observed these traits in his character, and concluded that he was a dangerous piece of property to keep; that his worth in money could be more easily managed than the man. Consequently, his master unceremoniously, without intimating in any way to John, that he was to be sold, took him to Richmond, on the first day of January (the great annual sale day), and directly to the slave-auction. Just as John was being taken into the building, he was invited to submit to hand-cuffs. As the thought flashed upon his mind that he was about to be sold on the auction-block, he grew terribly desperate. "Liberty or death" was the watchword of that awful moment. In the twinkling of an eye, he turned on his enemies, with his fist, knife, and feet, so tiger-like, that he actually put four or five men to flight, his master among the number. His enemies thus suddenly baffled, John wheeled, and, as if assisted by an angel, strange as it may appear, was soon out of sight of his pursuers, and securely hid away. This was the last hour of John Henry's slave life, but not, however, of his struggles and sufferings for freedom, for before a final chance to escape presented itself, nine months elapsed."
From the narratives of William Still, *The Underground Railroad,* March 31, 1863

From the Letters of Mathew Wilson, *New York Times*

"Philadelphia is the most progressive city of our time. It is also located within the most tolerant of all of the States. Historically, this achievement dates back to an earlier era. In 1780, more than eighty years before the Civil War, the State of Pennsylvania passed an emancipation law which was the country's first of its kind. The law declared that slaves born before that year were to remain as slaves, while persons born after that time would automatically become free after reaching their twenty-eighth birthday.

But there was more to the edict. The 1780 law also declared slave trading within Pennsylvania to be illegal; furthermore, it stated that slaves brought from out of state into the commonwealth would by virtue of their residence in Pennsylvania become free citizens after six months of continuous residence within the State."

The law had its intended effect over time. By 1800 slavery had been reduced to a limited practice in Pennsylvania; most slave owners, but for a few masters, had voluntarily manumitted their slaves and Philadelphia, its principal city, had become a haven for fugitive and free slaves, alike.

The city of Philadelphia was a base for many abolitionists and the Underground Railroad, as well. Both black men and women and white men and women shared in the operation of the rails.

WILLIAM STILL - FATHER OF THE UNDERGROUND RAILROAD

William Still helped as many as 60 slaves a month escape to freedom, interviewing each person and keeping careful records, including a brief biography/account of fugitives and the destination of each person he assisted, along with any alias that they adopted.

William Still

Still was in a unique position to provide board and room for many of the fugitives who came through Philadelphia before resuming their journey to Canada. There, he encountered many seeking freedom, including a former slave, whose identity was initially unknown, but later revealed to be his own brother, Peter Still; Peter had been left in bondage by their mother when she had escaped forty years earlier. William Still later reported that finding his brother led him to preserve the careful records that he did concerning former slaves, and which provided him a valuable source of material for his book The Underground Railroad (1872).

The Code. When Philadelphia abolitionists organized a vigilance committee to assist the large numbers of fugitives passing through the city after the Fugitive Slave Act of 1850 was passed, they named William Still as their chairman. And he served them well, in part, as a function of his own ingenuity, cleverness and resourcefulness, as well as his hatred for the trade. Foremost, among his efforts at aiding runaways was the development and dissemination of the underground railway code, a language employed in assisting fugitive slaves to escape from servitude.

It was a simple and effective communicative device in which Still devised and employed messages that were often encoded so that they could only be understood by those actively involved in the operation of the "railroad." For example, the following message, "I have sent via at two o'clock four large and two small hams," indicated that four adults and two children were sent by train from Harrisburg to Philadelphia. However, the additional use of the word via indicates that the "passengers" were not sent on the usual "train," but rather via Reading, Pennsylvania, an alternative routing channel. In this manner, using coded messages forged with deception, slave catchers could be tricked (if a message were intercepted) into going to the regular train station in an attempt to capture the runaways, while Still was able to meet escaped fugitives at the alternative station and guide them to safety. Once safe, fugitives could continue their escape to free northern territories and eventually, for many, Canada.

Two days before the Scobell party's scheduled departure from Philadelphia, on route to Lancaster, an unusual visitor arrived at the Wilson residence. He was a well-dressed black man with an equally well-attired companion. When Hunter announced his arrival, Dr. Wilson jumped from his chair in the sitting room and rushed to greet his visitor. It was William Still, the ardent abolitionist and humanitarian who served as a central figure in the Underground Railroad.

As a black man, Still was born free in 1821 in the Pine Barrens of New Jersey, the youngest of eighteen children. His father, Levin, had purchased his own freedom in Maryland in 1807. His mother, Charity, was also a slave. Lacking funds for her manumission, she escaped servitude, eventually joining her husband, but forced to leave behind their two oldest, enslaved sons.

Denied a formal education, as most blacks were at that time, Still was largely self-taught. When the Vigilance Committee of Philadelphia was formed after the Fugitive Slave Act of 1850, Still was ready to assume his task; subsequently, he was named the chairman of the group. In that role, working with others, he built an extensive covet organization with underground activities as far south as Norfolk, VA and Washington, DC. Among those Still assisted, and whose journey he recorded, was a young black man named Robert.

A Christmas Trip North

"Robert was about thirty years of age, dark color, quite tall, and in talking with him a little while, it was soon discovered that Slavery had not crushed all the brains out of his head by a good deal. Nor was he so much attached to his "kind-hearted master," John Edward Jackson, of Anne Arundel, Md., or his old fiddle, that he was contented and happy while in bondage. Far from it. The fact was, that he hated Slavery so decidedly and had such a clear common sense-like view of the evils and misery of the system, that he declared he had as a matter of principle refrained from marrying, in order that he might have no reason to grieve over having added to the woes of slaves. Nor did he wish to be encumbered, if the opportunity offered to escape. According to law he was entitled to his freedom at the age of twenty-five. But what right had a negro, which white slave-holders were "bound to respect?" Many who had been willed free, were held just as firmly in Slavery, as if no will had ever been made. Robert had too much sense to suppose that he could gain anything by seeking legal redress. This method, therefore, was considered out of the question. But in the meantime he was growing very naturally in favor of the Underground Rail Road. From his experience Robert did not hesitate to say that his master was "mean," "a very hard man," who would work his servants early and late, without allowing them food and clothing sufficient to shield them from the cold and hunger. Robert certainly had unmistakable marks about him, of having been used roughly. He thought very well of Nathan Harris, a fellow-servant belonging to the same owner, and he made up his mind, if Nathan would join him, neither the length of the journey, the loneliness of night travel, the coldness of the weather, the fear of the slave-hunter, nor the scantiness of their means should deter him from making his way to freedom. Nathan listened to the proposal, and was suddenly converted to freedom, and the two united during Christmas week, 1854, and set out on the Underground Rail Road. It is needless to say that they had trying difficulties to encounter. These they expected, but all were overcome, and they reached the Vigilance Committee, in Philadelphia safely, and were cordially welcomed. During the interview, a full interchange of thought resulted, the fugitives were well cared for and in due time both were forwarded on…".
From the Narratives of William Still, *The Underground Railroad*.

Escape attempts from the earliest periods of forced servitude and the inception of slavery had been planned and successfully advanced throughout the South. Many of these occurrences, however, lead to the recovery and resale of the unfortunate fugitives in flight, some of who incurred severe punishment upon being recaptured and/or death.

A Rescue Plan for Mae and her Boys

As he entered the room, Mr. Still is greeted by Dr. Wilson.

"Mr. Still, Mr. Still, welcome to my home. We are delighted that you could join us. Especially, since we are in the midst of planning an escape, where your consul and experience would be invaluable."

After introductions of Mr. Still are made by Doctor Wilson, all of the assembled guests take their places in the sitting room.

Doctor Wilson begins by addressing the group, "We know where Mae Hunter and her children are being held captive. They have been taken to a slave station in Maryland. As you might know, slave operations, like the Monroes use a series of way stations to "ship" their slaves further south and west. At these sites, where the standard of care is minimal, slaves are allowed to rest overnight and often longer, and are given food to keep them going. They are awful places, but that is part of the slave enterprise. Apparently, Mae has been used as a cook to feed fugitive and kidnapped slaves to be sold and transported further south.

"We have been trying to negotiate for the release of Mae and her boys, but without any success. It has become apparent to me that price is not an issue here. Her "owner" appears to want to keep them for none of the usual reasons slaves are kept."

"From what you are telling me," Wilson turned to face John and continued, "a hold over Hunter, and through him, privy to private discussions and Union business that might transpire in this household, and elsewhere, may be reason enough. Hunter also has many contacts that reside within the city and opportunities to gather information in the black community where they live and work. As you know, the use of spies in an important household has become another weapon in the arsenal employed by both sides and their allies."

Then turning from John to William Still, the doctor added, "John has volunteered his services to plan an escape for Mae and her boys."

"He has suggested that we use Hunter to set him up as a decoy in which he can infiltrate Mongo's slave trading operation, and free Mae and her children. If we send another man in it is likely that he will be sent far south immediately. And that might also occur if we send John in. However, a man like Scobell, if Hunter would serve as his accomplice, by creating the illusion that John is privy to Northern military strategy, would be of potentially far greater value to Mungo since John would have information that, once extracted, he could sell to authorities in the southern military."

"And securing a profit for their labors, whatever its source is the central concern of the Munroes," he said.

As John nodded in agreement, Wilson continued,

"What we would need to do first is to attract Mongo's interest in John. And I think that I know how to do that. First, we need Hunter to send a fake coded message to Mae, through Mungo."

"But how can we do that?" asked Mr. Still.

"We can't trust direct contact through a slave trader," he continued. "Moreover, anything Hunter passes to Mungo will be read by him first, if it is delivered at all," he added.

"You can count on that," noted John with a smile.

"And that is the point," said the doctor. "Mungo would entrap himself in our scheme," he continued.

"And since he would be the central force in this affair, he would likely be more willing to move our plan forward than if it were thrust upon him by us by some other means likely to arouse his suspicions."

"I would also imagine that having John as his prisoner, after his last encounter with him, would salve his ego. It would also probably take some of the pressure of defeat that he has incurred with John on that occasion and with which his family presently views him."

"But," added Emma, "wouldn't a plan involving John at that level be dangerous. After all, he has a history with Mungo that would alert Mungo to take precautions".

"Yes, that will occur, as we suspect," responded Dr. Wilson.

"However, if Mungo is forewarned, …and he will be by Hunter, and if our plan is not too obvious, we will avoid any bloodshed and safely place John in an environment in which he will be able to learn the extend of the Munroe slave operation, although he would be a captive at the same time".

"Mungo will be very interested in capturing John and in learning what John knows. He will also want to assess the monetary value of that information with southern military authorities. And that will buy John time to assess the slave operation he will be able to witness and, hopefully, enable him to rescue Mae and her children. If possible, he may also be capable of disabling the Monroes' ability to ply their trade through this channel in the future, at least temporarily. That is, if he can destroy their headquarters, perhaps, during the rescue," he added.

"This is a bold scheme. But, if John is willing it could work."

"But how do we put this plan into action? John must establish his listening posts, which will take several weeks."

"And he will need help," said Patrick." What do you think John?" he said turning to Scobell.

"Well, I could start to implement this plan in Lancaster, after I have completed the 'listening posts' assignment."

"Patrick can assist on those, as well as Big Jake," said Emma.

"They both could also assist in helping Mungo capture me and in aiding my escape," said John. "And there is Mr. Stevens and Mrs. Smith. Both will help, as well."

Author's Note: Representative Thadeus Stevens, was the most radical of his Republican colleagues. His noted accomplishments included passage of the Fourteenth and Fifteenth Amendments that abolished slavery and gave black men the right to vote. His less known accomplishments, preceding the war, included the hiring of spies to infiltrate slave operations and operating a safe house through the underground railroad. These "counter-underground activities" offered valuable information to the Union, and were helpful to slaves fleeing their captivity.

"Mae is a good Christian woman who reads her bible. By using a variation of several biblical phrases we want Hunter to write to her, admonishing her "to believe in God and that she will be saved". And that Hunter will send a man (savior) to her who, Hunter believes, can effect an escape for her and the children. That she should trust in him, as she would her God."

Relying upon several strands of recalled and paraphrased biblical verses, Hunter would write to Mae,

"Believe in me, and I shall send a savior unto you."

It was an innocuous message, but one that they all believed Mae would immediately comprehend. And in the intricacies of this cat and mouse game they fashioned, so too would Mungo Munroe; he too would understand the intent of the message. And hopefully, he would act in the manner anticipated. But, John would learn of that event as well, and he hoped, be prepared to deal with it, both when he walked into that den of inequity called "slavery" and when he left it with Mae and her children.

Elsewhere in Virginia, Another Meeting

It is early morning and there is a bite in the air. However, it promises to be another warm, late spring day. As Robert E. Lee contemplates his surroundings he is well aware that early summer was approaching, and it would be followed by more fighting, as the past two summers had been. This time, however, able to convince President Davis of the merits of his plan to invade the North, the Commanding General would bring the fight to Pennsylvania. He would take the war out of Virginia. At least, he would do so temporarily. That was the plan for the moment. And, he hoped that is would apply for later, as well. But aspiration and reality would take different paths. This battle in the heartland of Pennsylvania, as deadly and prophetic as it would prove to be, would not prevent a return to the ravaged fields of Virginia.

As he stepped out of his temporary headquarters, an old mansion requisitioned for Lee by his chief quartermaster, the general was met by his adjutant, Colonel Taylor.

A lone rider had arrived moments before to see the general. It was Harrison, the scout and confederate spy recruited and used by General James Longstreet, Lee's second in command.

Lee was familiar with Harrison's reputation, and trusted Longstreet's assessment of the man, although he was distrustful of the man, himself. His attitude stemmed from an old prejudice. The commanding general preferred to rely upon and use information gathered by his own soldiers, most notably sources employed by General JEB Stuart. Yet, Lee was no fool with respect to military information, recognizing that knowledge of the enemy was paramount to achieving military success. And he was also aware that as he prepared for Pennsylvania, that his knowledge of the terrain and countryside was limited.

Harrison, was an especially effective courier. As a lone scout, he could travel in unsuspected guise throughout the North. He could unobtrusively observe events, and gather relevant information of Northern troop movement that would elude a larger force of men; the latter were, by necessity, usually concerned with their own detection, as well as that of the enemy. Harrison, in contrast, could dispense with such precautions.

One other advantage associated with Harrison was that he had and continued to maintain a strong connection with other Southerners operating in the North, including the large network of fugitive retrievers in Pennsylvania. From these men he acquired information of military significance that he relayed to the high command. Lee may not have held Harrison in high esteem. However, he understood his value perfectly well.

As Harrison dismounted from his horse, he was hastily questioned by Colonel Taylor, as the latter escorted him to the General's residence. The colonel inquired where Harrison had been and what news he had for the commanding chief. Harrison, however, while amiable, as usual, kept his most important information for the general's ears. He was well aware of the low esteem in which he was held by formal soldiers, as well as recognized that his value resided in secrecy, rather than disclosure. He would report directly to Lee.

As he encountered the general, Harrison became aware of the fine lines drawn upon the general's face and the worn appearance of his body. The general always appeared elegant. And that was the case here. However, it was apparent to Harrison that the last year had been especially harsh upon the general, although Lee would quickly deny such observations. The general never sought excuses for his behavior, nor suffered them among others. It was part of his mystique and it served him well.

"Good day," said the general.

"General Longstreet has indicated to me that you have been in contact with the Federal army. Is that true?"

"Yes Sir. And they are moving north into Pennsylvania."

"The total Army of the Potomac?"

"Yes, Sir," replied Harrison.

"Do you have any information," inquired the general, "regarding the disposition of their leadership? They seem to be at the end of their supply of candidates for command."

"Well, yes sir! That seems to be the case. Mr. Lincoln has become exasperated, according to members of his inner circle, including Mr. Stanton as well, with their inability to find a worthy commander in the east."

"The latest information that I have been privy to," Harrison speculated, "suggests that he will appoint a new man to lead the Federals in Pennsylvania. Probably, a native, one of the Pennsylvania boys"

That would be Reynolds, or Hancock or Meade, thought Lee. All of them are worthy opponents, he reflected further.

"Yes, that is true. And they are all soldiers, rather than politicians."

"But, I have another reason for requesting this interview, Sir, if I may switch your attention to related matter. And it is one which, I believe, is of the utmost importance. One of my informants, a Mr. Max Monroe, a slave retriever and trader, by profession, has provided me with some very useful information. Mr. Monroe has an informant close to a very high source within the Federal Army itself."

"Apparently, the Federals in preparing for an advance of our army, suspect that you will be descending upon Pennsylvania. My source says that they have taken some steps to follow and report on the whereabouts and movements of the Army of Northern Virginia's as it makes its advance."

"They have employed some people to establish what I heard call are "listening posts" in order to report to their generals.

"Then they will know when we are coming," said the general, "and where we will be coming from, as well," he added.

"Not if we get there first."

"Or, if we round up their leaders and disrupt their operation," ventured Harrison.

"I would like your permission to authorize Mr. Monroe to use his resources and to capture and take John Scobell, their leader in Lancaster, as a prisoner. We probably cannot eliminate these spying centers. But, from him we can learn the location of these so-called "listening posts" and divert our troops around them."

"Yes, Mr. Harrison. That would reflect my thinking on the matter, as well."

"However, let me add, that I would hope that Mr. Scobell could be kept in near contact to us. He is likely to have additional information that we may need to possess in achieving safe harbor to our destination."

"The Army of Northern Virginia has proven itself a mighty military force. It has performed far beyond my best expectations. However, we do not have the resources available to us, as the North does, to continue indefinitely. If we win here, and I believe that we can, we may still draw outside support to our cause. And that would be crucial".

"This army, as you know, is our last best hope. We cannot afford to fail in this mission."

CHAPTER 3

THE CALL TO WAR FEBRUARY 23, 1862

"I have delayed in answering this letter in order that I might reflect on its contents. I have done so and come to the conclusion that if I do not participate in this war it will be the source of the deepest regret and disappointment in life. ... I rejoice that there is scarcely one of our name in all the South but who are engaged in some capacity in this glorious cause; and moreover, I hope and pray you will not allow it to be said that there was even one, capable of bearing arms, not on the list of his country's defenders."
University of Alabama student J. B. Mitchell in a letter to his father, October 12, 1862

"I went to Cambridge and resumed my studies with what zeal I could. During that week we heard that the rebel forces were pushing forward and Northward ... I assure you, my dear father I know of nothing in the course of my life which has caused me such deep and serious thought as this trying crisis in the history of our nation. What is the worth of this man's life or that man's education if this great and glorious fabric of our Union ... is so shattered to pieces by traitorous hands ... If our country and our nation is to perish, better that we should all perish with it."
Harvard University student Samuel Storrow in a letter to his father.

Killed at the Ford

He is dead, the beautiful youth,
The heart of honor, the tongue of truth,
He, the life and light of us all,
Whose voice, was blithe as a bugle-call,
Whom all eyes followed with one consent,
The cheer of whose laugh, and whose pleasant word,
Hushed all murmurs of discontent.

Only last night, as we rode along,
Down the dark of the mountain gap,
To visit the picket-guard at the ford,
Little dreaming of any mishap,
He was humming the words of some old song,
Two roses he had on his cap
And another he bore at the point of his sword.

We lifted him up to his saddle again,
And through the mire and the mist and the rain
Carried him back to the silent camp,
And laid him as if asleep in his bed;
And I saw by the light of the surgeon's lamp
Two white roses upon his cheeks,
And one, just over his heart, blood red!

Henry Wadsworth Longfellow

Divine Intervention

"My Uncle Peyton Harrison was a stanch Presbyterian, and when we met after the war, he said, 'Well, Randolph, you have left the Church of your Fathers.'

"'Yes,'" I replied, I have returned to the Church of my Forefathers." Randolph H. McKim, 1910. A soldier's recollections: *Leaves from the Diary of a Young Confederate.*

Each side, as might be anticipated, saw its fight as both preordained and sacred, with the outcome governed by Providence; independently they each embraced their God and prayed that their cause would prevail in this war so long sought, whose havoc would test their wills and beliefs as no other had before, or that would ever after do so in the course of their lives. June 19, 1861

A Prayer for Our Armies

Bishop Green of Mississippi

"Almighty God, whose Providence watcheth over all things, and in whose hands is the disposal of all events, we look up to Thee for Thy protection and blessing amidst the apparent and great dangers with which we are encompassed. Thou hast, in Thy wisdom, permitted us to be threatened with the many evils of an unnatural and destructive war. Save us, we beseech Thee, from the hands of our enemies. Watch over our fathers and brothers and sons who, trusting in Thy defense [sic] and in the righteousness of our cause, have gone forth to the service of their country. May their lives be precious in Thy sight. Preserve them from all the dangers to which they may be exposed. Enable them successfully to perform their duty to Thee and to their country, and do Thou, in Thine infinite wisdom and power, so overrule events, and so dispose the hearts of all engaged in this painful struggle, that it may soon end in the safety, honor and welfare of our Confederate States, but to the good of Thy people, and the glory of Thy great name, through Jesus Christ, our Lord. Amen."
Charleston Mercury

Mark Twain

Attempts to evoke divine intervention on behalf of their cause occurred on both sides. The great American humorist, Mark Twain, noting the call for support by each side in soliciting divine intervention as an aide to their purpose was inclined to mock the war in the most dramatic terms. Without patronizing either side, he saw the foolishness of calls for divine intervention and support as irrelevant and irreverent. His satirical comments include the following "battle cry":

"...O Lord our Father, our young patriots, idols of our hearts, go forth to battle-- be Thou near them! With them-- in spirit-- we also go forth from the sweet peace of our beloved firesides to smite the foe. O Lord our God, help us to tear their soldiers to bloody shreds with our shells; help us to cover their smiling fields with the pale forms of their patriot dead; help us to drown the thunder of their guns with the shrieks of their wounded, writhing in pain; help us to lay waste their humble homes with a hurricane of fire; help us to wring the hearts of their unoffending widows with unavailing grief... for our sakes who adore Thee, Lord, blast their hopes, blight their lives, protract their bitter pilgrimage, make heavy their steps, water their way with their tears, stain the white snow with the blood of their wounded feet! We ask it, in the spirit of love, of Him Who is the Source of Love, and Who is the ever-faithful refuge and friend of all that are sore beset and seek His aid with humble and contrite hearts. Amen."
The War Prayer by Mark Twain

The Protagonists—The Blue

Elisha Hunt Rhodes came a little late to the Civil War, but not by much. He enlisted, with his widowed mother's permission, underscored by his persistence in wanting to join the fray, on June 5, 1861. And he stayed to the end; he was discharged at the age of 23 as a seasoned veteran and as an officer on July 28, 1865. He was in uniform a bit more than four years. And he survived both Gettysburg and the remainder of the war. Many, of course, did not.

The following notes of his experiences of the war come from his diary of events that he observed and penned during the battle of Gettysburg:

Gettysburg - July 3rd 1863—"Our brigade marched down the road until we reached the house used by General Meade as headquarters. The road ran between ledges of rocks while the fields were strewn with boulders. To our left was a hill on which we had many batteries posted. Just as we reached General Meade's headquarters, a shell burst over our heads, and it was immediately followed by showers of iron. More than two hundred guns were belching forth their thunder, and most of the shells that came over the hill struck in the road on which our brigade was moving. Solid shot would strike the large rocks and split them as if exploded by gunpowder. The flying iron and pieces of stone struck men down in every direction. It is said that this fire continued for about two hours, but I have no idea of the time. We could not see the enemy, and we could only cover ourselves the best we could behind the rocks and trees. About 30 men of our brigade were killed or wounded by this fire."

And much later, toward the end of his encounter with this war of his generation, he writes:

July 28th 1865 –"...Today the 2nd R.I. Was paid off and discharged. The regiment met at 9 A.M. ...where they received their money and final discharge papers. ...I went home, took off my uniform and put on a citizen's clothes for the first time in over four years."
From the diary of Elisha Hunt Rodes, Private in Co. D, 2nd R. I. Volunteers.

An Immigrant's Tale

Simon Lauer immigrated to the United States from Wurtemberg {present-day southwest Germany}, in 1857. Just four years later, in October 1861, Simon, like scores of other immigrants found himself serving in the Union Army, in his case with the Maryland Volunteers. During a June 1863 battle, Simon was taken prisoner and held in Richmond, Va. for several months, until September of that year. Upon release, he was immediately hospitalized at the Regimental Hospital at Washington, D.C., for chills, fever, rheumatism and impaired hearing and sight.

By June 1864, however, Simon was back with his regiment and participated in the siege of Petersburg, Virginia. He left the army in October 1864. But duty soon called, and Simon reenlisted in February 1865.

On September 13, 1876, more than 10 years after his Civil War service ended, Simon Lauer was finally granted U.S. citizenship.

Author's Note: Patriotism – A prevailing motivation for Federal troops was, like that of their Southern counterparts, the idea/spirit of patriotism. Letters and diary accounts drawn from Union troops speak glowingly of the honor bestowed upon them in their pledge to defend the Union in the name of the nation's founding principles. Moreover, they, like Confederate troops frequently compared the present conflict in terms of the nation's earlier struggles.

One officer from the 101st Ohio correlated his current plight as an extension of that era, specifically, of those earlier soldiers, the patriots of 1776, in the following letter: "Our fathers in coldest winter, half clad marked the road they trod with crimson streams from their bleeding feet that we might enjoy the blessings of a free government." He continued by noting that, "our business in being here [is] to lay down our lives if need be for our country's cause." Unfortunately, he was killed two weeks later at the Battle of Stones River after penning this letter.

Many Union soldiers shared these sentiments, while others, often extended the depth of commitment that they undertook, or were determined to maintain in the name of patriotism; in some cases, they saw the present conflict as being of an even higher order than the causes/motives in favor of the original American Revolution. One Ohio lieutenant, writing in this vain, spoke of the higher responsibility that faced them relative to his predecessors in the following letter:

"Our fathers made this country, we, their children are to save it… and you should …experience a laudable pride in the part your {husband and brothers} are now taking to suppress the greatest rebellion the history of the world has ever witnessed… Why denounce the war when the interest at stake is so vital? … Union & peace our freedom is worthless… our children would have no warrant of liberty…[If] our Country be numbered among the things that were but are not, of what value will be house, family, and friends?"

Another Call to Arms

Among the many Irish-Americans that fought, another call, in this case to a distant patriotism, was frequently sounded. Among these men, many of whom fought on both sides, the parallels of the American Civil War to their age-old struggle against England were frequently drawn. To these patriots, the struggle for liberty here in America was a reenactment of past and continuing conflicts.

One private in the 28th Massachusetts of the famed Irish Brigade wrote in 1863, "This is the first test of a modern free government in the act of sustaining itself against internal enemies…if it fail then the hopes of millions fail and the designs and wishes of all tyrants will succeed… the old cry will be sent forth from the aristocrats of Europe that such is the common lot of all republics…Irishmen and their descendants have a stake in {this} nation…America is Ireland's refuge, Ireland's last hope… destroy this republic and her hopes are blasted."

Defending Home and Hearth

Among the many Irish-Americans that fought, another call, in this case to a distant patriotism, was frequently sounded. Among these men, many of whom fought on both sides, the parallels of the American Civil War to their age-old struggle against England were frequently drawn. To these patriots, the struggle for liberty here in America was a reenactment of past and continuing conflicts.

One private in the 28th Massachusetts of the famed Irish Brigade wrote in 1863, "This is the first test of a modern free government in the act of sustaining itself against internal enemies…if it fail then the hopes of millions fail and the designs and wishes of all tyrants will succeed… the old cry will be sent forth from the aristocrats of Europe that such is the common lot of all republics…Irishmen and their dependents have a stake in {this} nation…America is Ireland's refuge Ireland's last hope… destroy this republic and her hopes are blasted."

Defending the Flag - The 16th Maine

It was on the morning of July 1, 1863, the first day of the battle, when two divisions of the 1st Corps, Army of the Potomac arrived to enter a fight that had been raging all morning. {They joined the fray as Confederate forces were advancing on Gettysburg from the west and from the north.} Among them was the 16th Maine. The 16th regiment, along with the rest of the army, had been marching since June 12 from Virginia and Maryland toward southern Pennsylvania.

On July 1st, the 16th Maine fought bitterly for approximately three hours in the fields north of the Chambersburg Pike; but by mid-afternoon, it was evident that, even with the arrival of the rest of the 1st Corps and the entire 11th Corps, the position of the Union forces was untenable and could not be held. Correspondingly, they began to fall back toward the town of Gettysburg.

The 16th Maine was subsequently ordered to withdraw to a new position to the east of their previous battle station. However, they had been placed under precarious circumstances. "Take that position and hold it at any cost!" was the command. This meant that the remainder of the regiment [275 officers and men of the regiment among those who had not already fallen as casualties] was being asked to sacrifice themselves to allow some 16,000 other men to retreat. While an unlikely request, it was not an unusual one during the course of this war.

The 16th valiantly held their position, but they were soon overwhelmed and forced to surrender to the Confederates. While these men fought bravely, their attention shifted during the battle to the task of saving their beloved flags, especially when they realized that defeat was inevitable. {Flags marked the location of units on the battlefields amid the smoke and noise. To capture the enemy's flag was considered a great accomplishment, to lose one, a great shame.} As the Southern troops bore down upon them, the men of the 16th Maine spontaneously began to tear up their "colors" into little pieces.

Like other Union regiments, the 16th Maine carried an American flag and a regimental flag, known collectively as "the colors." "For a few last moments our little regiment defended angrily its hopeless challenge, but it was useless to fight longer," wrote Abner Small of the 16th Maine after the battle. "We looked at our colors, and our faces burned. We must not surrender those symbols of our pride and our faith." The regiment's color bearers "appealed to the colonel," Small continued, "and with his consent they tore the flags from their staves and ripped the silk into shreds; and our officers and men that were near took each a shred." Each man hid his fragment of the flags inside his shirt or in a pocket. The Confederates were thus deprived of the chance to capture the flags as battle trophies.

Their action demonstrated, as was noted many years after, that battle flags carried "very, very deep symbolism for Civil War soldiers", representing the "esprit de corps" of a regiment and "a larger entity - the country, the cause." Most of the 16th Maine survivors treasured the rescued remnants of their struggle for the rest of their lives, later bequeathing them to their descendants.

By sunset on July 1, 1863, eleven officers and men of the 16th Maine had been killed, 62 had been wounded, and 159 had been taken prisoner. Only 38 men of the Regiment managed to evade being captured and report for duty at 1st Corps headquarters. But the 16th Maine had bought precious time for the Union Army. Their comrades in arms, those whose retreat they had covered, were able to establish a very strong position just east and south of the center of the town of Gettysburg along Cemetery Ridge. During the night and into July 2nd, the 1st and 11th Corps were reinforced as other units of the Army of the Potomac arrived on the battlefield. For the next two days they would withstand successive assaults by the Confederates until the final repulse of Pickett's Charge, on July 3rd.

For these and other related feats of heroic behavior the Congressional Medal of Honor was created. It grew out of the need to recognize the valor exhibited by Union soldiers in the Civil War; and nowhere were actions of bravery and courage in the war better recognized than at the Battle of Gettysburg. In all, 63 medals were awarded to soldiers for their actions on the battlefields of southern Pennsylvania during that summer of 1863.

Mississippi played a pivotal, geographically strategic role in the Western theatre of the War. In addition, like many other states, its soldiers fought on multiple battlefields.

As the second state to secede from the Union, Mississippi's secession resolution, like those of the other southern states, clearly stated that its defense of slavery was its reason for leaving the Union. With a population of 791,000 people, Mississippi's slaves outnumbered whites 437,000 to 354,000. Maintaining the institution of slavery, disregarding its immorality as a human condition, therefore, seemed to be of absolute economic necessity for the state's agriculture-based economy.

White soldiers from Mississippi, most often reflected the state's position on slavery, but they fought for a variety of other reasons, as well. Some joined the military to defend home and hearth, while others saw the conflict in broader sectional terms. Formal declarations or other justifications withstanding, the soldiers' motivation, above all, was generally more personal than it was ideological.

One Soldier's Journey

Some soldiers took a rather circuitous route to battle; for them war was both an adventure and a quest. One of these men was John West, a resident of several Southern communities.

Gettysburg, July 1863: "I saw a great many wounded… who were mangled and bruised in every possible way, some with their eyes shot out,

some with their arms, or hands, or fingers, or feet or legs shot off, and all seeming to suffer a great deal".
Private John C. West, Company E, 4th Texas Infantry, and survivor of Gettysburg.

John C. West saw the war from a variety of perspectives. Although assigned to the Texas Infantry, he was born and educated in South Carolina. As an educated man and as a lawyer, he found his "fighting career" interrupted several times, including service he was called upon to perform as the district attorney for the Western District of Texas. This occurred on two occasions. However, he was determined to "see a fight" and "remain in the ranks, if necessary, until the close of the war". So in the early spring of 1863, he left his wife and two small children in Waco, Texas and set off to pursue his destiny. He had just turned twenty-nine years of age and was somewhat enamored, as were many, with the idea of war, recalling with fondness, one contemporary call to arms, in which Southern proponents observed, "We can't be whipped, but we may all be killed."

ANOTHER SOLDIER'S CALL TO ACTION

"I belong to the Charlotte Grays, Company C, First North Carolina Regiment. We left home for Raleigh. Our company is commanded by Capt. Egbert Ross. We are all boys between the ages of eighteen and twenty-one. We offered our services to Governor Ellis, but were afraid he would not take us, as we are so young; but before we were called out our company was ordered to go to the United States Mint in our town and take same. We marched down to it, and it was surrendered to us. We guarded it several days, when we were ordered to Raleigh, and left on the above date.

Our trip was full of joy and pleasure, for at every station where our train stopped the ladies showered us with flowers and Godspeed. We marched to the Fair Grounds. The streets were lined with people, cheering us. When we got there our company was given quarters, and, lo and behold! Horse stables with straw for bedding is what we got. I know we all thought it a disgrace for us to sleep in such places with our fine uniforms - not even a washstand, or any place to hang our clothes on. They didn't even give us a looking-glass." Louis Leon *Diary of a Tar Heel Confederate Soldier*

The average Confederate soldier was a young man who enlisted for the duration of the war. He was in his early 20s, unshaven, unkempt, gaunt, but tough from months of difficult living. The Rebel soldier's woolen hat and uniform was gray, ragged from either having been worn too long, or having been "handed down" from a dead soldier. It was not uncommon for the uniforms to be ill-fitting, with sleeves either too short or too long, and to have buttons missing. Uniforms, over the course of the war deteriorated, or were "replaced" by scavenging among fallen comrades or being salvaged from the dead (on both sides). In addition to this uncomfortable outfit, the soldier wore a white shirt. Those lucky enough to have a reasonably good-fitting pair of shoes would often nail horseshoes to them to prevent the soles from wearing down. While the confederate soldier's appearance was often shabby, it was his spirit that led him into battle.

The Rebel soldier carried a variety of muskets and rifles during the course of the war. As the war went on, more and more Rebels carried Enfield rifles that they had taken from dead Union soldiers. Once a Confederate had acquired such a rifle, he would wear its bayonet in a scabbard attached to the right side of his belt.

He kept his ammunition in a cartridge box also attached to the right of his belt. In addition, he carried a small rolled-up blanket, a haversack, a cloth-covered canteen, a tin cup, and a small frying pan.

As the war progressed the circumstances surrounding the welfare of the typical soldier grew more dire. He often lacked the basic necessities to carry on. Not only did the soldiers run out of ammunition, but often having not eaten meat in weeks, many fell ill from fatigue; starvation was common and living off the land was a widespread practice. Confederate soldiers were also poorly funded, and would sometimes have to wait months before being compensated for their service, usually impoverishing their families, who were left behind and waiting for support; some soldier's families would often go months without adequate nutrition. While not limited to either side, the desertion of many soldiers, many in response to family needs, and especially toward the end of the war, was common.

Both Northern and Southern soldiers suffered the harsh conditions of the war. Most tellingly, they suffered the harsh consequences of its direct assault on their lives and those of their families, as well as later, in the aftermath of the War. This was especially true, though not limited to

Southern families, both black and white, who lived most directly within and among the ruins of the war's devastation.

CHAPTER 4

The Rescue Plan

The rescue plan was imperfect. And John, based on his varied experiences as a spy, knew that to be the case as he examined conditions favoring its enactment and those arguing against its implementation. His advisors and allies in the scheme, both pro and con, and irrespective of position, nevertheless, each argued for prudence and caution.

As he was aware, it was a calculated gamble, one likely to tether precariously between success and failure at every juncture. It called for John to aid in his own capture in order to rescue a woman and her two sons, and then to escape successfully with them; it was, he thought, an outrageous scheme. But, he noted, that with an element of luck, coupled with careful execution, while clearly amidst uncertainty, it might just succeed. It was a plan based on the element of surprise and perhaps, for this reason foremost, it would succeed.

Planning would be essential to success. John recognized the implicit danger he would be placing himself in through this rescue mission. Mungo Monroe's capture and use of him, in order to obtain John's knowledge of Union operations, including his coordination of the listening posts, was problematic, but likely. Extracted information was a valuable product, one that would appeal to Mungo's sense of moral superiority, and reward him financially, as well. Moreover, his information was readily available. It could be attained easily under torture or the threat of its use. Most people, serving under the precarious whims of slavery, knew that resistance to compliance in the face of such conditions is often futile. And John knew the fortunes of slavery well.

After he was compelled to reveal details of northern military operations, which would only be a matter of time, there would be few constraints placed on Mungo from selling John to another trader who would send him further south into the most dreaded forms of slavery and into a short but often more than not, a certain, and deadly future. Few blacks escaped from the effects of such servitude.

"The Americans may boast of the rights of man, the great law of nature, as being the basis of their constitution; they may declaim against tyranny and oppression; yet every man who becomes a slave-holder in Missouri is a tyrant of their creation …The effects of slavery are truly appalling. Where slavery exists, virtue and morality are swept away as with a flood of corruption."
Issac Holmes (1823) – an account of the United States of America, derived from actual observation, during a residence of four years in the republic.

Mary Prince Tells Her Story

At its draconian worst, the cruelty and indifference of life lived under the yoke of slavery often proved to be a fate worse than death. The story of Mary Prince, a female slave, among countless others, dramatically illustrated this terrible inhumanity. In her own words, she describes her ten-year ordeal working the salt fields of Bermuda under slavery as follows:

"I was given a half barrel and a shovel, and had to stand up to my knees in the water from four o'clock in the morning until nine, when we were given some Indian corn boiled in water…We were then called again to our tasks and worked through the heat of the day; the sun flaming upon our heads like fire, and raising salt blisters in those parts that were not completely covered. Our feet and legs, from standing in the water for so many hours, soon became full of dreadful boils, which eat down in some cases to the very bone, afflicting the sufferers with great torment. We came home at twelve; ate our corn soup, called blawly, as fast as we could, and went back to employment till dark at night. We then shoveled up the salt in large heaps and went down to the sea where we washed the pickle from our limbs, and cleaned the barrows and shovels from the salt."
Mary Prince, 1831. *The history of Mary Prince, a West Indian slave. Written by herself*

John could not risk being caught without a means of escape or a deterrent from that fate. Timing would be critical in this mission, second only to preparation. And the latter would require some specialized assistance from others.

John reasoned that his task in completing a successful rescue would involve him completing a series of small, well directed, and carefully coordinated acts performed over a limited time period. And they would involve some small easily concealed weapons and deceptions. First, there was the issue of how to escape from the rope or chain bindings that he was surely likely to encounter. Mungo, after a number of failed attempts to capture John would not be inclined to treat him carelessly; he would be bound or imprisoned in some fashion and watched closely. And he would be severely punished if his attempt at escape failed.

In order to obtain a release from the constraints of rope binding, a likely means of confinement, John would conceal a small sharp file in his shoe. Sean had suggested, using an awl, that John dig a small opening in the heel of his right boot to hide a file that he may recover when it would be needed. Acting on this suggestion, John placed a thin, specially sharpened, fine-honed file in the small enclosure he had carved in his boot and applied black polish to conceal the opening. Then he looked for another means of escape.

If he were placed in chains, another possible event, depending upon Mungo's disposition and available resources, he would be put in a different, but equally difficult position. However, Patrick recommended that he help him secure a skeleton key or facsimile of a passkey from a locksmith that, he hoped, when properly modified, would suffice a release if he were placed in the standard assortment of padlocks in use at the time. The manufacture of locks at this stage of the war was of low order priority. Moreover, quality of product over the years had deteriorated as the interest in the production of such devices waned. It was also likely, they reasoned, that his iron binding would be of a primitive order, and dated, as well; any employed padlock would be older in origin and predate that of his key, affecting a favorable release, by the availability of such a device, from his bindings. It was a workable plan.

Both Patrick and John were also aware that any "defensive weapons" more sophisticated or apparent to the naked eye that he was likely to carry upon his person would be unlikely to pass close inspection by John's captors. His guards, under Mungo's direction, would be forewarned to be on the lookout for any deception and trickery. Hence, an additional layer of disguise was suggested.

His clothing, properly modified, as proposed by Aunt Amy, could also serve a special purpose. A further rouse, in the altering of the sizing of clothing John would be wearing could be employed in order to further disguise his appearance and the "escape" tools John would be carrying on his person. John's clothing would be refitted to reflect a few sizes too big, especially in select parts, such as his sleeves and leggings; this would allow further concealment of any additional objects he sought to hide. The small passkey that they had crafted, Patrick suggested, could be hidden in the binding of John's hat, held secure by some simple stitches Aunt Amy would sew in the crown.

The two devices John envisioned were in the realm of defensive weapons. They would be necessary to enable his release when the time for action occurred. But they were, according to his reckoning, insufficient. He now focused his attention on an offensive weapon, particularly one that would facilitate his escape with Mae and the boys. For this he would need the scientific knowledge and assistance of Dr. James Wilson.

Later that night, hopeful of obtaining some directions on this element of his plan, he approached Dr. Wilson who was in his study reading some papers by candlelight.

"Yes," John?

Good evening, sir".

"How are your plans coming along?" Dr. Wilson inquired.

"Well, I have been thinking of our means of escape," said John.

"I would like to insure this facet of the mission by carrying some small, concealed weapons into the slave compound that I could use during the escape itself. One idea that I would like to explore with you is the use of gunpowder to serve as a distraction, just prior to the escape. I have been thinking of a device that would take the form of a smoke bomb to conceal our activities."

"What type of devices have you been investigating? asked Dr. Wilson.

"I have been in contact with an artillery officer on General Hancock's staff, who has given me a simple formula for creating such a weapon."

"I have been told that such a device can be assembled using 75 percent saltpeter 15 percent carbon and 10 percent sulfur, easily obtainable materials. If I could sneak these chemicals into the camp, and assemble them later I can make a bomb to assist our escape."

"Well, that's true", noted Dr. Wilson, exhibiting a slightly hesitant, barely concealed expression of skepticism.

"John, I believe that I understand your reasoning, but what you propose is a highly risky venture", he added.

"The formula is sound, but, impractical. And, under the circumstances, dangerous, I might add."

"However, let us check on its feasibility and modify your approach, as needed, before we make a final decision," said Dr. Wilson.

A Change of Plans

The next day Dr. Wilson and John Scobell, went into town in purchase saltpeter and gather the other necessary ingredients for the smoke bombs. However, when he inquired of the pharmacist, in order to make his purchase he found that the anticipated store of ingredients that he requested had been depleted from his stock; the sulfur necessary to complete the project was gone. The normally ready supply that his pharmacy had stocked had been requisitioned by the army quartermasters corps for medical reasons. Apparently, new procedures were being implemented to employ the chemical; sulfur, a well-known curative, normally used in the treatment of skin disorders, was now being employed on a new experimental basis for treatment among burn victims. A modification creating the smoke bombs would be called for if John was to implement his plan.

Modification of the Plan

Upon learning of the unavailability of ingredients necessary to construct the smoke bombs, Dr. Wilson told John not to be discouraged. He suggested that there were other options available to them, which upon his recollection, might actually be of greater use in implementation. Consequently, the two returned to the residence to rethink the escape plan.

"I believe that there is another formula that we can use for your smoke bomb, said Dr. Wilson.

"And I would like to add one other suggestion to your agenda", he continued.

"I think that you will need some assistance in the final phase of your mission, someone who can secure proper transportation for Mae, the boys and yourself, from the site of your imprisonment. Have you thought about that phase of the project?" he queried.

"Yes", said John. "If he is willing, I would like to ask Jed Harper to accompany me. As a light-skinned black man, he has been able to move freely among whites (often passing for one) without raising suspicion. If he can keep track of my transfer, and the location of my imprisonment then he can discretely arrange for a wagon and some horses to be available for our escape at the proper time, and we should be able to complete the mission."

"He can also bring a supply of smoke bombs with him for your use, as well," said the doctor, "which", he continued, "would lessen your risk of detection."

"Moreover, there may be an easier formula that will serve your purpose, one less dangerous and equally potent. The formula I am thinking of is both less volatile and equally potent. And, it can produce an effective smoke bomb, as a screen, which will allow you a means of creating a distraction, a safe diversion, and disguising your escape more easily", he added.

"It consists of mixing together 30 parts potassium nitrate, 20 parts brown sugar and 5 parts liquid fuel (honey). The honey is not essential but makes a much better smoke mix.

"This method creates optimal thrust and is quite effective for your purpose. And it is easily manufactured. With this formula as a base, we will apply heat to the gathered ingredients. In the process of heating our material, using a saucepan, the sugar will be caramelized, and the quality of the bomb will also increase. In addition, we can control the rate at which the sugar caramelizes by controlling the heating of the pan, and by stirring the mixture as it heats up. If we place the saucepan over a low heat and stir it constantly, all the liquid will be drawn out and leave us with a light to mid-yellow paste.

"The paste then can be shaped into a mold and sized or be allowed to set beforehand, on its own accord. The drier, the better! It is as easy as that. There are no hard rules to follow, no complex formulas to apply or extensive instructions to abide by. The process can also be completed from start to finish in well under an hour either indoors or outside.

"I can supply you with some potassium nitrate from my lab and some dark brown sugar from the kitchen. How much you need is based on how many smoke bombs we want to make.

"I imagine that several, less than a dozen perhaps eight or ten, of sufficient size will do," he continued.

"Then I suggest that we build a sample 'bomb' and test it," added Dr. Wilson.

"By that means we can determine the size and carefully determine the number of 'bombs' that might be employed. If Jed Harper tracks you, he can carry the smoke bombs with him, freeing you from any likelihood of detection in having to conceal and carry them on your person."

But how would I get Jed and the 'bombs' into the slave compound?" asked John.

"Well, from what you have told me of your exploits together, I would imagine that Jed could pose as a buyer or seller of slaves. With sufficient funds he could enter and leave the compound under that guise. And, I'm sure that this Monroe character, from what you have told me, would be interested in selling from his "stock" of human freight. Or, we might provide him an opportunity of buying a slave, for that matter," said the doctor.

"If the price is right," John added, acknowledging Mungo's greed.

"And, Jed should also be able to bring a few small guns into the compound, as well as an accomplice, which may be needed," said the doctor.

John paused in order to assimilate the doctor's suggestions. Clearly, they had appeal to him. And they were also simple, as well as applicable, he thought, if scheduled carefully, within a timely framework.

With some guarded reservation and a bit of skepticism, John turned to Dr. Wilson and said,

"As you are aware, I will need to operate with speedy dispatch, putting this escape plan in action quickly. Probably, within a week of my capture, and no longer," John concluded.

"Anything beyond a week will shift the balance of control of this mission from us to them," he added.

"And at that point anything could happen, and doom it to failure."

A Discussion With Jed Harper

Within several days, initial preparations had been made to implement the plan. The blade and boot had been prepared and a special key crafted by a trusted locksmith was made. Aunt Amy had secured a set of clothes in his size and had modified them, incorporating several secret compartments within his garments, each according to John's specifications. At this point, John needed to speak with Jed Harper. Fortuitously, as he was in the midst of completing an assignment for Mr. Still, Jed was in Philadelphia at the time and arrangements were made for a meeting between the two friends.

The next day, John met with Jed Harper at a site arranged by Mr. Still. As he approached Jed, John was struck once more by the appearance of his light, fair skinned friend. Jed, was a mulatto, removed several generations from the seed of his origins. His appearance offered few slave-bearing signs. Yet, as a subject of the prejudices of two worlds, Jed was neither sufficiently black to be accepted by the black community completely, nor was he "pure" of blood in terms of the narrow definition offered by whites to be welcomed within and allowed access to the privileges of the white world. His mother was a "fancy girl", one of the light skinned slave women favored by rich white men, who sort companionship from this special class of black women displaying desirable physical attributes, with exotic overtones. Jed understood the malice of slavery in both worlds, although he was now a free black man.

Jed had assisted John on earlier missions under the guise of a white man. By adopting the posture of a slave trader he and John had been able to infiltrate the black and white communities and gather useful military information. They were among the many black and white people engaged in deceptive practices designed to aid fugitive slaves and foil their pursuers.

John explained the central components of the plan as Jed listened intently. Because the pair had worked together previously, Jed raised fewer questions than he would have with a companion whom he had little previous contact. However, he did inquire about the smoke bombs and requested that he and John test their use. Jed was particularly concerned about their effectiveness in providing for a shield of concealment during their escape. John, understanding Jed's concern in the matter, agreed that he should help with the construction and test of the "bombs".

Furthermore, Jed asked about weapons, both on entering the slave compound and in the rescue attempt. The former task would call for small arms while the latter would best be served with higher caliber firepower. These would have to be obtained from the army. The combination of arms to be employed was as follows:

For entrance to the compound, Jed suggested that they obtain small arms such as the colt derringer, which could be easily hidden on his person or in his clothing in the event that he were searched. Concealment of the weapon would be its main advantage in the immediate escape from imprisonment.

Colt Derringer

In contrast, to support their escape from the compound and for their journey home he recommended the use of the Spencer rifle, a short repeating rifle capable of rapid fire, without the delay of successive reloading. The benefit of the new Spencer rifle over the more traditional rifle would be in holding at bay a massive assault by several attackers at once. As John forecast, Mungo would be sure to mount an attempt at recapture of "his slaves" if they managed to escape the compound.

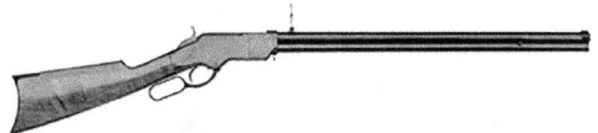

Spencer Repeating Rifle

One last element in the plan was requested by Jed, "I think that we may still need additional assistance. I would like to add another person to act as a lookout, and to ward off any dangers to our back."

"Do you have someone in mind?" asked John.

"Not at the moment", responded Jed. "However, I have heard you speak respectfully of Big Jake and wondered if he would be available to offer assistance. I understand that he is currently at home with his family in Lancaster. Do you think that he would help?"

"Well, I don't rightly know," said John. "However, he would be the right man for the job. And, I believe that he would help, if requested," he added.

"But we will have to journey to Lancaster to ask him directly", said John.

ANOTHER MEETING WITH GENERAL LEE

Meanwhile, in another place far from Philadelphia, the spy Harrison was meeting with General Lee to report on his recent activities within Pennsylvania. Harrison had news of John's plans, as obtained from Mungo, through his hold over Dr. Wilson's butler Job Hunter, husband of Mae and father to her children. Henry Harrison was anxious to report on the latest developments to General Lee, recognizing that his information would be, if he judged correctly, of significance to the general. As he approaches the general, he greets him with the following information,

"Sir, I met with Mr. Munroe and have arranged for his cooperation in the capture of the spy Scobell. Apparently, according to his source within a prominent Yankee household, the spy Scobell will be attempting a rescue mission of some blacks being held in custody by Mr. Monroe. Monroe thinks that he will have an excellent opportunity, if that activity comes to pass, to retrieve Scobell outside of Lancaster. However, he is not at liberty to share details at the moment."

"Well, that is welcome news. Any knowledge of the enemy's troop movement at this time could prove advantageous to us as we move north," asserted Lee.

"Yes Sir," Harrison responded.

"Mr. Monroe has been made aware of your interest in the spy Scobell", Harrison adds.

"I am assuming," continued the general, " that you have been in contact with General Longstreet on these developments. As we advance further north, you will keep him informed."

"Yes Sir," acknowledged Harrison.

"Before we end this discussion, however, I also want to impart to you one more piece of instruction, in the form of a caution, Mr. Harrison. Please instruct Mr. Munroe that no harm must come to Mr. Scobell. He is far too valuable a source of information to us, at this point, to allow him to be placed in harm's way," added the general.

CHAPTER 5

THE KILLING FIELDS

"We killed each other in bunches.
And, after that, nothing else really mattered at all."
Anonymous Soldier

April 20, 1861

"This war is not going to be the ninety days affair that papers and politicians are predicting. ...Both sides are in deadly earnest, and it is going to be fought out to the bitter end...For your cause there can be but one result. It must be lost. Your whole population is about eight millions, while the North has twenty millions. Of your eight millions, three millions are slaves who may become an element of danger. You have no army, no navy, no treasury and practically none of the manufactures and machine shops necessary for the support of armies, and for war on a large scale. You are but scattered agricultural communities, and you will be cut off from the rest of the world by blockade. Your cause is foredoomed to failure."

Letter written by West Point graduate Lieutenant James B. McPherson of Ohio (class of 1853) to his young friend, West Point graduate E. Porter Alexander of Georgia (class of 1857). Alexander, later became one of the chief artillerists in the Army of Northern Virginia.

Lieutenant McPherson, was promoted numerous times in the course of a brilliant, but short-lived career, created primarily in the Western theater. In a meteoric ascent through the officer ranks, he attained the rank of Major General in the Union army and was placed in command of the Army of the Tennessee while still a young man.

Unfortunately, however, General McPherson was killed in July of 1864 at the age of thirty-five outside of the city of Atlanta while serving under Major General William Tecumseh Sherman. General McPherson was shot and killed by enemy soldiers under the command of Confederate General John Bell Hood of Texas. Earlier, and before the war, at what might appear to have been some distant time, General Hood was a West Point classmate of General McPherson.

The Gathered Armies

"Well, it is five weeks ago night before last, since we left the South side of the Rappahannock [River] and we have marched some two hundred and eighty miles, besides what other work we have done since then. The first four days of the march I was quite sick all the time, and how the devil I got along is more than I can tell, but I managed to be up with the Regiment every night. After we got to Fairfax Court House, and got a chance to rest for a few days, I got quite smart again, and have been very well for the rest of the time."
Henry B. Parsons, 10th Massachusetts Infantry, July 13, 1863

❖ ❖

"We received orders to be ready to march at 7 O'clock. Soon we were in marching order and left for the scene of action. Passing through Cashtown and marching one hour we came in sight of Gettysburg, Here we rested in an old field until 2 0'clock, at which time we left to attack the enemy. After passing through a very heavy shelling for 20 minutes we rested and then formed a line of battle…"
Thomas Ware, 15th Georgia Infantry, July 2nd, 1863

They came from all directions. And they came at different times, some came early, some came late, some came and rested; most of those who came were exhausted from vigorous marches to this small, largely unknown agricultural community. Some had been there from the start, at the beginning of hostilities, others were new comers to the War. Some wanted it to end here, some wanted to continue until the very end, whenever that may be. And they all came, this enormous multitude of men and their horses and machines of war that came to Gettysburg; almost 170,000 of them eventually came, (approximately 93,000 soldiers from the Union and approximately 73,000 soldiers from the Confederacy), more than ever before assembled for one purpose, to fight. And, above all, they came to kill one another.

It was, in some ways, a war like all wars, fought in support of contrasting ideologies, as well as contrasting perspectives that could not be resolved at the bargaining table. But there was more to distinguish this conflict from most others; it was a war, on all fronts, fought within a family of known combatants. These included, especially in the border states of Maryland, Delaware, and Missouri, where conflicting loyalties within each state played a crucial role in the choice of national affiliation, brother against brother, friend against friend, and neighbor against neighbor.

❖ ❖

Mathew Wilson, correspondent, special to the *New York Times*

"The fighting around Culp's Hill (on Meade's right line) was fiercely lethal, as observed yesterday, on the third day of the Battle of Gettysburg. The 1st Maryland battalion of General Steuart's Confederate brigade attacked the 1st Maryland Eastern Shore Infantry of General Lockwood's Union brigade. Soldiers from each brigade had been recruited in the same section of Maryland; each had relatives and friends, or perhaps, former friends, in the other; cousins served in opposing color guards. The battle was decisive. Colonel James Wallace of the Union's Eastern Shore.

In his report he wrote that, "The 1st Maryland Confederate Regiment met us & were cut to pieces." He added that, "we sorrowfully gathered up many of our old friends & acquaintances & had them carefully & tenderly cared for."

As Steuart's men were forced to retreat to a more secure position, the distressed Steuart was heard to bemoan. "My poor boys! My poor boys!". Those soldiers caught between the lines had to surrender."
July 3, 1863, Gettysburg, PA

A Discovery of Kinship

Combatants with kinship ties, but differing loyalties, were there. These affiliations were known, but others, were occasionally discovered in the midst of conflict; and unforeseen circumstances often intervened on both sides. As the following incident illustrates, "strangers" with conflicting ideologies, but close personal ties, often met by chance.
July 1863

Oscar Reid was a Sergeant in Company A of the 6th Virginia Confederate Calvary. In a battle with the Union cavalry just outside the small town of Fairfield, Pa., a few miles from Gettysburg, he was wounded and captured by federal forces.

The circumstances of his engagement were a bit unusual. During a skirmish at a farmhouse between Union and Confederate lines, bullets flew in all directions. As the Union gained the upper hand, the Confederates fled, leaving behind their wounded, including Sergeant Reid. Through the course of circumstances surrounding the battle, Union officers decided to make use of the farmhouse-battleground as a field hospital, in which they could attend to their wounded Union troops and to those of the enemy Confederate soldiers, as well.

The family of the farmhouse's owner, in spite of conflicting loyalties, graciously cared for both groups of wounded soldiers. In the course of ministering aid they asked the sergeant his name. When he replied "Oscar Reid", they were taken by surprise, since they shared a common surname. Further inquiry revealed that they were, in fact, cousins from different regions of the country; yet, they had never met before this encounter.

Sergeant Reid, was cared for by his cousins, and then taken to a prisoner of war camp. Nevertheless, he was not abandoned by them. His newfound relations in Fairfield, PA. continued to express their concern for his well-being and for his welfare; after his departure they sent him clothing and other personal items to help ease his adjustment to prison life.

A Domestic Conflict

This was a war that was fought on home soil, within the confines of family and farm. Family members, as well as soldiers on the battlefields were, as letters to and from soldiers testify, frequent victims of the hostilities, physically, and most often economically and spirituality. These conditions, intentional or accidental, often added additional burden to the soldier's plight. The surviving soldiers, of course, returned to their homes at the end of hostilities. However, and especially in the South, they often returned home to vast devastation, previously unknown and largely unimagined.

Many people carried weapons for the first time. Others, came to war well-prepared, bringing their own weapons and occasionally, among the Calvary troopers, their own horses. These latter soldiers, especially in the South, were experienced hunters and trackers. Many, particularly in the North, during the initial phases of the war, were not. Most people believed in, what was a common idea at the time, a romantic illusion of war, with visions of bravery, gallantry and glory; they embraced the notion of war as affording its participants opportunities for fame and celebrity. Others, in a similar vane, thought that the war would be fought quickly, in heroic manifestations of manhood, and then settled decisively. The concept of a protracted conflict, that would change in intensity and form over time, was unforeseen by most, both combatant and civilian. Clearly, these were special people, called at this time, to decide their nation's fate and its future. But, who were they? Why were they there? How did they link their fortunes with the aims of the North and the South?

Many people took part in this war, above all, the soldiers, whom by count, numbered in the hundreds of thousands, (eventually several million in the North), on both sides. And they were changed inexorably over the course of their service, returning after four weary years, many from the beginning, as different men, both physically and spiritually, from when they first left for war. And they returned to a different country, as well.

Revolutionary and Civil War Combatants

Soldiers, in response to conflict, and period, will embrace different ideals, and often display contrasting characteristics of commitment and merit. During the Revolutionary War, it was observed, most pointedly declared by Washington himself, that the "quality" of soldier enlisted to fight in the War was less than ideal, and even deteriorated over time. As he reported to Congress in 1778, many of his men were initially of "the middling sort", and later, as the war dragged on, those that signed up, in most cases, did so because they had no brighter prospects. Washington, the realist, held few romantic illusions about his army.

The soldiers that fought during the Civil War, in contrast, were somewhat different. Most were literate, both in the Northern and Southern armies; more than 70 percent of Confederate soldiers and more than 90 percent of Union soldiers could read and write. Most of them were also volunteers, whose motives for involvement were often complex, consisting in part ideology, part patriotism, part romanticism, part obligation and part community via friendships and kinship to those of whom they fought along side.

Most were also highly sensitized to political issues and events. The median age of men at the time of their enlistment was twenty-four, which meant that many had voted in the critical 1860 election. Moreover, they continued to vote, for regimental officers, and in state contests, and even in national elections. (The participation of Northern soldiers in the 1864 elections proved critical to Lincoln's reelection.)

Complementing their high literacy rate, these soldiers were more informed and politically aware of their times and events than soldiers in most armies and in previous eras. Americans, at the time of the war, were the world's most prominent newspaper readers. Soldiers of all ranks continued their pursuit of news and avidly sought information from all available sources, especially newspapers. Moreover, on the Eastern front (where the course of the War was most avidly followed, as well as reported) there were many reporters covering the major events of the day, mainly the war, and many newspapers that printed the news from the front. War was a staple in the lives of an intelligent and learned readership, combatant and civilian, alike.

But it was the war that drew their attention foremost, and this fact was reflected in the most base of human motives. This is apparent in the following statement of one combatant.

"I intend to fight them to the last ... I will kill them as long as I live even if peace is made I never will get done with them".
John Collins, Confederate soldier from Virginia, 1862

IDEOLOGY AND BELIEFS

Two ideas, liberty and republicanism, both part of the great national experiment in our attempt at constructing a new nation, formed the initial core of beliefs and later misunderstandings that subsequently led to Civil War. In the beginning, upon our nation's founding, the interpretation and refinement of each of these themes was left inconclusive. This absence of definition was part of the founders' original intent (to create a living, and functionally adaptable form of government, subject to debate and modification over time) a necessary feature of their unique experiment, as Madison and other founders argued.

However, there were also different, more often, than not, irreconcilable interpretations of these seminal ideals. And, of course, added to the mix were the distinct perspectives-beliefs of the participants, often, as not, spiced by competing interests; these, events, were marked by debate, but not resolution. With the passage of time, somewhat unforeseen, the serious omissions and defects in the unfinished American agenda became apparent. Our constitution excluded too many details and created too many "what-if" type issues in application. In addition, it relied upon the successors of the original covenant to resolve issues, such as the disposition of slavery, especially its expansion into the new territories, that was unforeseen at the time of the nation's initiation or which eluded the founders themselves.

Finally, many of the issues that were to emerge in the next century were only partially evident, or they too were resistant to change by the members of the Constitutional Congress that were witness to, or participants in the original debates. Noble causes often have many interpretations, as well as limitations in means of application. And that was certainly the case here. The origins of the subsequent conflict were not apparent at the time; however, they emerged quickly and were in full debate by the early to mid nineteenth century. How to form a more perfect government was a theme frequently discussed throughout the latter part of the 18th century and beyond. Yet, it appeared illusive to those men and those that followed them. The context of divergent, prevailing ideas at the time are examined for us by Mathew Wilson, a *New York Times* war correspondent, from a rather unique perspective.

"I wasn't there, of course. That was two generations ago, in 1787, in Philadelphia. But my family was well represented. My grandfather, James Wilson was a prominent member of the constitutional delegation from Pennsylvania along with Franklin, the Morris's and several others. Moreover, he contributed to the debate and to the political maneuvering surrounding the convention.

"As an immigrant from Scotland, my grandfather embraced his newly adopted country with vigor, and was determined to see it survive. His concern was to insure that the new government was representative of the people's interests, that it was based on that illusive, new found entity, democracy. Correspondingly, he argued that "As all authority was derived from the people, equal numbers of people ought to have an equal number of representatives." However, his plan (favoring proportional representation based on population), while supported by Massachusetts, Pennsylvania and Virginia, which held almost half of the nation's population at the time, could not pass on its own accord. He needed southern support. And the price that he was forced to pay was the acceptance of slavery.

"With slave-favoring delegates as allies, he attempted to establish the first functional, if imperfect, democracy. And in the process he made a pact with the devil; he accepted the fiction that the southern states could be partly represented while maintaining their ties to slavery. He proposed a three/fifth compromise, as we know it, which insured passage of a constitution, but led future abolitionists to denounce his Faustian bargain as a "covenant with death". He, and his allies, spoke for their time, but not for mine."
From the correspondence of Mathew Wilson

Many young men, more than ever gathered before, fought in the war. They fought for varied reasons, for pride, for country and, if truth be told, as an expression of their emerging manhood.

In their correspondence with their families they frequently revealed the reasons underlying their beliefs. Some encompassed emotions ranging from patriotism to honor and duty, as well as community. One such message is expressed here.

A Letter Home

In the following footnote, some of the arguments for engagement in the war as advanced at the time are summarized in an exchange of correspondence pertaining to the reenlistment of a sixteen-year-old boy over his father's objections. In this report, the Virginia Valley newspaper reprinted their corresponding letters, relying on these letters, as it suggests, "To show the spirit of our " brave soldier boys," we publish an extract from the letter of a boy only sixteen years of age in reply to a letter from his father requesting him not to re-enlist--This boy is from Staunton, and belonged to the "West Augusta Guards," which has been recently converted into an artillery company, and he is now a member of the "West Augusta Battery." His letter breathes the right spirit, and we have no doubt that he expresses the feelings of a large majority of the soldiers from Augusta county.--He is an only son, and as his Father thought it probable that he (the father) would be drafted in which event there would be no one to support the mother of this young solder, his Father appealed to him not to re-enlist. This certainly was a strong appeal, and the boy no doubt felt the full force of it, but it was not strong enough to induce him to lay down his arms when his country needed his services. In reply to his Father's letter, he wrote:

"You and Ma are opposed to my re-enlisting in the army. If every parent gave such counsel, what would become of our country? I cannot consent to leave the army and quit the service when my country is bleeding and my countrymen are struggling for independence, and to leave my comrades to battle with the foe in their efforts to drive them from our land. It may be that you think that there are many who have staid (sic) at home who should take my place. If they act the coward and will not come out as freemen and declare they will have their rights, and will not shoulder their muskets and march in defense of their native State, but would rather stay at home, enjoying the luxuries of life and speculating off the poor soldiers who are in the service, guarding their homes,--if they act in this way, is that any reason why I should do the same. No, NEVER. I want to be one of those who, to the last, will rally around our standard to defend our noble and glorious cause, and, with our bright colors waving over us and with our brave General Jackson at the head of us, and with the motto - "Victory or death" - with stout hearts and determined minds, strike an effective blow for the preservation of liberty and the defense of our country. If the soldiers should not re-enlist, we would soon have no country - no home. They would be dishonored and disgraced, and the finger of scorn would be pointed at them. I for one would rather suffer banishment and exile - I would rather fill a soldier's honorable grave and sleep peacefully beneath the green sod of the Valley. These are my true feelings and sentiments. I cannot see how you or any one else can advise his son not to re-enlist - especially at this time, when the tide of success is setting against us."

CHAPTER 6

Adversity and Friendship in War, Part I

An Army Corps on the March

With its cloud of skirmishers in advance,

With now the sound of a single shot snapping with a

Whip, and now an irregular volley,

The swarming ranks press on and on, the dense brigades press on.

Glittering dimly, toiling under the sun – the dust cover'd men,

In columns rise and fall to the undulations of the ground,

With artillery interspers'd – the wheels rumble, the horses sweat,

As the army corps advance.

Walt Whitman

Other motives to fight were evident, as well.

Among these was the belief that the war, to the South, represented a defense of home and hearth in the face of perceived "Northern aggression," as different sources of propaganda urged and other explanations or justifications for the war, were stressed.

One soldier wrote home, expressing this idea in the following statement, "We are fighting for matters real and tangible…our property and our homes." And in comparison with Northern sentiment, he noted "…they for matters abstract and intangible."

And another wrote adding, "…the Yankees are sacrificing their lives {for ideals}; we, ours for home, country, and all That is dear and sacred… Every one seems to know that their liberty and property are at stake, hence we never can be whipped."

Even Northern soldiers came to recognize the fierce determination and ready willingness of their enemy in defending "home and hearth". As one Northern officer wrote home to his wife, "They are fighting from different motives from us. We are fighting for the Union…a high and noble sentiment, but after all a sentiment. They are animated by passion and hatred against invaders…It makes no difference whether the cause is just or not. You can get up an amount of enthusiasm that nothing else will excite."

The determination of Southern soldiers to fight was well-known and respected. Frank Haskell, a Union officer and combatant at Gettysburg, wrote about the Army of Northern Virginia in the following commentary, "This army of the Rebel infantry, however … is good – to deny this is useless. I never had any desire to – and if one should count up, it would possibly be found that they have gained more victories over us than we have over them, and they will now, doubtless, fight well, even desperately. And it is not horses or cannon that will determine the result of this confronting of the two armies, but the men with the muskets must do it – the infantry must do the sharp work."
Frank A. Haskell, The Battle of Gettysburg.

Fueling the Southern view suggesting that confederate soldiers were fighting in support of "a higher cause," was the perpetuation of the notion of "northern aggression" as a principal cause of the war. Clearly, Northern soldiers did not perceive themselves as "hordes of Northern Hessians" (a clear reference to Revolutionary War mercenaries), "lecherous Northern hirelings" (a reference to draft substitution practices favored in the North), "Abolition incendiaries" (perpetrators of black liberation), nor as "the thieving hordes of Lincoln" (blaming Lincoln for the initiation of hostilities and ravages to follow). However, the message and blame for the war, for the typical southern combatant was clear; the North created this calamity.

Interestingly, while a test of the varied and comparative commitments, or will to fight of Southern solders versus Northern soldiers relative to their respective causes cannot be made with any degree of accuracy, some observers, as in the case below do offer, as in this case, a disapproving and less favorable view of the Northern peoples perspective/commitment to the war.

January 2, 1963

"What we need is to feel that we are fighting for our lives and liberties; that is the way the rebels feel: they think that if they don't win, they will lose every liberty. Our people seem to be in an indifferent state,...; they would like to see the South conquered, if it could be done by any moderate means; but when it comes to every man and woman making some great sacrifice, they don't think it worth while, and would rather have a disgraceful peace...They don't seem to see that in case of such a peace, to be a native of the North would be sufficient to disgrace a man, and that we should always be considered a whipped nation."

Major Charles Fessenden Morse, Second Massachusetts Infantry

REVENGE AND VENGEANCE

As the War progressed, with its accompanying widespread destruction and hardships, other motives emerged. Aside from the normal fuel furnished by the heat of battle, the frustration of fighting a long and drawn out conflict, as well as, toward the end, the likelihood of defeat, even (perhaps especially) under a highly regarded, venerated leader such as General Robert E. Lee, revenge and vengeance became prominent motivational forces.

Often, in the face of accumulated, festering hatred, and as an act of revenge, surrendered combatants were shot down (especially emancipated black soldiers fighting under the Union banner), rather than taken prisoner, after they had given up their arms in defeat. As one officer wrote home to his wife, instructing her with the responsibility of inculcating in their children the motive for war, he offered the following message, that she should teach the children, "a bitter and unrelenting hatred to the Yankee race" insofar as they "invaded our country and devastated it…and murdered our best Citizens…" adding "…If any luckless Yank should unfortunately come into my way he need not petition for mercy. If he does I'le give him lead if he ask for bread…[I intend] to Massacre the last one of them ever has or may hereafter place his unhallowed feet upon the soil of our sunny South."

Community and Friendship

Men under arms, on both sides of the battle line often "fought for each other" as a community of like-minded combatants. This often occurred since regiments were recruited from each of the individual states directly, and within these states by local communities; soldiers were responsible for each other both before, as well as during the war, often through the perpetuation of bonds established previous to the war.

In addition, many new bonds of friendship were created or effectively forged during the War by an acknowledgment of their common needs or the desperate response of soldiers to one another's perilous experiences. This is illustrated in the case of artillery Captain John Bigelow and Corporal Charles Reed, his bugler, during their common plight on July 2, 1863 at Gettysburg.

A Friendship Forged in Fire and Fury

"He is worse than any regular that ever breathed." was how Charles Reed described Captain John C. Bigelow, the new commander of the 9th Massachusetts Battery at Gettysburg. The arrival of Captain Bigelow occurred in late February 1863. Under his command, he changed the lax and seemingly carefree lives of the men in the 9th Massachusetts Battery; within days of assuming his command, the men of the battery thought their new commanding officer was a tyrant. As Reed reported, "He don't have...the feelings for his men as a slave owner for his slaves. He has been order[ing] eight roll call's a day. In fact they are regular dress parades which precede all the drill call's[,] stable, and water calls." Reed did not perceive at the time that Bigelow's discipline and rigorous drill schedule would later save the lives of many of his fellow artillery gunners at the Battle Of Gettysburg.

John Bigelow was a veteran soldier with significant experience in the war. Early, in December of 1861, Bigelow had received an appointment as Adjutant of the 1st Maryland Artillery Battalion. He also served in a similar capacity in the Peninsular Campaign under the command of General George B. McClellan. At Malvern Hill his left arm had been shattered, and he had returned home to recuperate. Sometimes later he rejoined his battalion that autumn, and was with the Army of the Potomac at Fredericksburg. After a bout with malaria, briefly sending him home for rest and recuperation, he returned once again to the war in January of 1863. Subsequently, he received an appointment by Governor Andrews of Massachusetts, that lead to the command of the 9th Battery.

On the second day (June 2, 1863) at Gettysburg, John C. Bigelow and Charles W. Reed faced an unpredictable destiny together. In the midst of battle they had repulsed an initial Confederate attack around the Trostle farm. However, the situation remained critical for all of McGilvery's batteries, which included Bigelow's unit. Confederate General Kershaw's men quickly rallied and were "not long in taking...revenge." Closely watching the shifting Confederates, Bigelow found that "as soon as the woods were reached, [they] sent a body of sharpshooters against us." Reed later wrote that the men "advanced on us giving us such a shower of small balls that it was dangerous to be safe!" In their position on the far left, the 9th Massachusetts Battery received the brunt of the Confederate fire from the front and left. The Confederates, "came up on my left front as skirmishers, pouring in a heavy fire and killing and wounding a number of...my men," Captain Bigelow recalled. At his battery post, Private David Brett was horrified: "We could hear the bullets pass us[.] finily a man dropt about 6 foot to my right another right behind[.] 6 men were killed within a rod of me...."

Fighting raged in the Wheatfield east of the 9th Massachusetts Battery and along the front. Conditions continued to deteriorate until, shortly after 6:00 P.M. when the situation reached a critical point. At that time, the growing Confederate assaults reached the salient angle of Sickles' line at the Peach Orchard. Under the relentless advance of the Confederate brigades of Brig. General William Barksdale and Brig. General William T. Wofford, the Union line began to crumble. Though making a determined stand, the Union infantry slowly melted away from the "compact mass of humanity" of Barksdale's regiments. This stand allowed Union artillery in the orchard time to escape, though the right door was now open putting McGilvery's line under fire. McGilvery ordered two of his batteries to retreat while his last two, those of Phillips and Bigelow, continued to thunder away at Kershaw's men. Meanwhile, Barksdale's regiments advanced through the orchard after hitting the Union line located there, and prepared to rush down the slope into the unsuspecting artillerymen.

McGilvery first rode on horseback to Phillips and ordered him to retreat, intending to have his remaining batteries, "retire 250 yards and renew their fire," probably hoping to reform the broken line, or somehow strengthen the resolve of fleeing soldiers and stem the flow of retreating Union troops. But the situation was unraveling too rapidly. By the time McGilvery reached the 9th Massachusetts Battery he was ordering his batteries back to Cemetery Ridge. Bigelow's men had been steadily working their guns in a futile attempt to hold back the increasingly successful Confederate pressure being applied from the left and front. In the noise and confusion of battle, Charles Reed took no notice of the other batteries withdrawal as "we were so intent upon our work that we noticed not when the other batterys left." It was Captain Bigelow who spotted the new threat coming from the direction of the orchard: "Glancing toward the Peach Orchard on my right, I saw that the Confederates (Barksdale's Brigade) had come through and were forming a line 200 yards distant, extending back, parallel with the Emmitsburg Road, as far as I could see... Colonel McGilvery rode up, at this time, and told me that (all of Sickles') men had withdrawn and I was alone on the field, with no supports…{and that I should} limber up and get out."

Bigelow realized the order could not be carried out, for without infantry support and with Confederate skirmishers so close, "every saddle would have been emptied in trying to limber up." Making a swift decision, the captain petitioned McGilvery to "'retire by prolonge and firing,' in order to 'keep them off.'" It was a maneuver in which the cannon was joined to a rope that used the recoil of the cannon by pulling it as the men continued firing. This bold decision obviously revealed the confidence Bigelow placed in his men, as attempting such a maneuver was extremely risky, especially with untried troops. Many obstacles and problems could develop that may result in disaster for the battery. McGilvery also must have realized the risk, but in the heat of battle quickly "assented [to the request] and rode away." Whatever the reason, orders were quickly given, prolonge ropes fixed and the battery began to withdraw. "No friendly supports, of any kind, were in sight; but Johnnie Rebs in great numbers," Bigelow recalled. "Bullets were coming into our midst from many directions and a Confederate battery added to our difficulties. (The) Battery kept well aligned in retiring, (moving) with a slow, sullen fire." Drivers coached their straining horse teams as they dragged the heavy guns through the pasture south of the Trostle farm buildings. Gunners rammed charges down the hot muzzles as they moved, stopping briefly to fire the weapons, "keeping Kershaw's skirmishers back with canister, and the other two sections bowling solid shot towards Barksdale's men."

The men of the 9th Massachusetts together with the rest of the cannoneers along the Wheatfield Road were able to check the surging South Carolinians under Brigadier General Joseph Kershaw in the undulating fields around the Rose Farm. Firing double canister, Bigelow's men forced the rebel troops to seek the comparative safety of a section of woods now called Stony Hill.

The South Carolina troops first had to drive the Union infantry from the area after which they began snipping at the Massachusetts battery, killing both men and horses. As the battle raged the smoke obscured the field. If the billowing sulfurous clouds would have suddenly dissipated, Bigelow's men could have seen the precarious situation beginning to unfold around them.

Lt. Colonel McGilvery galloped to the rear in order to regroup and reorganize his withdrawing batteries along Cemetery Ridge. Reaching the higher ground beyond, however, McGilvery was shocked to find a huge gap in the center of the Union line. In his mind, "The crisis of the engagement had now arrived," and he knew that Bigelow's gunners would have to buy time for his other cannoneers. Spotting the 9th Massachusetts Battery, which had just halted under cover of a slight knoll near the Trostle farmstead and was beginning to limber up in preparation for retreat, McGilvery spurred his horse, "alone, in the midst of flying missiles" toward the battery. His horse staggered, being "shot four times in the breast and fore shoulder," as he reined up in front of Captain Bigelow he said, "Captain Bigelow, there is not an infantryman back of you along the whole line which Sickles' moved out; you must remain where you are and hold your position at all hazards, if need be, until at least I can find some batteries to put in position and cover you!"

Cannon in Battle

McGilvery and Bigelow both knew the consequences of these orders. Bigelow realized, "the sacrifice of the command was asked in order to save the line," and could only manage a weak reply that he would try.

The men of the battery were equally stunned and Reed knew, "we were left in a critical position." Bigelow found himself in a, "position...which... was an impossible one for artillery. The task seemed superhuman, for the knoll already spoken of allowed the enemy to approach as it were under cover within 50 yards of my front, while I was very much cramped for room and my ammunition was greatly reduced." The exhausted battery was trapped in the angle of two stone walls, making retreat impossible. Yet the men of the 9th Massachusetts Battery did not hesitate as Bigelow ordered his men to prepare for action. Most of the soldiers in the battery were just like Charles Reed who, though from common origins were, according to Bigelow, "Without exception... soldiers only from the highest sense of duty" and fought for a cause in which they firmly believed. Though earlier given a chance to safely leave the fight, Reed just "couldn't see it," and had "disobeyed orders" by returning to his battery. One of the battery's corporals best summed up the feelings of all the men in the battery when he later proudly wrote, "We the Glorious-young 9th Mass- Battery in Splendid Organization and for the first time in an engagement - stood the ground and were Willing to die for the Country."

Realizing that desperate circumstances required desperate actions, Bigelow took his chances. Risking the danger to his own men, the captain ordered all the ammunition laid beside the guns for "rapid firing." Utilizing every means possible to slow the advancing Confederates, he then ordered his four guns in the center and right, to "commence...firing solid shot low, for a ricochet over the knoll" and into the infantry beyond {a risky procedure considering the limited trajectory of his guns}. With his six pieces loaded and arranged in a semi-circle, with the limbers and horses crowded into the corner of the stone walls, the battery soon fell silent to await the onslaught. "The moments seemed like hours," Bigelow recalled, the guns prepared "not a moment too soon...for almost immediately the enemy appeared over the knoll. Waiting till they were breast high, my battery was discharged at them(,) every gun loaded...with double shotted cannister and solid shot, after which through the smoke [we] caught a glimpse of the enemy, they were torn and broken, but still advancing. The enemy opened a fearful musketry fire, men and horses were falling like hail.... Sergeant after Sergt., was struck down, horses were plunging and laying about all around...."

The tenacious advancing troops consisted of approximately 400 men of the 21st Mississippi Infantry, which struck the right and front of the battery. At the same time skirmishers from Kershaw's Brigade, who had doggedly followed Bigelow's guns, threatened from the left front. Flushed with victory, the Mississippians pushed onward, "yelling like demons," as "Again and again they rallied." Directing the battle from his horse, Bigelow witnessed, "The enemy crowded to the very muzzles [of the guns] but were blown away by the canister. Notwithstanding their insane, reckless efforts not an enemy came into [the] battery from its front. (The) rapid fire recoiled the guns into the corner of the stone-wall, (which) more and more cramped my position." Canister ammunition began to run low as Bigelow, still willing to take risks, ordered case shot with the fuzes cut short to be used, "so that they would explode near the muzzle of [the] guns. (Yet the Confederate) lines extended far beyond our right flank, and the 21st Miss...swung without opposition and came in from that direction, pouring in a heavy fire all the while."

Caught in a "withering cross fire," and with his left section entangled among some large bowlders" and the stone wall, Bigelow ordered the guns to retire. After quickly limbering up the crews headed for their only escape, an opening in the stone wall opposite the Trostle farmyard. The first gun, however, upon reaching the gateway, overturned and blocked it. While the men of this gun scrambled to right it, the crew of the trailing gun looked in desperation for a way out. A few men "tumbled the top stones off the wall" before the drivers headed "directly over the wall." Aghast at the spectacle, Reed remembered the "horses jumping and the gun...going over with a tilt on one side and then a crash of rocks and wheels" as the piece made its successful flight.

Desperately Bigelow gave orders for the remaining crews to prepare for a general retreat and "rode to the stone wall, hoping to stop some of [the] cannoneers and have them make a better opening, through which I might rush one or more of the remaining four guns...." But with the left section gone, Kershaw's skirmishers "being unchecked, quickly came up on [the] left and poured in a murderous fire." At his captain's side, Bugler Reed, recalled "I saw the enemy skirting down the stone wall... and called to the captain to look out," while at the same time "throwing his horse back on his haunches." Bigelow never heard the warning as six skirmishers opened fire and the captain "caught two bullets, my horse two, (and) two flew wide."

CHAPTER 7

ADVERSITY AND FRIENDSHIP IN WAR: PART II

As his horse staggered to the rear, Captain Bigelow fell dazed near the wall. Reed and Bigelow's orderly were quickly drawn to their commander's side. As he leaned against the wall, Bigelow saw "the Confederates swarming in on our right flank." Hand to hand fighting soon engulfed the battery, with the men employing handspikes and rammers as improvised weapons to defend their guns. The odds against them were overwhelming; with all the remaining officers and many of its sergeants either killed or wounded from battle, with the air alive with missiles, and the battery caught in a turmoil of confusion, the resistance of most units would collapse.

The men of the 9th Massachusetts Battery, however, did not flinch; instead they stood by their guns, their discipline holding them together. "We fought with our guns until the rebs could put their hands on [them]," wrote Private David Brett. "The bullets flew thick as hailstones...it is a miracle that we were not all killed...not a man run[,] 4 or 5 fell within 15 feet of me."

Bigelow witnessed the melee, Confederates "standing on the limber chests, and shooting down cannoneers. Not even then did the batterymen cease their fire. Longer delay was impossible, (and) having thus accomplished what was required of my command," he gave the order to retreat. "The men abandoned the death trap and made their way to the rear, leaving behind the shattered remains of the battery and a sacrifice of three of four officers, six of eight sergeants, 19 enlisted men, 88 horses and four of their six guns."

In the midst of the chaos, Reed remembered his wounded captain, that "told...the orderly and myself to leave him and get out as best we could. (I) didn't do just that." Reed again disobeyed orders.

Years afterward, Bigelow could not forget the actions of his faithful bugler: "He remained with me...called my orderly and had him lift me on to his horse; then taking the reins of both horses in his left hand, with his right hand supporting me in the saddle, took me at a walk [to the rear]."

"Then we tried to get away," Reed wrote. "Some of the confederates saw us...and several of them tried to take us prisoners. They did not fire at once, but tried to pull us from the horses' backs, but were unsuccessful, as the horses kicked and I was able to do some execution with my... saber.... We were still struggling when an officer, who saw his men were about to fire, told them not to murder us in cold blood. Then I started for the northern forces."

Escaping From Harm's Way

The wounded captain and his bugler were now between the battle lines, "the shells of the Enemy...breaking all around us." They had over 400 yards of open ground to cross before reaching safety. " Before I was half way back" Bigelow remembered an officer was sent "urging me to hurry, as he must commence firing." The captain's painful wounds, however, prevented the horses from moving at anything faster than a walk, so Bigelow told him to "fire away." Now caught between the fire of both lines, {North and South} Reed also had to contend with the orderly's frightened horse, which was difficult to control. Bigelow later praised Reed's conduct: "Bugler Reed did not flinch; but steadily supported me; kept the horses at a walk although between the two fires and guided them, so that we entered the Battery between two of the guns that were firing heavily....

Less than four months earlier, Reed had labeled his commander "a regular aristocrat," feeling he was worse than a slave owner. Yet in the heat of battle, the bugler twice disobeyed orders and willingly risked his life to save his captain. Bigelow never forgot Reed's "gallantry," writing to him thirty-two years later that, "the obligation still remains with myself." Bigelow felt so strongly about Reed's acts of bravery that in 1895 he submitted Reed's name for a Medal of Honor, citing his "distinguished bravery and faithfulness to duty at the Battle of Gettysburg." When the medal was awarded later that year Bigelow acknowledging Reed's bravery noted, "I feel the Government honors itself in honoring you." On a more personal level, Bigelow felt Reed had not only saved him from a stint in a Confederate prison but, more importantly, had also saved his life. The captain later wrote, "Even though the Mississippians would probably have spared me, Dow's (6th Maine Artillery) searching canister and Shells would not have done so."

Aftermath

The experiences of John C. Bigelow and Charles W. Reed at Gettysburg, were to linger throughout the remainder of their lives. But is was not their heroism that caused these lasting memories, but rather the pain and suffering of their fellow soldiers to which they had borne witness. As Charles Reed wrote home afterward of his fallen comrades::

"During the din of battle my feelings were curious and various but the one idea I entertained could not be shaken off until the fight had ceased for the day. It appeared to be a grand terrible drama we were enacting and the idea of being hit or killed never occurred to me, but when I saw the dead, wounded, and mutilated pouring out their life blood...then the terrible sense of reality came upon me in full force. The novelty had vanished. I could only turn my thoughts to him who sees and controls all, with silent thanks giving and weep for the many, many dead and maimed."

Not only had Charles Reed lost many of his comrades, but he had also lost his innocence, as well. The terrible consequences of war had changed him, as it did for so many others. And it changed them all, forever.

Hancock and Amistead: Generals Caught in the Maw of War

The men who fought in the fields and within the valleys of Virginia and later upon the hills of Pennsylvania were caught up in the immediate demands of their task as soldiers. Many were also trapped by their past associations of kin and friendship. And they were not alone. Their officers, at all ranks, suffered the consequences of past affiliations and previously established bonds of friendship, as well. Among them, one special friendship, of Union Major General Winfield Scott Hancock and Confederate Brigadier General Lewis Addison Armistead, stands out.

When Fort Sumter was bombarded by Confederate artillery in April 1861, Armistead and Hancock were stationed in Los Angeles, California. As regular army officers who first met at West Point as students, and subsequently fought together in the Mexican War, they, like so many others, were forced to choose sides, to align with the North or the South. Some like Hancock of Pennsylvania would fight for the Union. Others like Armistead, of Virginia, with loyalties to the South, would fight for the Confederacy.

On the night of their departure, those officers going south bade a tearful farewell to their comrades. Among them, Armistead gave Hancock's wife, Almira, also a close friend, his prayer book with the slogan, "Trust In God And Fear Nothing" inscribed inside. To Hancock, he gave a new major's uniform.

Throughout the war, Armistead did not cross paths with Hancock -- that is, until Gettysburg in July of 1863. Now there they were - two old friends just a bit over a mile apart, but on opposite sides of a battlefield, leading their men, each side poised to kill the another.

Their destinies meet on July 3, 1862. General James Longstreet had opposed Lee's plan for an offensive charge on the third day at Gettysburg, and told him, quite bluntly, that not even 15,000 troops could take the well-entrenched Union position on Cemetery Ridge. Longstreet believed that it would be a massacre. But Lee was inspired by the deeds of his men and when George Pickett petitioned Longstreet for permission to move his troops forward, Longstreet could only bow his head in an acceptance of the inevitable.

Eager to acquire fame and notoriety, the flamboyant Pickett shouted to his men "Charge the enemy and remember old Virginia,", waving his hat to the troops in his division. In an instant, 15,000 butternut-clad troops began marching across an open field, a potential graveyard, lacking even the most rudimentary cover, clearly reminiscent of Fredericksburg in December of 1862, and likely to have similar consequences. They were ordered to travel about a mile from their position on Cemetery Ridge and into a potential inferno where the Union army awaited them.

The carnage was appalling. The Confederates marched steadily into the face of Union fire and were slaughtered in alarming numbers. Armistead led his troops gallantly, his campaign hat skewered on the tip of his sword, and held high for all to see. By the time the Confederates reached the wall, however, fully two-thirds of their number was wounded or lying dead. As Armistead crossed the wall, he too was shot down.

As he lay bleeding, resting against the wheel of a cannon, Armistead asked after Hancock and was told that his friend was also wounded. "Not both of us on the same day!" Armistead cried. Then he said to Captain Henry Bingham, Hancock's aide, "Tell General Hancock from me that I have done him and you all a grave injustice."

Although Armistead's wounds were not considered life threatening at the time, he died two days later in a field hospital. He was worn out and mentally exhausted as he lay dying. It was said afterward of him that Lewis Armistead simply died of a broken heart - the most tragic irony of all.

Hancock, on the other hand, lived to fight another day.

CHAPTER 8

The Blue and the Gray

By the flow of the inland river,
Whence the fleets of iron have fled,
Where the blades of the grave-grass quiver,
Asleep are the ranks of the dead:
Under the sod and the dew,
Waiting the Judgment Day:
Under the one, the Blue,
Under the other, the Gray.

These in the robings of glory,
Those in the gloom of defeat,
All with the battle-blood gory,
In the dusk of eternity meet:
Under the sod and the dew,
Waiting the Judgment Day:
Under the laurel, the Blue,
Under the willow, the Gray.

Francis Miles Finch (1867)

The colors worn by the combatants, like the flags they displayed were significant elements of the pageantry. The costumes added to the anticipated glamour of the War. And they were varied and often, magnificent. The flags, moreover, had strategic significance in maneuvering troops marching into battle and additional tactical relevance in helping them locate units already engaged in battle.

The colors worn also lent identity and spectacle to the events that were to transpire. At least, initially, with the first flush of excitement at the outbreak of War [and little awareness of its multiple horrors], color added to the anticipated festivities of events to come. Costumes and parades were also part of the panorama. And music, was composed for the occasion, as well.

The Bonnie Blue Flag

We are a band of brothers

And native to the soil,

Fighting for the property

We gained by honest toil;

And when our rights were threatened,

The cry rose near and far-

"Hurrah for the Bonnie Blue Flag

That bears a single star!"

Harry McCarthy

There were many variations within the pageantry. There were brightly clad Zouaves [North and South soldiers who emulated the costumes of native North African troops serving in the French Army in the 1830's [who wore uniforms consisting of a fez and turban, baggy red pants, a vest and a short jacket with a one button clasp at the throat and a sash as well as leggings] from Louisiana to New York and Pennsylvania. These men distinguished themselves in both costume and ferocity. And in all probability their brightly-clad uniforms served as well-defined targets on the battlefield, as well.

Both the North and South adored parades and the Zouave costumes worn by parading soldiers contributed to the festive atmosphere and the romantic feel in the air. Yet, in spite of all the banners and the costuming, the purpose of the War was clear to all: to kill as many of the enemy as possible. And it did.

Killed at the Ford

He is dead, the beautiful youth,
The heart of honor, the tongue of truth,
He, the life and light of us all,
Whose voice, was blithe as a bugle-call,
Whom all eyes followed with one consent,
The cheer of whose laugh, and whose pleasant word,
Hushed all murmurs of discontent.

Only last night, as we rode along,
Down the dark of the mountain gap,
To visit the picket-guard at the ford,
Little dreaming of any mishap,
He was humming the words of some old song,
"Two roses he had on his cap
And another he bore at the point of his sword."
We lifted him up to his saddle again,
And through the mire and the mist and the rain
Carried him back to the silent camp,
And laid him as if asleep in his bed;
And I saw by the light of the surgeon's lamp
Two white roses upon his cheeks,
And one, just over his heart, blood red!

Henry Wadsworth Longfellow

Union Soldiers – Motivation

Previously, we examined some of the reasons why soldiers on both sides fought this terrible war. However, earlier the focus was placed upon soldiers from the Confederacy. Were Union soldiers as well motivated? Did they also need to prevail, as Southern men claimed (as was their special challenge), in order to maintain their property, their country, and their freedom?

Patriotism – A prevailing motivation for Federal troops was, like that of their Southern counterparts, the idea/spirit of patriotism. Letters and diary accounts drawn from Union troops speak glowingly of the honor bestowed upon them in their pledge to defend the Union in the name of the nation's founding principles. Moreover, they, like Confederate troops frequently compared the present conflict within the bounds of the nation's earlier struggles.

One officer from the 101st Ohio correlated his current plight as an extension of that era, specifically, of those earlier soldiers, the patriots of 1776, in the following letter: "Our fathers in coldest winter, half clad marked the road they trod with crimson streams from their bleeding feet that we might enjoy the blessings of a free government." He continued by noting that, "our business in being here [is] to lay down our lives if need be for our country's cause." Unfortunately, he was killed two weeks at the Battle of Stones River after penning this letter.

Many Union soldiers shared these sentiments, while others, often extended the depth of commitment that they undertook, or were determined to maintain in the name of patriotism; in some cases, they saw the present conflict as being of an even higher order than the causes/motives in favor of the original American Revolution. One Ohio lieutenant, writing in this fashion, spoke of the higher responsibility that he faced relative to his predecessors in the following letter:

"Our fathers made this country, we, their children are to save it… and you should …experience a laudable pride in the part your {husband and brothers} are now taking to suppress the greatest rebellion the history of the world has ever witnessed… Why denounce the war when the interest at stake is so vital? … Union & peace our freedom is worthless… our children would have no warrant of liberty…[If] our Country be numbered among the things that were but are not, of what value will be house, family, and friends?"

Men were called from all parts of the country and and they responded in force.

A Call to Arms

Among the many Irish-Americans that fought, another call, in this case to a distant patriotism, was frequently sounded. Among these men, many of whom fought on both sides, the parallels of the American Civil War to their age-old struggle against England were frequently drawn. To these patriots, the struggle for liberty here in America was a reenactment of past and continuing conflicts.

One private in the 28th Massachusetts of the famed Irish Brigade wrote in 1863, "This is the first test of a modern free government in the act of sustaining itself against internal enemies…if it fail then the hopes of millions fail and the designs and wishes of all tyrants will succeed… the old cry will be sent forth from the aristocrats of Europe that such is the common lot of all republics…Irishmen and their descendants have a stake in [this] nation…America is Ireland's refuge Ireland's last hope… destroy this republic and her hopes are blasted."

DEFENDING HOME AND HEARTH

Because the war was fought on native soil, soldiers from each side felt a special duty to defend and protect their farms, family and friends from perceived hoards of invading attackers; their enemies might have been distant neighbors, but they were also in effect, "foreigners." Soldiers at Gettysburg, especially men of the 83rd Pennsylvania, were now fighting on native soil. In other battles, most conflicts took place south of the Mason–Dixon line, in Virginia or Maryland or in the West. In Pennsylvania, Northern troops were called upon to fight for their homes and families, as Confederate troops had in Virginia and Maryland. As Captain Amos Judson noted, as his troops entered Pennsylvania, having marched north some days before the battle, "they were about to enter the threshold of their native State and fight upon her soil" where "their enthusiasm knew no bounds". Underscoring this attitude, one soldier, Private William Brown of the 44th New York added, that the Confederates "have made a mistake invading old Pennsylvania."

The blood lust of Northern troops inspired by an invasion of their "home territory" by the Army of Northern Virginia was also noted by Charles Salter of the 16th Michigan. Specifically, he was bewildered by the hatred, venom and brutality that he found at Gettysburg. Yet, in a letter written after the battle, he remarked that, "It seemed as if every man, on both sides, was actuated by the intense hate, and determined to kill as many of the enemy as possible, and exerted up an enthusiasm far exceeding that on any field before that we have been engaged in."

Even after the battle of Gettysburg, as soldiers began to assess the events that transpired there, their role as defender of an invaded countryside was held in special regard. This perspective was especially important for the Army of the Potomac, an army that had been outsmarted and out generaled as well as frequently defeated, in most previous battles.

Interestingly, the theme of home emerged once again in Charles Salter's remarks after the battle, in which credit for the "victory" at Gettysburg was being assessed. He writes, "All the papers that I have seen yet seem to lay the blame of our former defeats to our former generals, and give the credit of the victory to General Meade. But our army knows this to be not the true state of affairs, for we will fight better in Pennsylvania and Maryland than we will in Virginia, for in the present case we are defending our own soil and in Virginia we felt that we are invading rebel soil…And I contend that it was the Army of the Potomac that won the battle, not Gen. Meade, and we would have done just as well, or better, under McClellan, Hooker, or any other general. We are not fighting for generals, but for our country, and I hope that the Northern people give the credit of our fighting to the soldiers."

By sunset on July 1, 1863, 11 officers and men of the 16th Maine had been killed, 62 had been wounded, and 159 had been taken prisoner. Only 38 men of the Regiment managed to avoid being captured and reported for duty at 1st Corps headquarters. But the 16th Maine had bought precious time for the Union Army. Those whose retreat they had covered were able to establish a very strong position just east and south of the center of the town of Gettysburg along Cemetery Ridge. During the night and into July 2nd the 1st and 11th Corps were reinforced as other units of the Army of the Potomac arrived at the battlefield. For the next two days they would withstand successive assaults by the Confederates until the final repulse of Pickett's Charge, on July 3rd.

For these and other related feats of heroic behavior the Congressional Medal of Honor was created. It grew out of the need to recognize the valor exhibited by Union soldiers in the Civil War; and nowhere were actions of bravery and courage in the war better recognized than at the Battle of Gettysburg. In all, 63 medals were awarded to soldiers for their actions on the battlefields of southern Pennsylvania during that summer of 1863.

Mississippi – The Deep South

Mississippi played a pivotal, geographically strategic role in the Western theatre of the War. In addition, like many other states, its soldiers fought on multiple battlefields. As the second state to secede from the Union, Mississippi's secession resolution, like those of the other southern states, clearly stated that its defense of slavery was its reason for leaving the Union. With a population of 791,000 people, Mississippi's slaves outnumbered whites 437,000 to 354,000. Maintaining the institution of slavery, disregarding its immorality as a human condition, therefore, seemed to be of absolute economic necessity for the state's agriculture-based economy.

White soldiers from Mississippi, most often reflected the state's position on slavery, but they fought for a variety of other reasons, as well. Some joined the military to defend home and hearth, while others saw the conflict in broader sectional terms. Formal declarations or other justifications withstanding, the soldiers' motivation, above all, was generally more personal than it was ideological.

Some soldiers took a rather circuitous route to battle; for them war was both an adventure and a quest. One of these men was John West, a resident of several Southern communities.
Gettysburg, July 1863.

Private John West

"I saw a great many wounded… who were mangled and bruised in every possible way, some with their eyes shot out, some with their arms, or hands, or fingers, or feet or legs shot off, and all seeming to suffer a great deal."
Private John C. West, Company E, 4th Texas Infantry, and survivor of Gettysburg.

John C. West saw the war from a variety of perspectives. Although assigned to the Texas Infantry, he was born and educated in South Carolina. As an educated man and as a lawyer, he found his "fighting career" interrupted several times, including service he was called upon to perform as the district attorney for the Western District of Texas. This occurred on two occasions. However, he was determined to "see a fight" and "remain in the ranks, if necessary, until the close of the war". So in the early spring of 1863, he left his wife and two small children in Waco, Texas and set off to pursue his destiny. He had just turned twenty-nine years of age and was somewhat enamored, as were many, with the idea of war, recalling with fondness, one contemporary call to arms, in which Southern proponents observed, "We can't be whipped, but we may all be killed".

Other Players

Just as in every war, here too, some men carried the torch, more often than others, while their less dedicated or disillusioned comrades sought to avoid active combat – both Union and Confederate, alike. During the Civil War, only about half the men on active duty were actually engaged in fighting. Many others, excluding those whom were clearly ill (suffering the consequences of a variety of diseases) or unable to fight as a function of incurred battle-related injury, as well as those that lost faith in their cause (a considerable number, especially, toward the waning days of the

War) were referred to as beats or dead- beats, skulkers, sneaks, stragglers, or coffee-coolers. During the fighting these men were absent, or elsewhere.

There were other classes of noncombatants as well. In both armies, many were able to attain "bombproof" jobs – those positions safely out of range of ongoing hostilities, such as clerk, supply personnel within the quarter masters corps, as prisoner guards, teamsters, or as hospital service workers.

Other noncombatants included those who were able to pay for military exemptions by hiring a military replacement (an acceptable practice in the North), and those who were exempted from the draft (in the South) through the enactment of laws that deemed their positions vital to the War effort. In October of 1862, one such law, the Twenty-Negro Law, a much detested and maligned statue, exempted from Confederate conscription any white man on a plantation that contained twenty or more slaves whose employment he supervised.

Other men, who sought to fight were often prevented from doing so because of extraordinary family responsibilities. Private William C. Jordan of Company B, of the 15th Alabama Infantry was one of these soldiers. When called to serve by the governor of Alabama in the spring of 1861, he was voted out of his military unit, because of his unusually heavy personal family responsibilities. As the time he was a planter, in charge of his own holdings, as well as those calling for his administration of those responsibilities associated with the estates of his late father-in-law, brother-in-law and brother, all of whom had died preceding the initiation of hostilities.

As he wrote: "So I was then guardian or representative of a widowed sister with eight minor children, a widowed sister-in-law with four minor children, a widowed mother-in-law and two minor children, a wife and three children and a dear father; in all, consisting of three widows, a wife, seventeen minors and over one hundred slaves that had to be hired out or otherwise looked after."

Private Jordan came late to the War. He was, according to his own testament, a devoted Unionist, but who like others of similar background and persuasion, decided to do his duty and serve the cause of his birthplace. In April of 1963 he finally received his long-awaited opportunity, joining the 15th Alabama in Virginia. He was part of the gallant regiment that stormed Little Round Top on July 2, 1863.

There was, however, one more obstacle to be overcome before his quest could be realized. On his way to Gettysburg, Pvt. Jordan, received word that his only son had died of measles. He was devastated and was urged to come home. And he struggled with the dilemma of continuing onward or returning home. In the end, he decided against returning home, just then. Instead, he continued his march to Gettysburg, to his fate with destiny at Little Round Top. As a survivor of Gettysburg, he observed later, sometime after the War, of his journey into the heartland of Pennsylvania, recalling, "I don't believe that a better army ever trod the earth than the one which followed General Lee to Gettysburg."

Whether they believed in their cause, perhaps even more so than their Northern adversaries, as some claimed, or in their fight, in which they had been remarkably successful relative to their size and access to material support for the war, there was little evidence that the soldiers of the Confederacy ever faltered in their belief in their leader, General Robert E. Lee. After the third day at Gettysburg, when Lee claimed responsibility {which was his by virtue of position and command} for the ill-fated, failed advance at the Union center {Pickett's charge}, a disaster of monumental proportions and clearly an ill-timed strategy, in spite of his acceptance for the consequences of questionable generalship, his men refused to hold him responsible or hold him up to blame. It was a two edged sword in some ways. General Robert E. Lee, after the immediate preceding victories at Fredericksburg, followed by Chancelorsville and the Seven Days, came to believe in the might of his army and their capacity for making war. And they, in turn, in spite of their losses and heavy suffering, came to believe in him as an inspired, clairvoyant leader. As John West of the 4th Texas, wrote home after the third day's battle at Gettysburg, "General Lee, never would have attacked the enemy in their position on the mountain side except for the splendid condition of his army and his confidence in its ability to accomplish anything he chose to attempt." Regarding the issue of blame, other men, for other reasons, not the least being, a failure of faith, were later assigned to play that role.

GETTYSBURG

From the silence of sorrowful hours
The desolate mourners go,
Lovingly laden with flowers
Alike for the friend and the foe:
Under the sod and the dew,
Waiting the judgment-day,
Under the roses, the Blue,
Under the lilies, the Gray.

So, with an equal splendor,
The morning sun-rays fall,
With a touch impartially tender,
On the blossoms blooming for all:
Under the sod and the dew,
Waiting the judgment-day,
Broidered with gold, the Blue,
Mellowed with gold, the Gray.

So, when the summer calleth,
On forest and field of grain,
With an equal murmur falleth
The cooling drip of the rain:
Under the sod and the dew,
Waiting the judgment-day,
Wet with the rain, the Blue,
Wet with the rain, the Gray.

Sadly, but not with upbraiding,
The generous deed was done,
In the storm of the years that are fading

No braver battle was won:
Under the sod and the dew,
Waiting the judgment-day,
Under the blossoms, the Blue,
Under the garlands, the Gray.

No more shall the war cry sever,
Or the winding rivers be red;
The banish our anger forever
When they laurel the graves of our dead!
Under the sod and the dew,
Waiting the judgment-day,
Love and tears for the Blue,
Tears and love for the Gray.

Francis Miles Finch (1867)

CHAPTER 9

THE LISTENING POSTS

Leaving Philadelphia, on a frosty morning in the middle of March, John and his colleagues set off on their journey to Lancaster. They arrived within several weeks, avoiding the natural impediments likely to be incurred during that difficult traveling season, as well as avaricious slave retrievers that might be encountered along the way; fortunately, using a network of safe roads and allies, their journey occurred without incident, or misfortune.

Upon their arrival in town they proceeded, after several inquiries, to Big Jake's house, as they had agreed upon earlier. Jake's home was a modest dwelling surrounded by a small parcel of workable farmland, which was located on the fringes of the black section of town. What the house might have lacked in elegance in appearance, it compensated for in quiet simplicity and an air of functional domesticity.

Later that day the group met with Jake and his wife Eva and their two small boys, Ned and Owen. The greeting they were given by the household was rather extravagant under the circumstances, yet understandable. As Eva explained, she and the boys were grateful to John and the others for rescuing Jake, who had previously fallen into the hands of Smithy and his slave "rescuer" henchmen. On that earlier misadventure, Jake was kidnapped and beaten. He was scheduled by Smithy to be taken south and sold, in spite of the fact that he was a free black man. A person's skin color, unfortunately, marked not only his or her station in life, but whether he or she would be indentured for life, in spite of their accomplishments or status. The imprisonment of black people, whether free or slave was a recognized, if contemptible, business venture at the time, and one destined, before his rescue, to condemn Jake to forced servitude for the remainder of his days.

On this occasion, however, there was cause for joy and celebration, and thanksgiving. Jake was home and with his family once more. And Eva opened their home willingly, and with gratitude, to all the members of John's party that had insured his freedom, once again.

After dinner, with the boys sent to bed, the adults sat down before a fire in the great room of the house to discuss recent events and future plans. Jake, with funds provided by Congressman Stevens, had found places in the communities designated to serve as listening posts, for the teams of observers set to occupy the dwellings located in each of the settings selected.

Eva, with the assistance of Representative Stevens companion Mrs. Lydia Hamilton, had recently begun to stock the houses with food and bedding, as well as other essential goods. As Eva explained, "the houses are ready, and good, trustworthy folks, well-known in the community have been identified to help with establishing the households and other tasks".

Jake added that, "several of these folks volunteered to deliver messages from one community to the next in the event that the Southerners are spotted within their community, or if they are alerted to do so by any of us. All communications will be filtered by way of Lancaster, where John will be coordinating our initial efforts."

After opening remarks were exchanged, a number of questions, regarding procedures, were raised by members of the group. Patrick asked how the aides would be identified and Jake indicated that code names and phrases, known only to the couriers, would suffice as a second level of security. The listening post aides would adopt communication patterns derived from the practices employed previously by members of the underground railroad. These communicative interchanges had been used in a variety of escape plans, over time, with a high degree of success. During the discussion a number of other issues were also raised and addressed. One of these concerns involved John's quest for security regarding their perilous undertaking.

Ever alert to the nefarious behavior of slave traders within a community, and there were many operating in Pennsylvania at the time, John asked whether those selected to the task could be trusted as reliable informants, likely to maintain fealty to their roles. Jake responded by informing the group that those selected to participate were now free, but former slaves, unlikely to support Southern aspirations, or to be diverted from the mission before them. Moreover, Jake reiterated to John that he was careful to select men, and some women, as well, who suffered under the yoke of slavery, and bore its scars before escaping the inevitable dehumanization of the system. He also indicated that many still had relatives that were captive to the practice and continued to toil under the injustices of slavery. As a group, he noted, that the people selected to participate were committed to working toward freeing those still held captive and to the destruction of slavery. Several of them, it was reported further, possessed weapons and were awaiting the call to join the Union ranks as combatants when, as they anticipated, the call to arms and the recruitment of black soldiers would be made by the government. As they correctly anticipated, the call would come shortly.

GETTYSBURG

If the muse were mine to tempt it
And my feeble voice were strong,
If my tongue were trained to measures,
I would sing a stirring song.
I would sing a song heroic
Of those noble sons of Ham,
Of the gallant colored soldiers
Who fought for Uncle Sam!

In the early days you scored them,
And with many a flip and flout,
Said "these battles are the white man's
And the whites will fight them out."
Up the hills you fought and faltered,
In the vales you strove and bled,
While your ears still heard the thunder
Of the foes increasing tread.

Then distress fell on the nation
And the flag was dropping low;
Should the dust pollute your banner?
No! The nation shouted, No!
So when war, in savage triumph,
Spread abroad his funeral pall-
Then you called the colored soldiers,
And they answered to your call.

And like hounds unleashed and eager
For the life blood of the prey,
Sprung they forth and bore them bravely
In the thickest of the fray.
And where'er the fight was hottest-
Where the bullets fastest fell,
There they pressed unblanched and fearless
At the very mouth of hell.

Paul Laurence Dunbar

By the summer of 1863, many states in the North, including Ohio, Rhode Island, Connecticut, Maryland, and Pennsylvania began to organize black (AKA colored) regiments. These efforts met with great success. By the end of October of 1863 there were fifty-eight regiments of Negro troops in the Union Army with a total strength, including white officers, of 37, 482 men. These troops came from eight Northern states, seven Confederate states, and the District of Columbia.
July 11, 1863

"We fight for God, liberty and country, not money. We will fight fearless of capture, as we do not expect quarter so shall give none. It is infinitely more honorable to die upon the battlefield, than to be murdered by the barbarians of the South. Promotion we will not ask, until we have earned it; and when we have, this nation shall know no rest until those in authority have crowned the brow of our heroes with wreaths of living green, until the highway of advancement is open to the dusky sons of America, as well as those of paler hue."
Editorial published in the *Anglo-American*, September 4, 1863

"We stand as ever on the side of the Government, and pledge to it "our lives, our property, and our sacred honor," in its efforts to subdue the rebellion of the slave oligarchy of the country, in its determination to emancipate the slaves of all rebels, to establish freedom in the District of Columbia and the National Territories,… to recognize the citizenship of the native-born colored American, and to protect the colored soldiers, who, taking the American musket and bayonet, have gone forth at the call of their country to do and die for the Government and the Union."
Resolution of Black Citizens, Xenia, Ohio

Among antebellum free blacks, and those recently released from bondage, black soldiers joined the Union's ranks with zeal; after all, they were fighting, for pride and freedom. They had done so before, aboard slave vessels and within the restricted opportunities afforded them across the many plantations where they were held in servitude. The opportunities then were fewer, and the odds of success were exceedingly long. However, as illustrated in the following examples, they had fought for freedom, if not for liberty, then for personal dignity, even within the limited confines of slavery, as opportunity afforded them.

Recruitment of Black Soldiers

BLACK DEFIANCE

In the following incident, Solomon Northup, identified earlier as a free black man tricked into slavery, displays his contempt for the system of forced servitude into which he has been condemned and, specifically, the perpetrators of his plight. On this occasion, in response to the his "master's" order to remove his clothes and accept punishment for a perceived minor transgression, Solomon Northup recalls for the reader the following story,

"Master Tibeats," said I, looking him boldly in the face, "I will not". I was about to say something further in justification, but with concentrated vengeance, he sprang upon me, seizing me by the throat with one hand, raising the whip with the other, in the act of striking. Before the blow descended, however, I had caught him by the collar of the coat, and drawn him closely to me. Reaching down, I seized him by the ankle, and pushing him back with the other hand, he fell over on the ground. Putting one arm around his leg, and holding it to my breast, so that his head and shoulders only touched the ground, I placed my foot upon his neck. He was completely in my power. My blood was up. It seemed to course through my veins like fire. In the frenzy of my madness I snatched the whip from his hand. He struggled with all his power; swore that I should not live to see another day; and that he would tear out my heart. But his struggles and threats were alike in vain. I cannot tell how many times I struck him. Blow after blow fell heavy upon his wiggling form. At length he screamed – cried murder – and at last the blasphemous tyrant

called on God for mercy. But he who had never shown mercy did not receive it. The stiff stock of the whip warped around his cringing body until my right arm ached."
Solomon Northup – *Twelve Years a Slave.*

Many other blacks fought for their dignity within this system of denigration. Another narrated incident, appearing within a novel based on an actual occurrence, involved the escape of former slave George Harris. In this episode George Harris was approached by a party of fugitive slave hunters seeking to "retrieve" and return him and his family to slavery. And again, we see evidence of resistance and defiance.

"Gentlemen, who are you, down there, and what do you want?"

"We want a party of runaway n-----," said Tom Loker. "One George Harris and Eliza Harris, and their son, and Jim Selden, and an old woman. We've got the officers, here, and a warrant to take 'em; and we're going to have 'em too. D'ye hear? A'nt your George Harris, that belongs to Mr. Harris, of Shelby county, Kentucky?"

"I am George Harris. A Mr. Harris, of Kentucky, did call me his property. But now I'm a free man, standing on God's free soil; and my wife and my child I claim as mine. Jim and his mother are here. We have arms to defend ourselves and we mean to do it. You can come up, if you like; but the first one of you that comes within the range of our bullets is a dead man, and the next, and the next; and so on till the last."

"O, come! come!" said a short, puffy man, stepping forward, and blowing his nose as he did so. "Young man, this ain't no kind of talk at all for you. You see, we're officers of justice. We've got the law on our side, and the power and so forth; so you'd better give up peaceably, you see; for you'll certainly have to give up, at last."

"I know very well that you've got the law on your side, and the power," said George bitterly. "You mean to take my wife to sell in New Orleans, and put my boy like a calf in a trader's pen, and send Jim's old mother to the brute that whipped and abused her before, because he couldn't abuse her son. You want to send Jim and me back to be whipped and tortured, and ground down under the heels of them that you call masters; and your laws will bear you out on it, - more shame for you and them! But you haven't got us. We don't own your laws; we don't own your country; we

stand here as free, under God's sky, as you are; and, by the great God that made us, we'll fight for our liberty till we die."
Harriet Beecher Stowe – *Uncle Tom's Cabin*

The above incident reflects a composed narrative of a reported event, rather than a directly observed, or personally experienced, factual one. It is, nevertheless, based on the actual experiences in the life of a free former slave, Josiah Henson. Josiah Henson spent thirty years on a plantation in servitude in Montgomery County, Maryland. He escaped from slavery through Ohio (a free territory) to Canada, after his owner reneged on a promise allowing him to purchase his freedom (a common practice, albeit one that relied upon the dubious integrity of the slave owner or his heirs.)

Henson became a Methodist preacher, abolitionist, lecturer, and founder of a cooperative colony of former slaves in Canada. His memoirs, "Uncle Tom's story of his life", published in 1849, provided Harriet Beecher Stowe with the model for her best selling book, Uncle Tom's Cabin, and the story for her historic novel.

From "Cargo" to Contraband

Initially brought to the Americas as freight or "cargo", to be treated within the context of servitude as slaves, the events of the Civil War created still another category of black people, that of war-seized "contraband". In terms of definition, contraband refers to hidden or stolen property seized by another party usually within the context of war and its spoils. The unique nature of the civil war created a still further class of contraband that of displaced and dispossessed black people, who were not the spoils of war, as commonly defined, but its forced labor in support of Confederate war aims. Some unforeseen victims of the war were among the many displaced blacks refugees. Many were escapees. Others found themselves people caught in a maelstrom of events abandoned by the plantation system and escaped the confines of slavery without benefit of home or sustenance.

The use of the term contraband was first employed as a means of accounting for black people who fled from servitude, as opportunity afforded them, during the course of the War into Union ranks. Initially, since no Northern provision or policy existed in order to care for such persons, nor guidelines regarding what role they might play in the conflict, impromptu recommendations and practices were adopted (usually as a discretionary or improvised action), often initiated on the part of a commander/administrator of a Southern district captured and held by a Union army. However, as the war progressed and large numbers of slaves fled toward Union lines, a policy was needed.

In May of 1861, three escaped slaves arrived at Fortress Monroe, on the tip of the Virginia peninsula. The Fortress was in Union hands, at that time, under the command of General Benjamin Butler, formally a Massachusetts lawyer and politician. According to the men, their master compelled them to work on digging a Confederate battery, obviously, an aid to the Southern war effort. In their escape they appealed to Butler for sanctuary.

Butler, an astute lawyer, and politician from Massachusetts before the war, saw some interesting possibilities for obtaining needed workers by employing these men. Although unauthorized to do so, he offered them protection. He reasoned that since they were aiding the enemy in its war effort against the Union, it was proper to seize them as contraband.

Sometime later, when a Confederate officer demanded that Butler return the runaways under existing state laws, Butler refused his request. Butler argued that since these men were being employed in work directed against the United States government, they had become legitimate contraband of war and were eligible for confiscation.

Butler's action ignited similar responses from fellow officers faced with increasing numbers of black refugees seeking asylum within their columns. Shortly thereafter, on August 8th, the United States Congress authorized, under the idea of "military necessity", the seizure of all Southern property employed "in aid of the rebellion". The contraband law became official government policy. And while the contraband policy was still a far cry from the full liberation of slaves, or the arming of former slaves to fight for the Union cause, it was one of several steps eventually leading to that event.

Black Men Enter the War

Frederick Douglas

"Who would be free themselves must strike the blow...I urge you to fly to arms and smite to death the power that would bury the Government and your liberty in the same hopeless grave. This is your golden opportunity."

"Once let the black man get upon his person the brass letter, U.S., let him get an eagle on his button, and a musket on his shoulder and bullets in his pocket, there is no power on earth that can deny that he has earned the right to citizenship."

Earlier, at the beginning of the War and upon the initiation of hostilities in 1861, free black men, and later with the inauguration of the Emancipation Proclamation on January 1st, 1863, former slaves were able to fight for their rights as free men and potential citizens. Then, as at the time of the Revolutionary War, and once again during the War of 1812, black soldiers were to play a prominent role in this war, as well.

Black men began to enlist as Union soldiers in 1862 and by the end of the war almost ten percent (180,000 men) of the Union Army consisted of black soldiers. Moreover, they performed well; contrary to the prevailing treatment accorded them, as well as the perpetuation of persistent myths and stereotypes regarding their alleged willingness to fight, the actions of black soldiers proved critical to the Union cause. As the War terminated, twenty-one black soldiers were granted the Congressional Medal of Honor in recognition of their heroism during the War. Nevertheless, their role and participation was often maligned; existing conditions forced black men to earn their places of honor in spite of encountering numerous obstacles outside and within the armed forces.

Racial prejudice was a fact of life for the black soldier. Initially, when black men tried to enlist they were told that it was, "a white man's war; no blacks need apply." As the war progressed, however, with few victories on the eastern front, the necessity of black participants was contrary to the prevailing treatment accorded them, as well as the perpetuation of persistent myths and stereotypes regarding their alleged willingness to fight; the actions of black soldiers proved critical to the Union cause.

Initially, many white officers saw little value in the black soldiers, exhibiting implied and overt hostility to their participation. Aside from direct ridicule, they instituted harsh punishments, assigned them to hazardous duty more often than whites, and demonstrated neglectful practices relative to their well-being. Black officers (which were few in number) were as badly treated as those in lower rank.

Equal Pay for Equal Sacrifice

As black soldiers entered the Union ranks they suffered more inconvenience, discrimination, and disbelief than any other ethnic group of soldiers.

As the following letter attests, the plight of the black soldier was especially troublesome for the family he left behind. These circumstances were especially burdensome, relative to the disparate salaries offered black versus white soldiers, a practice that continued to devalue the value of the black man well into the war.
February 20, 1864

"I am a soldier, or at least that is what I was drafted for in the 6th USCT {United States Colored Troops}; have been in the service since Aug., last. I could not afford to get a substitute, or I would not be here now and my poor wife at home almost starving. When I was at home I could make a living for her and my two little ones; but now that I am a soldier they must do the best they can or starve. It almost tempts me to desert and run a chance of getting shot, when I read her letters, hoping that I would come to her relief. But what am I to do? It is a shame the way they treat us; our officers tell me now that we are not soldiers; that if we were we would get the same pay as the white men; that the government just called us out to dig and drudge, that we are to get but $7.00 per month. Really I thought I was a soldier, and it made me feel proud to think that I had a right to fight for Uncle Sam. When I was at Chelton Hill I felt very patriotic; but my wife's letters have brought my patriotism down to the freezing point, and I don't think it will ever rise again; and it is the case all though the regiment. Men having families at home, and they looking to them for support, and they not being able to send them one penny…"

Bought and Sold

Most black men faced racism in the army, at times, often similar to that which they had encountered under servitude, as well as those in their roles as private citizens. Some adjusted, while others fought racism in various guises, and still others refused to submit to it at all. Lieutenant Robert H. Isabelle was of the latter persuasion.

Lieutenant Isabelle was one of three black officers in the Union army. He was a member of the second Louisiana Native Guards selected as an officer by his men. He was an educated man whom, as a volunteer, chose to serve in the Union Army when Federal troops took New Orleans in 1862. However, he resigned from the army with other black officers during the course of his service. Racism, as he reported, prevented him from serving his country. He wrote his commanding officer Captain W. Hoffman on March 3, 1863, offering him the following explanation,

"I joined the United States Army…with the sole object of laboring for the good of our Country, …but after five or six months I am convinced that the same prejudice still exists and prevents that cordial harmony among officers which is indispensable for the success of the army."
Second Lieutenant R. H. Isabelle

Racial prejudice existed in 1961 in varied form, both within and outside of the army. And it existed throughout the war in all theaters of battle and their surrounding environs. Nor was racism confined to the South; freedom from victimization among black people in the North was always a tentative condition, even among those with abolitionist leanings. In the hands of white slave retrievers, and their conspirators, in both the South and North, it was also a precarious state.

The army did not change or screen out prejudice from the lives of black soldiers; it merely reflected the views and behavior of the wider society within which it functioned. One, unfortunate way, in which this occurred was in the poor treatment of wounded black soldiers. In the following incident reported by George W. Hatton, Orderly Sergeant, 1st USCI, Hampton (Virginia) Hospital, we find the practice of racism within the hospital system designed to care for wounded troops. As his letter attests, Sergeant Hatton's desire to return home to recover from injuries incurred after a battle {a common and frequently granted request} in Petersburg, Virginia, was subject to a very different disposition than that of a fellow white applicant.

July 16, 1864

"I have been silent for a long time, but today I must speak, for it is a day long to be remembered by me, a wounded soldier of the U.S. Army.

I was wounded at the battle of Petersburg on the 15th of June last, and arrived at the Hampton Hospital on the 20th. On my arrival there, I wrote to my father, stating that I was wounded and that I would like him to come and see me, and if possible, take me home, where I should have the attendance of my kind and loving mother. My father complied with my request, and arrived at Fortress Monroe on the 30th. I was overjoyed to see him.

Today he departed with a hung-down head, leaving me with an aching heart. I must state the cause of my trouble. It is as follows:

On my father's arrival at the hospital he stated the object of his visit to the doctor in charge, who, very short and snappish, referred him to Dr. White, one of the head surgeons. Father immediately proceeded to Dr. White's office, where he expected to receive a little satisfaction, but to his heart-rending surprise, received none. After making every exertion in his power to get a furlough, he failed in so doing, without receiving the slightest shadow of satisfaction.

All of this I was willing to stand, as I had discharged my duty as a soldier from the first of May, 1863, up to the time I was wounded, for the low United States' degrading sum of $7 per month, that no man but the poor, down-trodden, uneducated, patriotic black man would be willing to fight for. Yes, I stand all this; but the great wound I received at the hospital was this: A white man, whose name I did not learn, came from Washington with my father for the same purpose, to see his son and carry him home. His success needs no comment; let it suffice to say that he was white, and he carried his son home.

Such deception as that I thought was crucified at the battle of Fort Wagner {July 18, 1863}; buried at Milliken's Bend {June 7, 1863}; rose the third day, and descended into everlasting forgetfulness in the Appomattox River at the battle of Petersburg.

Mr. Editor, when, oh! when can one of my color, and in my position, at this time, find a comforter? When will my people be a nation? I fear never on the American soil; though we may crush this cursed rebellion." George W. Hatton, Orderly Sergeant 1st USCI

Another account of inequality within the Army, coupled with the expressed hope for an initiation of equitable civil rights for the black soldier, was penned by Corporal John. H. B. Payne, a school teacher from Ohio. He wrote on May 24, 1864:

"…I am not willing to fight for anything less than the white man fights for. If the white man cannot support his family on seven dollars a month, I cannot support mine on the same amount.

And I am not willing to fight for this Government for money alone. Give me my rights, the rights that this Government owes me, the same rights that the white man has. I would be willing to fight three years for this Government without one cent of the mighty dollar. Then I would have something to fight for. Now I am fighting for the rights of the white man. White men have never given me the rights that they are bound to respect. God has not made one man better than another; therefore, one man's rights are no better than another's. They assert that because a large proportion of our race is in bondage we have a right to help them.

I want to know if it was not the white man that put them in bondage? How can they hold us responsible for their evils? And how can they expect that we should do more to blot it out than they are willing to do themselves? If every slave in the United States were emancipated at once, they would not be free yet. If the white man is not willing to respect my rights, I am not willing to respect his wrongs. Out rights have always been limited in the United States. It is true that in some places a colored man, if he can prove himself to be half-white can vote. Vote for whom? The white man. What good do such rights ever do us - to be compelled always to be voting for the white man and never to be voted for?

CHAPTER 10

THE COLORED SOLDIERS

"Jake", said John, sitting in Jake's great room, his back to the roaring fire set earlier by Eva, "As you are probably aware, judging from the guns and supplies we carry, and Jed's and Hunter's presence, that our mission here in Lancaster is more complicated than it would seem. It is, and at this point, it still is, twofold. The first, setting up the "listening posts" is, thanks to your work, well underway. With the trusted volunteers you have found, and the help of Aunt Amy, Patrick and Danny, these may be monitored and not demand any additional attention beyond my initial presence.

The second task is more personal and demands our immediate attention. Hunter, Jed and I are traveling south in several weeks in order to set in motion a plan to rescue Hunter's wife Mae and his two boys. The three of them were captured earlier, and are being held captive by Mungo, as leverage over Hunter. As things stand, we have reason to believe that after Mungo has exhausted his use of Hunter that he will sell Mae and the boys and have them sent south. He has assured Hunter that he will release his captives, but based on our knowledge of Mungo, and our last adventure with him and Smithy, there is little reason to assume that he will keep his promise.

I know that it is somewhat unreasonable to ask, but we could use your help. Your knowledge of the countryside could prove invaluable. And you are a good man to have in a fight You proved that in the rescue of Danny. Will you join us?"

"Jake, No! No! You can't go," exclaimed Eva in a pleading voice, expressing both her sense of anger, and resentment.

"By the grace of god, you were just returned to us. If you go on this mission, I know that you will never return. I feel it in my bones. You will be tempting fate once more. And this time you will lose to whatever force dictates our destinies. And, you barely escaped eternal punishment earlier."

"I would not ask," interjected John, sensing the direction of the discussion and his need to intervene, "and I will understand if you refuse, but I must ask for your help. Aside from William Tall Tree and Sean O' Conner, who are recovering from their wounds under the care of Dr. Wilson and Ms. Emma Pruitt in Philadelphia, you were the best fighter with a rifle that we had.

Unfortunately, I suspect that we will need that skill once again." he added.

As John spoke, Eva once again pleaded with Jake.

"No you can't risk everything that we have, the boys, myself to go off on this …adventure. Can't you see that…"

Resisting the entreaties of his wife, Jake declares, "But, I must. Don't you see that," responded Jake, turning toward his wife.

"John and these other folk risked themselves for me and I am in their debt. Beyond that, these folk need me and I could help," he continued.

"But what about the boys? How can you leave them? Or me?" argued Eva.

"Yes, I reckon that it does come down to them, and you, …and my honor, responded Jake. "But, how can I refuse this request …and still face my sons? I don't need to be a hero to them, but how can I tell them that I refused to help another person held in captivity like I was, to be branded and sold like cattle, or pigs, when it is in my power to stop that atrocity?

"Black folk have a different path to take in these current matters than white folk. And, it appears to me that we don't have much choice.

"Don't you realize that we are all tied up together in this struggle?" he continues. " Mr. Douglass says to us, it is a Gordian knot that can only be severed by a group of men, large enough and determined enough to wield the sword of justice. The struggle is too great to be trusted to any one man, or any one isolated group of people."

"But I couldn't stand to lose you again," cried Eva.

"I understand that, but we are caught in this time and in this place. White boys have been fighting this war for the last two years. Now it is our turn to come to the fight. And I can contribute, irrespective of the consequences, to our struggle, as John has done. I can do no less".

A Short Conversation

The year is 1863. It is early spring and the soil is wet and ripe from a recent rain. It is planting season, a time to renew, once again, the productivity of the fertile earth in this part of the land. The place is an isolated field in rural Pennsylvania where two young black men are tilling the soil in preparation for the yearly planting, when one drops his rake, sighs, and turns to his companion, then says to him:

Peter – "When are we going?"

"They need us and I can't wait"

Jack – "My God. You sound like one of them white boys".

"Just can't wait to get your head blown off."

Peter – "Well, we've been waiting a long time and now it's our turn".

Jack – "That it is. I agree. And I hear tell that once we get in, it will only be a couple of months before it's all over."

Peter – "Well I hope I get there before it is."

Jack – "You will. Many of us will also. The black man will be heard from. It is only a matter of time."

WILL THEY FIGHT?

The presence of Black Soldiers was felt

Among the many questions associated with arming former slaves, as well as free blacks, was whether they would be willing to fight, and how well they were likely to conduct themselves on the battlefield. In the Civil War, wide-spread skepticism and exclusionary attitudes on the part of whites {who saw the war, at least initially, as a conflict of contrasting political ideologies, rather than in support/abolition of slavery}, led to the need for a renewed validation of the black man's willingness to assume an active role in this more recent conflict; the distinguished service performance of black men in the nation's previous wars (the Revolutionary War and the War of 1812) was either forgotten or disregarded. Compounding this pessimism, was the need (as Lincoln professed in his initial hesitation to use black troops) to keep the border States (who still practiced slavery in many places) within the Union. The arming of black men and former slaves could be a defining catalyst leading to the shifting of their value from a source of labor supporting the conflict to that of a potential army.

And they came, in unprecedented numbers. And their presence was felt.

Yes, they will Fight: Black military heroes

Fort Wagner, South Carolina, July 18, 1863
Within two weeks of the Army of the Potomac's victory at Gettysburg and General Grant's victory at Vicksburg, in July of 1863, a large Union force gathered outside the walled Confederate fort on the beach at Fort Wagner. From the bay, six ironclad Union ships began their bombardment. Lying on a sandy beach within 1000 yards of the fort were members of the Union infantry, including the 600 men of the 54th Massachusetts Colored Infantry. Behind them was the 6th Connecticut; however, on this day it would be the black soldiers of the 54th who would lead the perilous assault, followed by the Connecticut 6th.

Robert J. Simmons, 1st Sergeant, Co. B, 54th Massachusetts Infantry, a black trooper was there and the following letter documents his experiences:

"We are on the march to Fort Wagner, to storm it. We have just completed our successful retreat from James Island; we fought a desperate battle there Thursday morning. Three companies of us, B, H, and K, were out on picket about a good mile in advance of the regiment. We were attacked early in the morning. Our company was in the reserve, when the outposts were attacked by rebel infantry and cavalry. I was send out by our Captain in command of a squad of men to support the left flank. The bullets fairly rained about us; when I got there the poor fellows were falling down around me, with pitiful groans. Out pickets only numbered about 250 men attacked by about 900. It is supposed by the line of battle in the distance, that they were supported by a reserve of 3,000 men. We had to fire and retreat toward our own encampment. One poor Sergeant of ours was shot down along side of me; several others were wounded near me.

God has protected me through this, my first fiery, leaden trail, and I do give him the glory, and render my praises unto His holy name. My poor friend {Sergeant Peter} Vogelsang is shot through the lungs; his case is critical, but the doctor says he may probably live. His company suffered much. Poor, good and brave Sergeant {Joseph D.} Wilson of his company {H}, after killing four rebels with his bayonet, was shot through the head by the fifth one. Poor fellow! May his noble spirit rest in peace. The General has complimented the Colonel on the gallantry and bravery of his regiment."

The Civil War was almost two years old when President Abraham Lincoln issued the Emancipation Proclamation to take effect on January 1, 1863. With that historic step, for the first time, black Americans were encouraged to enlist in the Union Army. And they came in large numbers: 180,000 strong.

Among the enlistees was a young man named William Carney. Born on February 29, 1840 at Norfolk, Virginia, William Carney's mother was a slave to Major Carney. Prior to the Civil War there were no functioning programs for educating young black men in the South. Yet, Carney, among a few, was fortunate enough at the age of 14 to attend a secret school where he learned to read and write.

Emancipated when his owner, Major Carney died, young William Carney moved to Bedford, Massachusetts and began preparing for a future as a minister. However, when volunteers were sought to join the Army, William Carney decided to temporarily set aside his plans to enter the ministry. He later stated, "I felt I could best serve my God by serving my Country and my oppressed bothers." He became a member of, and trained with, the 54th Massachusetts Colored Infantry's C Company. This first black company became the test case for assessing the commitment and capability of black troops in the Union Army and. It also answered the question of whether the colored troops would distinguish themselves.

The assault on Fort Wagner was to be the first real test of young black, volunteer, Union soldiers. Though the 54th Massachusetts was a federal unit, it was an entirely separate regiment. And despite Lincoln's proclamation and his acceptance of these "soldiers of color", prejudices and preconceived notions of blacks prevailed in the North.

Among those chosen to lead the assault on Fort Wagner was 23-year old Sergeant William Carney. It was a severe test for these young, inexperienced troops, as well as a momentous occasion filled with tense drama.

On the day of the attack, the troops were assembled in front of the battery. Upon receiving an anticipated signal to advance, the troops jumped to their feet and charged at a run towards the enemy stronghold. The Confederate defenders were prepared for them and cannon fire and bullets flew through the air, devastating the advancing 54th. Nevertheless, heedless of the danger and often fighting hand to hand, the 54th continued the advance. Ahead of them Sergeant John Wall carried the colors, the red, white and blue of the United States of America. Suddenly a rifle bullet dropped Sergeant Wall and the flag began to fall to the ground. As he observed these events, Sergeant William Carney threw his rifle aside and grasped the colors before they touched the ground.

As he retrieved the flag, another rifle ball sliced through the air, this one hitting Sergeant Carney in the leg. With soldiers falling all around him Carney gathered the strength to ignore the pain in his leg, raise the colors high in the air, and continue to lead the advance. Somehow he gained the entrance to the fort and planted the flag, ... only to find that at that startling moment that he was alone, ...everyone else either having been killed or wounded. Then, this solitary figure and his flag remained pressed against the wall of the fort for half an hour as the battle raged on. Suddenly, an attack to the right of the fort's entrance drew the enemy's attention away from him. Meanwhile, Sgt. Carney noticed a group of soldiers advancing towards him. Mistaking them for friendly troops, he raised his flag high. Again gunfire split the air as Carney realized, all too late, that they were Confederate soldiers.

At that moment Carney remembered the flag he was protecting. Rather than dropping the flag and fleeing for his life, he wrapped the flag around the staff to shield it and ran down an embankment. Stumbling through a ditch, chest-deep in water, he held the flag high. Another bullet struck him in the chest, and another in the right arm, and still another hit him in his right leg. Carney struggled on, however, determined not to let the flag fall to the enemy.

From a point safely in the distance of where they had retreated, what remained of the 54th Massachusetts Colored Infantry watched the Sergeant struggle towards safety. A retreating member of the 100th New York passed Carney and, seeing the severity of his wounds said, "Let me carry that flag for you." With his indomitable spirit and courage Sergeant Carney replied, "No one but a member of the 54th should carry the colors." Despite the sounds of rifle and cannon fire that followed him, Carney struggled on. Another enemy bullet found its mark, grazing his head, but Carney still wouldn't quit. Before turning over the colors to another survivor of the 54th, Carney modestly said, "Boys, I only did my duty; the old flag never touched the ground!"

Many Civil War medals were awarded for protecting and displaying the flag under fire, or for capturing enemy flags. Sergeant William Carney received one of his nation's highest honors for his bravery under fire; he was awarded the first Medal of Honor given to a black soldier, on May 23, 1900, nearly 40 years later. {More than half such awards from the Civil War were presented 20 or more years after the fact.}

The exploits of the 54th Massachusetts at Fort Wagner, extinguished any doubt of the value of black combatants in the field, or any lingering fears of a less than fully committed fighting force. Its courage was widely reported, as well as lauded in the Northern press. The New New York Tribune compared the actions at Fort Wagner with those that occurred 90 years earlier at Bunker Hill, noting that the former battle would stand as a symbol of black patriotism with the same reverence expressed for the latter among white Yankees.

One jubilant, public expression of the pride taken in support of the 54th, was offered by the abolitionist Angelina Grimke Weld in discussion with a friend. She asked her companion, "Do you not rejoice & exult in all that praise that is lavished upon our brave colored troops even by the Pro-slavery papers? I have no tears to shed over their graves, because I see that their heroism is working a great change in public opinion, forcing all men to see the sin & shame of enslaving such men."

Recognition of the extraordinary acts committed by the 54th regiment on the Fort Wagner battle field, also reached the highest levels of the government and the army. General U. S. Grant, shortly after the battle wrote the following private letter to President Lincoln:
August 23, 1863

"I have given the subject of arming the negro my hearty support. This, with the emancipation of the negro, is the heaviest (sic) blow yet given to the Confederacy. ... By arming the negro we have added a powerful ally. They will make good soldiers and taking him from the enemy weakens him in the same proportion they strengthen us. I am therefore most decidedly in favor of pushing this policy to the enlistment of a force sufficient to hold all the South falling into our hands and to aid in capturing more."

U. S. Grant, Major General

Perhaps, as important as official recognition of his value, the black soldier needed the support of white officers and other common soldiers in the field. His exploits on the battlefield, as evident in the following comment of one eyewitness, led to such deserved acknowledgment.

August 24, 1863

"… you have no idea how my prejudices with regard to negro troops have been dispelled by the battle the other day. The brigade of negroes behaved magnificently and fought splendidly; …could not have done better. They are far superior in discipline to the white troops, and just as brave".
National Intelligencer

Among his fellow soldiers, attitudes toward the black trooper slowly changed, as well. A letter from an anonymous private to William Lloyd Garrison, publisher of The Liberator, illustrates these changes.

July 15, 1864

"I thought you might be pleased to know that your principles were strongly represented in the department that loaded the 100-pounder gun that threw the first three shells at Charleston city, S.C. No. 1 {gunner} is a strong abolitionist and has worked well among the soldiers. This man puts the load into the gun. No. 2 is now in favor of emancipation, though he don't think the Negro is his equal. No. 3 was an old emancipationist years ago, and always took your paper. And the gunner is a Republican. The other members seem to go with the strongest party, but believe in extirpating slavery from the land at the present time."

Public recognition was equally forthcoming. Perceptions, by the public, at least in regard to the performance of black troops on the battlefield, were changing.

The *New York Times* published the following declaration regarding the recent performance by black troopers at the front:

"…this official testimony settles the question that the Negro race can fight…It is no longer possible to doubt the bravery and steadiness of the colored race, when rightly led."

June 11, 1863

Naval Heroes

When called upon, black soldiers distinguished themselves on many fronts. Less well known is that their efforts were complemented by black naval heroes and sailors, whose military value, (as a function of their earlier entry into the war), was realized well before those fighting on land-based campaigns was about to be recognized. Two such stories are reported here. May 19, 1862

When it occurred, it was referred to as "…one of the most heroic acts of the war" by the *New York Times*. It was also noted, as reported by a senior naval officer, as "one of the coolest and most gallant naval acts of war." It was that, as well as one of the most audacious actions committed on behalf of the Union cause. And it was highly celebrated at the time.

In 1900, a statute was passed by the United States Congress, in recognition of the heroic deed of Robert Smalls in the early stages of the war. The citation read, "Robert Smalls, on the thirteenth of May, eighteen hundred and sixty two, did capture the steamer Planter, with all the armament and ammunition for Fort Ripley, at the city of Charleston, taking her out and turning her over to the Federal blockading squadron off Charleston…"

Smalls was not a combatant at the time of his remarkable feat. However, he saw and seized an opportunity to aid the Union war effort, as well as to attain freedom for his family and himself. It was a daring and outstanding display of courage.

In the fall of 1861, in Charleston, SC, Smalls {an experienced, knowledgeable seaman} was wheelman (pilot) of the Planter, an armed Confederate 140 foot long side wheeler steamer, employed as a military/material transport. The Planter was a swallow draft vessel capable of navigating river channels in the hands of a skilled navigator.

On May 12, 1862, the Planter's three white officers decided to spend the night ashore. They believed that their vessel was secure, having posted twenty guards at the wharf during the night, with sentinels a few paces from the boat. In the early morning hours of the 13th, however, Smalls and several other black crewmen would seize the vessel and make a run for the Union vessels which formed a blockade of the port. In accordance with a plan previously devised by Smalls they planned to seize the Planter as opportunity dictated. On that night, Robert, who had learned to imitate the Planter's captain's demeanor through observation, assumed the helm of the Planter, as its "captain". (He was dressed in a captain's uniform and donned a hat similar to the captain's. Observers, several of whom spotted the vessel from shore, as it slowly passed by, did not notice anything amiss.)

The Planter backed out of what was then known as Southern Wharf around 3 a.m. The ship, then unexpectedly, and unobtrusively stopped at a nearby wharf to pick up a number of stowaways. These included Smalls' family and several other crewman's relatives; those rescued had been concealed in hiding on the shore for some time.

With his wife and children and this small group of other African Americans now on board, Smalls made his daring escape. The Planter not only had the "contraband" as passengers, but it also had four valuable artillery pieces aboard, besides its own two guns. Perhaps most valuable, however, was the code book that Robert had in his possession that would reveal the Confederate's secret signals and placement of mines and torpedoes in and around Charleston harbor.

Smalls piloted the ship past five Confederate forts which guarded the harbor, including Fort Sumter. {The renegade ship passed by Sumter at approximately 4:30 a.m.} It then headed straight for the Federal fleet, which was part of a Union blockade of Confederate ports, making sure to hoist a white flag. The first ship which the Planter encountered was the USS Onward, which prepared to fire until a sailor noticed the white flag. When the Onward's captain boarded the Planter, Smalls requested that he raise the US flag immediately. He then turned the Planter over to the United States Navy, along with its inboard cargo of artillery and explosives intended for the Confederate fort.

Robert Smalls "naval career" did not end then. Smalls became a pilot for the Union navy, and later for the Union Army. He returned to the Planter where he piloted plantation raids leading to the emancipation of black slaves. On one occasion, during an engagement with the enemy, the white captain of the Planter abandoned his post under an assault by a heavy artillery bombardment, forcing Smalls to take command of the vessel. Smalls did so, assuring the safe passage of the Planter. In response, the Federal government made Smalls the official captain of the Planter.

Although faced with racial injustice all of his life, Smalls made the best of those limited opportunities afforded him. After the war he became the first black U.S. congressman from South Carolina, where he served intermittent terms for a decade, helping to establish the Paris Island Marine Corps Training Depot, among his contributions. Above all, he demonstrated that blacks could provide the intelligence and manpower to push for a successful completion of the war.

Another dramatic incident of comparable heroism involved the sailor-gunner John Lawson (U.S.S. Hartford) at the momentous Battle of Mobile Bay on August 5th, 1864.

Early on August 5th, the U.S.S. Hartford, as flagship of the U.S. naval flotilla, was one of many Union ships gathered outside Mobile Bay, the last functioning Confederate naval port on the Gulf of Mexico. It was to be the scene of an historic battle. That morning, as John Lawson prepared the heavy gun on the berth deck, Admiral David Farragut (the old man of the Navy) had himself tied to the upper mast of the Hartford (to witness and direct the battle) as the fleet moved in to attack. There were four major obstacles facing the attacking fleet: Fort Morgan, which guarded the entrance to the bay; Confederate gunboats inside the bay; the massive Confederate ironclad, the Tennessee; and three lines of mines (torpedoes, as they were called at the time).

As they entered the bay, the Confederate ships and forts fired a massive barrage upon Farragut's eighteen-ship fleet. In the confusion, the fleet stopped, forcing the Hartford to steer around a stalled ship in front of it. As the Hartford headed into the mine field, a crew member shouted out a warning. Farragut, mindful of the danger, but intent on his mission, responded with his infamous cry, "Damn the torpedoes! Full speed ahead!"

Meanwhile on the deck of the Hartford, Lawson and his crew were exchanging cannon fire with gun crews stationed at Fort Morgan. During the fierce battle, a significant number of the Hartford's crew were killed or wounded. Lawson, himself was struck in the leg and thrown across the deck; he was badly shaken and told to go below deck to seek medical assistance. Lawson, however, disregarded those instructions and returned to his post. In spite of the terrible slaughter going on around him, he continued to fire away until the fleet had passed the Fort and the Confederate minefield. During the fierce fighting most of the rebel gunboats in action had been sunk and the Tennessee was captured. Finally, by ten o'clock that morning the battle had ended and Lawson could then have his wounds attended.

The next day, having witnessed Lawson's heroism, the captain of the Hartford, officially commended him for his bravery; for his fortitude and commitment to duty, he too, was subsequently awarded the Congressional Medal of Honor.

CHAPTER 11

Capture

Shortly after their arrival in Lancaster the Scobell party, under John's direction, began the work that would create and monitor the "listening posts" operation. The task itself was a simple one: Patrick and Danny, Aunt Amy and Hunter, Big Jake and lastly, John, himself would each assume responsibility for setting up a "post" using a cadre of independent resident-informers as operatives. Each unit would operate independently of the others, where possible, as well as in unison, as warranted, within an agreed upon system set up by John for gathering, assembling, and distributing information.

The process itself was twofold. On one level the varied groups were independent of each other. Yet, they were also interwoven within the whole. Each party would operate as a distinct quasi-secret entity maintaining its separate anonymity. This strategy would allow the unit to maximize its efficiency and safeguard the security of the enterprise in the event of detection.

Under the suspicion of observer reports of troop movements being conveyed to the enemy, the Army of Northern Virginia, contrary to General Lee's wishes, but supported by his staff, had began to develop a counter-intelligence service to deter similar efforts on the part of the Army of the Potomac.

Each unit was semi-independent of the others. However, each was also part of an integral system in which couriers attached to the unit in question, who were assigned on the basis of their geographical location, would travel among its composite parts gathering and relaying acquired information as it became available. John, with the assistance of Jed Harper, served as the chief coordinator and facilitator of these data. As such, the latter traveled among the coordinators of the independent units in order to gather together the varied components that hopefully, would comprise the mosaic that when stitched together would reveal the strategy and implementation of its military resources by Southern forces in support of the movement of troops and supplies committed by the Army of Northern Virginia to the forthcoming battle. Their work, as spies, would be viewed and interpreted as "treasonable" by the South military authority operating within its locale, and subsequently, punishable by firing squad. Consequently, it demanded extraordinary caution and attention to detail.

It was a good plan. However, it needed time to succeed. If permitted to be carried to completion, which would require a month or so, especially during the most active period of Southern troop movement, it would have allowed observers to secure the data necessary for the development and institution of a more acutely directed federal counter attack. At least, that was the hope, and it appeared to be a reasonable expectation for the initial period of the "listening posts" operation .

For the first several weeks, independent cadres of informers obtained information of value and were able to offer John data on the general pattern of southern troop movement. These data, as expected, came from disparate sources, but John, with Jed's assistance, was able to put together some of the bits of reported observations into a coherent pattern. He found, moreover, as before in other places, that black people along the routes taken by large bodies of troops, were especially good observers. And he knew that on this occasion, with the support of Generals Hancock and Reynolds, as opposed to his experience in the past, most notably at Antietam, that his reports would be heeded and acted upon, rather than ignored. However, as under earlier circumstances, fate would play a crucial role in this drama, unfortunately, before he could complete this mission.

John knew that his work with the listening posts would have to be completed quickly or through the efforts of others as his date with destiny approached. As anticipated, but occurring a bit sooner than he assumed would be the case, Mungo would intervene in their plans.

The Intervention of Mungo

It was scarcely to be imagined at the time; numerous intelligence reports were arriving almost daily from the widely scatterd "listening posts". And they were coming in from all directions. If early indications derived from his scouts were to be believed, as appeared to be the case, John was compiling an intelligence report sure to be of interest to Generals Reynolds and Hancock; the listening posts were actively gleaning data from their varied communities, as hoped. Moreover, the data suggested significant shifts in southern troop moment; the Army of Northern Virginia was on the move, coming from a variety of directions and heading, if they were reading the signs correctly, toward Harrisburg, Pennsylvania. Within several days, if confirmed, John would be able to file a report of significant value to the Army of the Potomac.

John, by working desperately with his cadre of informants estimated that he would need less than a week to confirm reports of initial sightings of large enemy troop advances. However, unknown to him at the time, his report would never be filed; John and Jed's early progress was to come to naught shortly.

It occurred early one morning as John was traveling on horseback on a familiar circuit within the confines of the boundaries surrounding the "listening posts". About halfway into his journey, he was approached on the trail by a lone rider heading in his direction. It was a figure familiar with his route. As the rider drew near John recognized that it was Jed and, as John assumed by his unexpected arrival, his friend carried unwelcome, but anticipated, news.

As he reined in his horse, Jed said, "I have just been in contact with Hunter. He informs me that Mungo has approached him and the time has come. We can expect that Mungo, with several of his men, to initiate your capture this afternoon. We need to be ready."

The meeting as related by Jed was short and precise. Mungo, with Noah, Hunter's son in tow, intercepted Hunter at a local inn that the latter frequented. Allowing for a short rejoicing between the father and son, Mungo set up conditions for John's capture and discussed further arrangements for the release of Mae and her younger son. In turn, Hunter was to accompany John that afternoon, on a route designated by Mungo in order to facilitate his capture. Hunter was to lure John to the site, as suggested by Mungo, in order to confirm a fictitious, unconfirmed sighting of a large contingent of Southern troops. Hunter was told to inform John that this sighting might be the main body of the First Corps, but would require his further confirmation. Noah was to be left in the care of friends and to rejoin his father later.

That afternoon Hunter and John set out for their expected rendezvous with Mungo. In preparation, John wore his special loose fitting clothing and hat. Each contained his hidden escape implements. He also decided to carry a small derringer, well hidden, as well.

Jed had gathered the smoke bombs prepared by John and himself with the aid of Dr. Wilson, the Ketchum grenades supplied by General Hancock, as well as four repeating rifles, and food and blankets, donated by Rep. Stevens and Mrs. Smith. He had stored them away in preparation for the journey in which he will track John and Mungo. With Big Jake accompanying Jed on horseback, the rescue team was ready. Jed would follow John and Hunter's trail about a mile behind them, with an armed Jake approximately a half mile in front of Jed, and to the rear of John and Hunter.

As Hunter and John reach a clearing their path is blocked. They suddenly find themselves surrounded by three armed men carrying rifles, who appear unexpectedly, from behind the scrub brush encircling the road. It is Mungo and two of his cohorts on horseback. "Pull up," shouts Mungo, "We have you covered." As anticipated, the plot for John's capture has been set in play and John takes stock of the scene.

He notes that Mungo has changed somewhat; physically he seems the same as John recalls. However, he also appears to be in be in a festive, receptive mood. With a rather sardonic smile on his face Mungo has pause for joy; with his armed men protecting him and limiting movement of his two captives, Hunter and John, he is in complete control and he relishes this newfound, power over his adversary. He has plotted and waited for this moment to arrive for some time, seeking redemption and revenge, and he obviously relishes it.

With his rifle aimed at John's chest Mungo says, "So we meet again. And under somewhat fortuitous circumstances, I might add. That is, for me."

John says nothing in response, and Mungo continues, "This time, I'm afraid, you will not escape from me or your fate. Certainly, not on my account."

"I have plans for you. None, of which you could have imagined."

John, aware of the need to keep the false screen play surrounding his capture alive and believable, turns to Hunter in feigned anger, and shouts, "You created this! You knew that he would be here! And you lead me to him. You damn traitor!"

"He forced me to betray you," shouts Hunter in mock response. "I had no choice. It was you or my family. And I choose them."

Mungo, although apparently amused by this heated exchange of verbal admonitions and recriminations, nevertheless, decides to terminate the fierce word play among John and Hunter. "That's enough of that. We have work to do. Hunter you may go, with my thanks. I will keep my end of the bargain. You can expect to see your wife and child shortly."

As Hunter turns to leave, Mungo turns to face John and directs the following orders to his men, "Miller, Parsons, tie him up good, and make sure that he is securely fastened to his horse. He's coming with us."

As Mungo continues south, Hunter turns in the opposite direction and proceeds north. Unknown to Mungo, once out of sight Hunter charts an alternative course and soon rejoins the team tracking John. He will accompany Jed and Big Jake in the pursuit of Mungo and his captive.

The three travel in tandem for several hours on the trail. Before long Jed stops to water the horses as they approach a stream, while Jake keeps account of Mungo and his party, riding ahead to keep track of his movement. Turning to Jed at this respite in their journey, Hunter attempts to explain his decision to join the rescuers.

"Noah wanted to join me", says Hunter. "However, I couldn't let him fall into Mungo's hands again. I promised him and myself, that I would see this through and return with his mother and younger brother. As John has made me realize, I can't trust Mungo's word in this matter nor his pledge to release Mae and my son. And John's friendship demands my loyalty and support."

Nodding his head in agreement, Jed moves the team forward.

Within a short time Big Jake approaches the wagon signaling Jed to stop the team. Apparently, Mungo has neared his slave compound. As Big Jake, Jed, and Hunter approach the road leading to the enclosure of Mungo's slave compound, they unexpectedly, encounter an old black man clothed in tattered garb who warns them that they are preceding on a 'pat down yonder where a black man ought not go, unless he's in chains."

The man, whose named, they learn is Ethan, informs them, "That white man (referring to Mungo) seized my boy, Chance. If you are going into that camp, I will help you. I was part of the gang of workers that helped construct it. At first, we didn't know what it was meant for. But, when we discovered what they had in min'd, we built part of one side with softer wood, and left a pry bar, so that it would be easier to force it down in the event of an escape."

"Yes. That's true", said Hunter. "My boy Noah told me to be on the lookout for defects in the wooden fence, having been told of several by one of the prison inmates in the camp."

Having reached their destination, the rescue party, with Ethan guiding them, they retreat from the road and make a "tentative" camp at a partial clearing close to the river's edge and out of sight. A guard is posted at a place overlooking the site. The first posted is Jake, followed by Jed and then Hunter. After precautions are completed the party beds down to rest. The next morning their plan for the rescue is reviewed and a sequence of action is proposed.

Previous to this juncture in the mission, John and Jed sketched out a timetable for the escape. Based on weather reports solicited from local residents, Jed and John purposed a schedule to coincide with prevailing climatic patterns. Their plan was to use nighttime cosmic signs for guidance that would correspond with astronomical sightings evident in the evening sky. At the moment the weather was cloudy, a contingency which occurred frequently in this part of the country and at this time of year. However, they also learned that this was a temporary phenomenon. Normally the night sky would become clear again within a brief period of time. That respite would provide an opportunity for the planned escape.

Meanwhile, John, under Mungo's control, is taken to the prison camp located at the end of the road and across a dry stream, navigated by Mungo and his cohorts. As they rode up to the enclosed structure set upon a small mound in the low lying hillside, across the river, John was struck by the enormity and barren-like atmosphere of the prison compound. It appeared to him to be an old mill that had, with minimal refurbishment, been converted into a fortress redesigned to hold a captive population.

Aside from its stone walls, surrounded by a high wooden fence encircling the entire compound, the fortress contained a warren of small cells designed to hold prisoners. John, upon Mungo's orders, was conscripted to one of these rooms. It was a quick transition, both physical and psychological, a dramatic change, transformative in its effect upon a prisoner, shifting him from the fresh, open air where he stood moments ago, to a darkened, foreboding enclosure emitting the foul mustiness and fetid smells of congregated souls held in captivity in a cramped space with limited sanitation and toileting facilities.

As he adjusted his eyes to the darkness of this new setting, John heard the sounds of other occupants. He quickly realized that he was not alone. However, he could not immediately determine the number of fellow inmates that were imprisoned with him. Nevertheless, from the scattered murmuring there appears to be at least half a dozen men and women of assorted ages.

Within a short interval he heard a voice, "Do not panic. You are not alone. There are several of us here. And there is no danger to you. My name is Samuel. Who are you?"

John identified himself to the stranger and learned that the voice he heard belonged to Samuel Goddard, until recently a former freeman, captured and brought to the compound by a team of Mungo's men. Samuel informed him that up until about a month ago he had resided on a small farm in Chambersburg, PA. Subsequently, he was kidnapped and taken prisoner by "slave retrievers". This information was somewhat welcome news to John, in spite of its tragic toll on Mr. Goddard and his family; it suggested that the slave compound , this gathering place of displaced persons where they were sequestered, bordered the lower tier of Pennsylvania, a distance not far from Lancaster. The journey between imprisonment and freedom was within reach, and perhaps, attainable for a number of the inmates that Mungo had imprisoned, as well.

Hungry and tired, but mindful of his mission as well, John asked when they would be fed. Samuel informed him that a young boy, Lucas, came around with his mother two times a day with a pot of food and some water for the inmates. "It would be Mae and her son", thought John. Fortuitously, he realized that this natural occurrence of events, a confluence of persons and circumstances, would enable him to establish contact with them shortly.

At the Clearing

The plan was set; the rescuers were ready and prepared to proceed, only awaiting the proper opportunity, likely a day hence. At that time, Jed and Jake would send forth a low level smoke signal from a "smoke bomb" tossed over the fence of the enclosure shortly before dusk at its least populated southern corner. It would be a signal to John indicating that they were ready to proceed. The plan would depend, in part, upon John locating and alerting Mae to be prepared to join him the evening of their departure. This would occur during Mae and her sons nightly round of distributing the evening meal to the incarcerated prisoners as the sun set. Mae would be at the distribution site, as always, and Jed and Big Jake would then loosen the outside fence, preparatory to their escape and in anticipation of the approach of the captives.

The Meeting with Mungo

The next day Mungo send word to his chief lieutenant to bring John to him at his residence, an old two-story former farm house that served as the compound headquarters.

As a precaution, he ordered that John be placed in an old set of chains and secured by his men when they retrieved him from his enclosure that morning. Mungo was determined to hinder any possibility of escape or any display of suppressed temperament or mismanagement on his part. His past interactions with John led him to regard his adversary with respect, an unfortunate oversight characteristic of most whites accustomed to underestimating the intellect and resourcefulness of blacks. It was a bow to white people's false confidence that those unfortunate souls held in servitude exemplified the worst features of the black race and by extension, justified keeping this underclass of the population in slavery. Mungo, as his past experience with John demonstrated, was far less likely to fall into this trap, as others have, and he cautioned his men to regard John with care and to show heightened vigilance around him; let fools, like Smithy, he reasoned, maintain their aloof posture toward blacks and correspondingly, suffer the consequences of their ill thought out beliefs.

As John was shuffled into his office, Mungo adopted a posed, self-contained civil attitude toward him. "Good morning Mr. Scobell," he said. "Please have a seat. We have some business to conduct and I thought it best to get it out of the way first thing." Characteristically, with a practiced, but disguised guile, Mungo had prepared himself for the interview he wished to conduct. He had decided beforehand that a cordial, as opposed to an adversarial approach, would serve his interests best. However, he did not anticipate John's reaction at this initial meeting where he was met with an oppositional, angry response by his adversary.

"I don't believe that I have any business to conduct with you. You kidnapped me, a free black, in free territory and are obligated to release me," said John, adding "That is the law."

"Well, Mr. Scobell, that may be how you choose to view your situation here", said Mungo, maintaining his temper, "but you are no longer in federal territory nor under the jurisdiction of the laws of the state of Pennsylvania. In this sovereign place, where slavery is protected by decree, I am the law," introjected Mungo.

"So let's do business."

"I am prepared to make an exchange. I want information on the whereabouts of your "listening posts", and the nature of your activities in Pennsylvania. I also want to know the latest information about Federal troop movement. And I will offer you a reasonable exchange. I will be willing to release you somewhere south of here when I leave this locale in order to pursue other business in several weeks hence."

"No!" shouted John. "I will not help you undermine our war efforts. I am a prisoner of war and should be treated as such."

"Well, again you misread your situation here," responded Mungo.

"You are a spy, Mr. Scobell. And according to the rules of warfare, I have every right to hang you. Moreover, since the high command of the Army of Northern Virginia has been informed of your presence here, I can obtain official sanction for my actions at any time, especially, if it is warranted. So, as you can see, your position here is quite untenable and only of temporary stability. Your fate, your very life, I might add, is in my hands. You probably have surmised this some time ago."

"You are lying", said John. "You have no such authorization, either to release me or to retain me. If that is the case, show me some written proof to the contrary."

Mungo is a bit perplexed by John's response to his offer. "Written proof?", he reiterates the phrase and thinks to himself.

While Mungo would normally dismiss John's request as further evidence of his impudence, usually with a taste of the whip to keep him under control, he decides that the "lawyerly" approach that John suggested might help sooth the injured pride that he felt in John's presence, particularly after the recent incidences they shared.

"By damn," he thought, "I can out think and get the better of this uppity darkie. And, I will."

"Alright, Mr. Scobell", said Mungo. "Since we appear to have some time before we need to settle this matter, I will get you the authoritarian you seek. I am meeting with a representative of the Army of Northern Virginia later tonight (the spy Harrison, presumably). He will provide any "necessary" authorization of my authority in this matter. Then, we can meet again and perhaps come to some reasonable accommodation."

John's bid for time, by delaying action by a suspicious, self-aggrandizing Mungo, as he had hoped to do, would succeed. As expected, Mungo's self-satisfaction in capturing John and his over-confidence in his ability to turn him would work against his hold over John. The escape attempt would occur that night, as John anticipated, at a time when Mungo would be gone and unable to direct any counterattack or retrieval of his "captives". His lack of vigilance, by his absence would further hinder Mungo's immediate plans to maintain John as a captive or to secure military information from him.

Further Developments that Afternoon

That afternoon John would met with Samuel and other "cell block" leaders. Recognizing that there was a substantial number of captives that could assist in an escape effort, by creating confusion and mayhem, possibly leading to their own freedom, as well, he planned to request their assistance.

Typically, each afternoon the maintenance of the prisoners well-being permitted, according to camp procedures established by Mungo himself, a limited, but relatively free exchange of contact among the inmates. The usual arrangement was to allow for two cell blocks, of about 50 inmates each, to use the enclosure at different times for one hour. That afternoon, however, with Mungo gone, the chief guard, in a misguided attempt at efficiency (and sloppy adherence to the rules, if truth be told) allowed all four cell blocks of 200 prisoners access to the enclosure at the same time. The head guards, in Mungo's absence (Miller and Parsons) decided that since the main object of the afternoon courtyard experience was to permit prisoner exercise, they were inclined to ignore the potential threat of free assembly. Permitting all four groups to congregate at the same time appeared to them as a time-saving opportunity, which it normally would be. But, not today. Those congregated would also be offered an opportunity that they could not resist.

At a number of improvised, sporadic meetings in the penal-like courtyard, Samuel introduced John to the various cell block leaders. As John explained to each of them, at sun set an escape attempt will be staged. To aid this process, they were encouraged to send their people out of their cell blocks upon a given signal, to seize weapons, where possible, and to cause havoc within the compound. There were thirteen well-armed guards stationed to prevent a slave insurrection. However, there were over 200 inmates under their collective charge. As John explained, his colleagues would loosen the fence on the southern fringe of the compound, that evening, allowing those prisoners that were able to reach the terminus of the property to escape.

John's plan was greeted by surprise and a ray of hope was raised among the participants who had gathered. However, several of the cell-block leaders, upon hearing the plan, nevertheless, remained skeptical. They argued that other, less dramatic smaller escapes had been attempted in the past, but with limited success. The cell-lock leaders were especially concerned over safety and asked how their people would be protected from the guards, especially as they proceeded to the fence. John, in response, spoke to them about the two surprise weapons that would be employed to counteract their concerns. He noted, "To disguise the escape attempt smoke bombs will be thrown within selected areas, and previous to a rush to the fence."

"If all works well, the smoke bombs should disguise our movements and confuse the guards by adding to the general mayhem I hope to create" he continued. "At this time", he also informed them that "a number of hand tossed grenades, a new explosive device, like a miniature bomb, will be tossed by my colleagues, Big Jake and Jed, to be thrown upon and into the major buildings that compose the compound." "These weapons", he added, "each have high explosive power and should ignite a number of the buildings, as we make our escape.

"I would also suggest that men familiar with horses race to the corral where they will find horses that they may use to aid them in fleeing from here."

"But what about guns?" inquired one man. "Will we have any?"

"My men will have a number of repeating rifles that will be used to shade and protect those of us that make it to the fence. However, you and your men will need to obtain any stored weapons in the compound or wrestle away arms from the guards, where possible. While Mungo's men may shoot potential escapees, remember that since they view us as property, as does their "owner", and as especially valuable property, I may add, they will not want to lose any of us in a gun fight. Then they will have to explain the loss of his "property" to Mungo when he returns. And, as they knew, Mungo will not tolerate that occurrence."

CHAPTER 12

Into the Woods

As nightfall descended, the escape plan was set; at this point, it only awaited a final call, a strategically placed spark to be ignited by the efforts of a coterie of players, among them John and Jed, accompanied by Big Jake and Samuel, who would appear shortly facing each other on opposite sides of the fence that sealed the enclosure.

Upon the surface a gentle calm appeared to settle over the prison camp; it was early evening, and as usual, the prisoners gathered in place within their respective cell blocks, preparing for the last roll call of the day. However, belying the apparent serenity, the atmosphere within the camp was underscored by a brittle, foreboding tension in which John and his colleagues, both within and outside of the compound, were set to initiate their respective roles.

The restive atmosphere reflected the heightened state of safeguards that had been initiated by the guards. Precautions, somewhat more elaborate than usual, had been set in place. A suspicious Mungo Monroe had mandated them for he had learned his lessons well at the hands of John Scobell somewhat earlier. Before he left for his meeting with Harrison, a necessary encounter in the scheme of things, Mungo relayed directives to his chief lieutenants, setting forth orders designed to secure the compound. Guns were locked in a strong box in the main building, horses were corralled, the prisoner's cells were checked, and the guards' schedules were reviewed and modified, as required. As a further precaution, Mungo ordered that John be locked in chains overnight in order to prevent any precipitous activity on his part; although confident of his operation, perhaps a bit overconfident, Mungo was not taking any chances this late in the game.

A Run for the Fence

As the sky darkened, John initiated the escape plan. He was alone, locked in an enclosed, smaller cell within the main body of his cell block. With some effort he removed his specially prepared key from his clothing and began working it into the old lock that fastened together the chains that secured him. Aside from obtaining the key from its hidden location, he needed to maneuver his body into place in order to allow his fingers to reach the partially-rusted lock binding his chains. It was only a matter of time, however, before he was able to discretely locate the lock with his finger tips, shifted it into place, insert the key and twist it into service and remove his chains. Within a half an hour he was able to set himself free.

His cell block, like all of the others in the compound, was held in check by one sentry, who patrolled the grounds in a semi-circular pattern of movement around the perimeter starting with an area immediately fronting the block. After releasing himself, John was tempted to call the attention of the guard patrolling his cell block, to overpower him and to force open his cell door. However, he hit upon an alternative idea after examining the door lock. Apparently, all of the locks in the compound were crafted by the same manufacturer, probably purchased at the same time, as suggested by a similar correspondence in design. John while examining the door lock wondered whether his skeletal key would work in the door lock, as it had on the chains that were used to bind him. Carefully, slipping his key in the lock, and jiggling it slowly as the guard turned the corner of the block, he was surprised to find that his observation was correct; he was able to open the lock and correspondingly, the cell door with ease.

Signaling to Samuel to call the guard as he neared the door, John rushed it open to the surprise of the sentry and was able to subdue and wrestle him to the ground, cuffing his mouth from any outcry before the guard was able to sound an alarm and alert others to the activity that transpired. Using the chain that bound him, and wrapping it around the guard's body several times, John was able to secure the guard's compliance with little difficulty. As a final gesture to prevent him from calling out, a rag was stuffed into the guard's mouth as he was gently lowered to the ground. A belated struggle by the bewildered sentry was met with a swift kick to his stomach, and then, silence ensued.

Handing Samuel the guard's rifle and powder, as well as a revolver, John peered outside the cell block and noted that the sky had cleared. Slowly he crept to the south end of the compound. Within several minutes of reaching his destination, he noted smoke coming from the south side of the fence, in the direction of a storage building closest to the outer limit of the compound. It was the signal from Jed and Big Jake that the escape plan was in effect. With a whispered hint to them that he was on the other side of the fence, Jake swinging the end of a heavy shovel at the wooden posts that retained the sidewalls tore down a part of the structure. The exposed opening in the wall widened under his continuing efforts.

Within several moments, John witnessed a barrage of smoke bombs to follow the breach in the wall. Jed and Big Jake had entered the compound each carrying a container full of explosives, Jed with a cloth sack filled with smoke bombs and Big Jake with an iron bucket filled with Ketchum grenades.

The noise generated by their activity was awesome. Adding to the smoke created by the bombs, the flurry of escaping prisoners running toward and past Jed and Jake through the opening in the gate, created a noise far exceeding that of the compound only moments ago. A stampede of souls was on and the pattern of turbulence created by this massive number of people moving in the same direction, at the same time, was only exceeded by the destruction of the facility itself. While the smoke bombs created a foggy image of the mass of activity that was created by the fleeing prisoners, the exploding Ketchum bombs added a second layer of commotion.

The high volume of smoke that was generated masked the direction that many of the prisoners, informed by Samuel and the other cell block leaders of where the escape would take place, had sought. In addition, as anticipated, the smoke bombs decreased the ability of the guards to locate the direction of the fleeing prisoners, or to organize a concerted response to the escape itself. They were befuddled and confused, lacking direction and focus. Not knowing how to suppress the crowd and being uncertain whether to fire their guns or not, the few guards that attempted to quell the crowd, by getting in front of it, were run over by the mass of fleeing prisoners. And in the process they often lost or were stripped of their weapons. Whether Mungo would have been able to lead a successful counter attack by the guards being able seal off the fence and stem the escape effort is a matter of conjecture. Nevertheless, his lieutenants could neither focus nor direct their charges. Some of them, it was observed, fled themselves, while others were paradoxically captured and taken prisoner by the inmates.

The Ketchum grenades were another matter. Tossed under the guidance of Jake's strong right arm they created both confusion and destruction. The latter effort was especially apparent as Jake selectively employed the use of his arsenal. One grenade was used to bring down the main guard tower, where three guards had climbed to the top then proceeded to rain down bullets upon escaping prisoners in an effort to dissuade them from reaching the fence. Their efforts proved in vane, however, as the tower blew up, spewing forth its splintered timber in all directions and the guards that spilled out of the enclosure unprotected by its housing unit, in a loud explosion. In truth, the guards had little protection from the flying debris created by the grenades or from the inmates who often sought them out for retribution.

Other grenades were thrown in the vicinity of buildings that held the compounds main structures; in this fashion the escape team was able to destroy Mungo's lodgings in the main house, the guards sleeping quarters, adjacent to it, and the horse corral at the far end of the compound just after some prisoners released the animals held within its confines.

Ketchum Grenades at Work

THE FATE OF THE GUARDS

It was inevitable, perhaps, that several of the inmates, particularly those that had been subject to harsh punishment at the hands of the guards, would seek retribution. Such was the case at the southeast end of the enclosure. In that corner of the compound a number of guards were cornered and stripped of their weapons by an onslaught of inmates.

As a small crowd of two dozen former inmates, some with guns seized from the guards, most with rakes and improvised weapons, descended upon three of the trapped guards they were surprised to find Samuel among them. Defying the crowd Samuel had inserted himself between the guards and the mob.

As one of the mob, a lean tall black man with a noticeable limp and clutching a rake in his right hand moved forward in a menacing fashion, Samuel stepped out in front of him and said, "Abel, stop! You are about to commit an abomination against your fellow man."

"My fellow man?" answered Abel.

"This bastard is not my fellow man. If truth be told, and I couldn't speak before without fear of a beating, he is a mean, poor excuse of a man. He was sent by the devil to inflict harm upon poor, defenseless, black people. And he has done so, repeatedly. To me, and to many others", he continued.

"He has no sense of fellowship. Nor, is deserving of our mercy. He is evil and we all know it, especially him.

"He deserves it." "You all know it," shouted Abel at the crowd.

"Look at my leg. This man is responsible for my being crippled. His negligence, his arrogance led to this limp. Now, look at him, crawling on the ground, seeking mercy. Did he offer any to me? Or, to any of you."

"And what about Charlotte and her baby?" cried another.

"This man tormented her until, out of desperation, she took her own life and that of her baby by running into the fence after dark, knowing that the guards would shoot her down like a dog, which they did.

Where was the justice there, I ask you?"

"No! This is not a man who earned the right to be judged impartially. Neither, at our hand, nor any of the courts that currently operate to protect him and others like him".

"But, you are not him, nor are we", interjected Samuel. "You are not cut from the same cloth. You are better. And you are responsible to a higher being."

"But, why let him escape justice?" asked Abel.

Why not shoot him down for the mad dog that he is?" continued Abel.

"Probably because vengeance resides in the hands of God, not us," said Samuel. "And whatever reckoning that will come, will come from another hand."

"Are we not better than our task masters?" asked Samuel.

"Are we not better than the sons of Ham?" he continued.

"Let us not break the vow with our maker that we will conduct ourselves on a higher plane than have the white folk that we have been forced to serve under."

"And let us not succumb to a level of vengeance that has been ascribed to us by those very same folk."

"Amen," said the crowd, clearly swayed by Samuel's argument, while setting down the weapons that they were menacingly carrying during and previous to Samuel's comments.

As they disassembled two men from the group led the frightened guard, a quivering man by the name of Adams, to one of the cell blocks and bound him in chains. As one of them said as they left him, "We will leave you unharmed, Adams. But, you will have to answer for your crimes in the future. For now, that will be to Mungo, who I suspect will bare you little tolerance. And later, you will have to face your maker, who hopefully, will shown you a bit more."

Meanwhile, at the other end of the compound a different story was emerging. In that vicinity, a group of six guards had assembled with their weapons in hand to deter the escape effort. Lead by Mungo's nephew Leroy, the men stationed themselves around the ammunitions supply house, sealing off access to weapons and munitions from the unarmed inmates.

Leroy, in a surprising demonstration of leadership, unhesitatingly ordered his colleagues to assemble behind three wagons that were dragged out and placed so as to offer an effective wall separating the prisoners from the guards. The wagons, now stationed in front of the supply house, served as protective barriers that limited prisoner access and further movement. This maneuver also created a formidable obstacle between the inmates and the supply of stored weapons; from there, Leroy and his men were able to control a wide area of the compound and to hinder the path of the inmates and prohibit their exodus, as well.

It was an excellent, improvised tactic that temporarily stemmed the massive flow of bodies seeking escape by crossing the compound in order to reach the opening in the southern fence and freedom. Trapped by this maneuver, in which the guards could resort to their weaponry, as well as maintain an effective firing line, many of those in flight stopped running, while others were turned around to flee in the direction from which they had recently fled.

Wisely, as Mungo would counsel (in keeping the property value of the potential escapees in focus) and as he would have directed him, Leroy had ordered the men to aim their weapons in order to inflict injury and to avoid major casualties. In addition, Leroy had two men roll out a stored cannon, a Whitworth Breechloader from the supply house in order to create an added sense of panic among the fleeing crowd. His stalemate had succeeded. But he would not prevail, at least, not for long.

The Whitworth Breechloader

It was evident that Leroy's actions were causing panic to erupt among the inmates as they sought direction and escape from certain capture. This latest reaction was, of course, noted across the field, with some dismay. From his vantage point, at other side of the compound, the barricade and counterattack had first been observed by Samuel who, sensing the problem, but at a loss for an immediate solution, sought out John in order to find an answer to the impasse.

As he raced toward John, he shouted, "They have erected a barricade and put a big gun in the path of the people seeking to cross the yard. What can we do?"

Author's note: The Whitworth was a rifled Civil War cannon that fired an elongated 12-pound shell. It was imported from England by both sides during the Civil War. However, only the South actually employed this weapon during the war. One feature made this gun unusual; it was a breechloader offering its crew more protection than that of the typical cannon. Other cannons at the time were muzzle (front) loaders. Among its attributes the Whitworth was also extremely accurate and could fire a solid shot beyond 2,800 yards (about half a mile). Moreover, the gun made a distinctive shrill as the shot flew overhead.

❖ ❖

"I think that we need to use some grenades to clear them out. It would seem to be the only thing that could stop them and the gun. I was hoping to limit casualties and to avoid injury to any of Mungo's men. However, that seems unavoidable now", said John.

"Jake seems to have done considerable damage here at the gateway. Perhaps, I can guide him to the other end of the compound."

Just then, John spotted Jake in a clearing engulfed within a group of frightened women and small children. He was busy directing several groups including a short black woman with a small child. They were standing in the midst of a haze created by the smoke bombs. As Jake turned toward the site where John stood, John signaled him in order to draw his attention.

As Jake raised his hand in acknowledgment, John ran to Jake, calling, "We need to disable that gun and allow those folks an opportunity to come this way, through the fence. Do you think that you can accurately toss a couple of grenades in that direction? Or, is it too far a throw?"

Jake sized up the distance in his mind and answered, "No, I think that I can do that. Stand back while I toss this grenade." And with that slight warning, he stepped forward with his left leg and with his opposing right arm threw a grenade approximately a hundred and fifty feet in the direction of the wagons.

It was an arduous toss, clearly a herculean effort beyond the competence of most men . However, it landed slightly off target. Nevertheless, while he missed the cannon in front of the right side of the barricade, he hit the near end wagon that had been anchoring the barricade. As the grenade exploded, it created a horrendous roar causing people around it to drop to their knees and to clasp their ears. Others, most of whom were able to avoid injury, ran from the explosion and sought shelter out of harm's way.

The blast, and the subsequent fire caused to the wagon as it absorbed the concussion of the bomb, escalated the fight. It alerted the men manning the Whitworth gun to turn the muzzle of their weapon toward the source of the grenade and to fire a round in John and Jake's direction. Their aim proved good; but fortunately, in the scheme of events, it was not deadly. John and Jake were shaken by the return discharge, as were others around them. However, they were also able to escape injury and find suitable cover nearby. It was a narrow escape, worth avoiding.

Meanwhile, as the gun crew hurried to load another shell in the breech of the Whitworth, Jake and John ran forward, seeking to gain a position closer to the gun in order to increase the accuracy of a second attempt at disabling the unit. This time, they were more successful. Jake tossed two grenades in rapid succession. The first grenade backed the crew up in light of its implosion, as they sought to avoid flying scrapple. The second grenade, tossed shortly thereafter, landed on target. Its muzzle smashed, the gun was disabled and its crew disbursed. As the people in the area of the blast became aware that the gun was now out of commission, they once again left shelter and raced across the field in an effort to reach the break in the fence.

As many people slipped through the fence, John sought out Mae and her younger son. The tumult was great and the smoke and fires overwhelming. However, John persisted, inquiring of several people and at last, located them. Mae was huddled behind one of the storage sheds, having experienced the rude eruption of noise and tumult created by the Whitworth. However, she readily recognized John as a rescuer and proceeded to follow him as he directed them to safety through the fence. The first facet of their escape was now well under way, proceeding according to plan. Hopefully, with a bit of luck, John and his colleagues could continue to follow the strategy initially set for the rescue and bring Mae and Lucas home. But, that hope was based on little more than a wish for an end to this adventure that eventually would demand the strenuous exercise of guile, courage and intelligence.

Mungo Returns

Within an hour the majority of fleeing inmates had succeeded in making their escape from the compound, some on horses stolen from the compound, most on foot. Their paths varied. As they had been kidnapped and assembled from many different places, they fled in a variety of directions as well, making their recapture less certain and also less probable. While many would succeed in reaching the northern territories, fleeing from their present location north to Pennsylvania and beyond, others would travel on to Canada; nevertheless, many, lacking appropriate resources, and help, would be recaptured in the forthcoming days.

The plights of their guards varied, as well. Many, unfortunately, caught in the mélange while trying to block the mass of escapees, in their attempt to curtail the tide of fleeing prisoners, had been subdued by the inmates, themselves. Others were beaten in random confrontations, with prisoners, some severely. Subsequently, all of the guards that were taken captive during the escape were locked in the cell blocks that they formerly patrolled as a precaution against a pursuit of the fleeing prisoners. Others, unwilling to face the assumed wrath of the inmates fled the compound in fear of retribution as it became apparent that the prisoners held the upper hand; the escape was a success, reversing the fortunes of the former captives and those assigned to insure their imprisonment. In a strange twist of fate, the keepers were transformed into the kept.

Other guards feared that there was more to come. Among those that had fled having failed in their attempt to prevent the exodus, several would ultimately have to answer to Mungo, perhaps, as viewed by some, a fate worse that being taken prisoner by the inmates themselves. They knew that Mungo could, and would be less forgiving than the prisoners themselves.

As the camp laid in ruins, many of its buildings still smoldering from a combination of fires set forth by the inmates before they fled and the Ketchum grenades explosive force, it was apparent that some explanation of the recent series of events that had transpired would be necessary.

Several hours after the burning wreckage of buildings laid in embers, presenting a view that could be observed several miles from the site, Mungo returned to witness the scarred remains of his compound directly. His initial reaction was one of incredulity, followed by a state of anger and outrage. His first response, subsequent to experiencing the shock borne by witness to the destruction of his enterprise, was to seek out his lieutenants and obtain from them an explanation of the events contributing to the current state of affairs. Mungo would not allow this outrage to go unpunished. He would extract his revenge, among those that permitted his empire to fall and among those who caused its destruction.

CHAPTER 13

The Pursuit

Mungo's anger could barely be held under control; moreover, his inclination, upon seeing the destruction around him, was not to control it at all. His compound was destroyed and his business, his livelihood, as it were, lay in ruins. His years of hard work had been disrupted and clearly, his future prospects were likely to be diminished, if recoverable, at all. In addition to his physical property, his capital outlay, which was invested primarily in the form of "slave property", was lost, perhaps, forever. He was distraught and a bit deranged, as well. Deep within his soul, at a place thought unattainable, and beyond his apparent depression and frustration, there was a cry that sought revenge: in Mungo's world, someone would pay.

Mungo Returns: Part 1

As Mungo leads his mount closer toward the compound he is dismayed by what he is witnessing. There, he finds several dozen bodies, primarily former slaves, dispersed around the compound. Randomly scattered among them are a number of dead guards. Yet, there are no weapons among either the dispersed bodies he views nor within the ruins he observes. Apparently, they have been collected and seized by the escapees. As he gallops past the facade of the main building of what was formerly his home, but now is only a half-timbered shell, a fire bombed ruin left smoldering in ashes, he dismounts from his horse and goes in search of Leroy, his nephew. He knows that there are a few people among those semi-isolated, lingering souls, several of whom he spotted walking half-dazed around the grounds, that he could trust to offer an acceptable account of the mayhem that had taken place in his absence.

Fugitive Slaves

As he strolls past the coral that once held his prize horses, in front of a nearby cellblock, he hears shuffling sounds. Peering into the enclosure he finds Leroy bound and struggling in chains. As he approaches the sound, Mungo finds Leroy, in spite of his fears, alive and bruised but otherwise, unharmed.

Leroy is gagged and chained. But he is neither suffering the ill effects of having been beaten, as some of the guards had been, nor has he been injured or killed in the outburst, as apparently several others were. Removing the gag from his mouth, Mungo finds Leroy coherent and willing to tell his story.

Like the guards left to maintain the compound, Leroy explains that he was subdued and chained by the inmates after his resistance to the uprising was foiled. When the big gun was decommissioned he was taken prisoner and then dragged to one of the cell blocks where he was left as Mungo found him. However, he was witness to a variety of different occurrences among the events that transpired before his incarceration.

Mungo's head buzzes with a number of questions. He asks Leroy, "What happened here? Where is my property? Where are my men? Who is responsible for this destruction? Why weren't we able to contain it?"

Leroy shakes his head and responds, "As you can see there was a prisoners revolt, a riot. It came as a complete surprise and we weren't properly prepared to deal with it. I'm not right sure that you or any of us could have done anything to prevent that from happening. The escape was not an inside arrangement, although it profited from inside help. It was well planned and came from the outside being pulled together by strangers. But they were well organized; it was intelligently planned beforehand, with weapons, smoke bombs and those new grenades. I don't think that anything of that sort could have been predicted."

"Yes, we were unprepared, and perhaps, lax. It is also true that we took too few precautions before the attack, while our response to the assault was mishandled when it was evident what was happening. They had the element of surprise working for them, which served their purpose well. But we were lazy and less prepared than we should have been."

Incredulous upon hearing Leroy 's account of the escape, Mungo responds, "But you had a good number of guards and ample weapons to handle this, didn't you?"

To which Leroy answers, "Perhaps. But it was an event that was simply waiting to happen. I don't know if it could have been prevented, or if we could have limited the damage. I do know that we contributed somewhat to the ferocity of the attack by the inmates, once they were able to act on their own volition. I also think that the guards would have been treated better if some of our men, like Adams, had not previously misused and abused the inmates. It seems to me that Adams' presence, along with Greene and Martin, among several others, led some of the prisoners to take on a mean look. And that led to a few summary executions, and to some of the worst beatings I witnessed. I would think that if it were simply a random outburst by some hotheads, I would have been treated in a similar fashion, being your nephew. And I would have faired far worse than the rest had if that had been the case. But, that wasn't so."

"How did our men act when the prisoners were released from the cell blocks?" asked Mungo. "Could we have prevented it? What about Miller and Parsons, the men that I left in charge? Were they up to the challenge?" he inquired further.

"Well, they didn't help things", I reckon", said Leroy, turning away, displaying disdain, and obviously exhibiting an ill-disguised reluctance to inform on them.

"Look", responded Mungo, somewhat exasperated by his detection of a lack of credulity and misdirection in Leroy' response and in his attempted evasion of Mungo's inquiry, "As a Munroe, this is your enterprise, as well as mine. We cannot hope to get things up and running again, if we don't sort this out or if we repeat the same mistakes. And we need to flush out those responsible as soon as possible. And now's the time to do it."

"Well, there were some mistakes made", suggests Leroy, "where … I think, we could have done things differently."

"I reckon that Miller & Parsons should never have allowed the open congregation of all segments of the population, and the mingling of inmates within the compound that afternoon previous to the escape. That was not our usual procedure, as you know, but they were just trying to hurry up the exercise period, and get the prisoners bedded down. Unfortunately, that change in procedure, I believe, offered the prisoners an opportunity to gather among themselves and plan their escape."

Mungo, exasperated, blurted out his dismay, "Those fools! I purposely ordered limited contact among the prisoners to prevent collaborations of that nature, in order to limit events such as a planned escape from happening. What were they thinking? Didn't they realize that?"

"What about the leaders? Who were they? Did this involve Scobell?" Mungo continues.

"Well from what I could gather, the failure of the guard to conduct an adequate search of Scobell's clothing appeared to allow him access to a devise, likely a special key, that he carried in with him, and that permitted him to escape his chains," says Leroy. "And, as near as I could tell, that was the start of it."

"But, I warned them to be extra careful with him. Damn them," blusters Mungo in response.

"What about the sentries? Did Miller or Parsons post guards outside the compound, or did they direct the attention of the sentries in the tower toward the detection of a presence of outside intruders? That precaution would have prevented the attack," he added.

"Well, Scobell and his two, well-armed associates stationed outside the compound pulled this off. And they were lucky," said Leroy. "But, unfortunately, they were more than just lucky," he added.

"They were prepared and they were heroic, I guess, especially the big black one. He was responsible for the grenades. When I had several men put out the big gun, I was able to halt the break, but only temporarily. The crowd stopped their advance in the face of the breach loader. But, the big black one, after assessing our position, rushed us and destroyed our weapon with a series of well-aimed grenades. Even after we temporarily stopped him, he was able to inflict damage. He is probably the most dangerous of the bunch and he certainly does not appear to fear white folk," noted Leroy. "At least, not us," he adds.

"Well, we need to make plans to recover our property," responds Mungo. "Now here is what we are going to do. We don't have time to deal with those that have failed us. We will at some point, I promise you that, but not now."

Mungo quickly turns and starts a short journey around the compound to assesses his remaining assets, particularly his contingent of remaining men. He finds that a number of guards were shot in the riot, while others were beaten with sticks and assorted implements. Other men, but not all of them, fled for their lives after some of the prisoners seized weapons and when it became apparent that the prisoners were in control of the compound. Still, Mungo is left with eight guards, a sufficient number to start rounding up some of the stranglers. After gathering those able men that he could, he will use his resources to restore the fencing to the compound and to hold the recaptured escapees that he will set out to find and retrieve. However, he recognizes that he will also need to recruit additional replacements as soon as possible if he is to mount an effective search and recovery of his assets.

His first act is to compose a notice of his intentions, several of which he will have one of his men post immediately in the nearby towns. The posts are a call for men to act as slave retrievers which he will organize as a posse aimed at retrieval of "his slaves". In the notices, Mungo offers each man $ 100 for every slave or black person that he retrieves alive, $25 for each captured slave that has been wounded and returned and $ 5 for each dead slave brought back to the compound. The latter, he anticipates, will be buried in a large pit, dug by the retrieved slaves themselves, to fit that purpose, and to serve as a warning to other slaves who might attempt a similar escape in the future.

It is a busy day for Mungo. Upon questioning several of his guards, Mungo learns that Adams mistreatment of his slaves provided them an incentive for the dispersal of their anger and the destruction of his property. In response, Mungo vows to himself that he will deal with Adams and the guards that failed to protect his property, as well as those that deserted the compound in the face of the riot. Their responsibility for the losses he suffered will not be easily dismissed.

Already several deserters have been identified with the names of several others expected to follow. The Harrop boys, two brothers from Alabama were among them. He expected that they will be traveling south beyond his reach at this time, and he will need to deal with them later. The Browns, three cousins from Mississippi, and equally culpable as deserters, will likely flee south and west and that will leave their disposition pending, as well. But the slave retriever community was a small one, and word of mouth alone will alert him to their activities as well as his opportunity to exact revenge. His reaction will be anticipated as members of this sordid community would expect, and it would be swift and it would be just. If he had his way, which was likely not to be the case, to his chagrin, it would also be final.

That had been the case with Adams, the guard accused of mistreating his "property." Upon finding him bound and beaten in one of the cell blocks, Mungo had him released and attended to by a local physician. Adams' gratitude, however, was short lived when Mungo had him publicly whipped subsequently for his failures, both previous to and after the escape. Nevertheless, Adam's narrowly escaped his final judgment when he passed out and remained unconscious for some time. His subsequent dismissal and lose of employment following the whipping, added to the public humiliation accompanying his failures. It had been a swift and, according to Mungo, just response, although perhaps, according to his reasoning, less than was deserving.

Fleeing Mungo's Wrath: Part II

As Mungo took account of his situation and attempted to resurrect his business enterprise, other related activity, somewhat distant from the compound itself, was simultaneously occurring. Among the fugitive slaves, John, Jed and Jake had already fled with the other inmates. As the revolt terminated, John quickly organized their party for the escape; Mae and Lucas were led to the wagon brought earlier to the compound by the rescuers and boarded without incident and, as space permitted, they brought along a number of others with them, including their newly found ally Samuel Goddard, as well as Miles Freemont, a tall black man from Lancaster, his cousin Sidney Bousey and his companion Pearl Bennett. The latter three persons, as John learned, had an intimate acquaintance with the roads and byways around Cashtown and Lancaster. That knowledge would be useful, John reasoned, as they made their way toward those communities. Moreover, as long term residents in the area before their seizure he assured himself, their friendships with neighbors would help secure food and other supplies, as needed during their journey.

Unfortunately, there was no more room for additional passengers, although several others had requested passage. While people fled in mass, it was generally recognized that some would be recaptured, probably shortly, while some would die in their escape to attain freedom, and that some, a fortunate few, enough possibly to sustain hope in others, would escape.

As the group occupied places within the wagon, with Samuel driving and Jed sitting beside him with a repeating rifle as his side, John and Jake mounted the horses that they would ride upon allowing them to serve as scouts, accompanying the wagon north. They too were well armed, carrying the repeating rifles brought by Jed and Jake on the mission south.

Using maps , some hastily constructed from information of roads and travel routes, which was supplemented by available oral reports of current weather conditions, Jed had formed an escape route. He believed that this information would prove invaluable since slaves knew of alternative pathways often used to elude pursuers, including kidnappers. He was also aware that Southern troop movements toward Pennsylvania could easily deter them, if they were detected, from their principal aim, to get to Lancaster safely and to report the latest information obtained from the "listening posts" to the federal central command. As usual, they were operating under precarious circumstances. If the Army of Northern Virginia caught up with them they would be turned south, possibly returned to Mungo, himself. Great care and guile might be necessary to accomplish their mission. But they knew the risk and they were prepared.

Unless otherwise prevented, by delay or deterrent, the route home was well-conceived and plausible, with slight variations; the journey north would take Scobell and his colleagues to Hagerstown, Maryland, then by rail (if they could secure passage and assuming that the rails were running) to Chambersburg, Pennsylvania, then on to Cashtown, through Gettysburg and on to York and then by rail to Lancaster. They would travel on the tracks and on the heels of the Army of Northern Virginia, but with luck, avoid serious contact, a difficult, but not impossible task.

Regarding Mungo, the odds changed considerably. With Mungo, some form of confrontation was almost inevitable. The Monroes, as John, as well as Jed and Jake knew from past engagements, would pursue Scobell and his colleagues as a primary goal, seeking revenge, as an all, but consuming passion sustaining his anger. It was evident, in no uncertain terms, to all parties that the rescuers were at this time beyond the jaws of renewed captivity, but only barely.

The success of this phase of the escape plan would rely upon finding hidden routes north where possible, and a self-defined, well-thought out deception, to be employed, where necessary. And a deception, at this stage, similar to a sleigh of hand, would be called for. Fortunately, it was part of the plan. The latter occurrence, based on precedent used earlier among fugitive slaves, was incorporated in their detailed thinking on the onset; it reflected an infrequently observed practice thoughtfully applied among some blacks, and amplified in this case, by their own ingenuity.

John, whose experience and penchant for planning was well recognized, was responsible for this element of the plan. Using his experience as a union scout and spy, as well as knowledge of past practices, John created a rescue scenario based on deception; and, his secret planning for this part of their mission was well thought out and done in advance of their initial incursion south.

A successful escape from hostile territory to freedom, he reasoned, would rely upon a plan that would be available and applicable to the times. It also would have to be workable, and indeed, beyond the vagaries of luck or chance. Indeed, it would require the employment of an unsuspecting guise, one that had proven successful among prior fugitives so endowed and equally empowered. In accord with his deception, he determined to place the fate for its success in the hands of his most trusted fellow traveler;

it was the unique blend of circumstance and talents within the disposition of Jed Harper, John Scobell's long-term friend and fellow conspirator upon which the scheme depended.

Jed Harper, a rather inconspicuous man of 31 years, had the distinction of being a light-skinned black man, who bore the imprint of two opposing benefits, a mixed racial ancestry at birth that was reflected in an unusual soft "peaches and cream" facial complexion, as the saying goes, that blurred common racial distinctions between blacks and whites at the time, and a kind tutor that he had encountered in his youth, who taught him to read and write, a considerable advantage for a black man. But, even here his education was rather distinct, if not exceptional. In addition to his acquisition of a keen command of the written and spoken language, well beyond that of most black people, his astute teacher taught Jed to speak and act like a white person. In fact, to a remarkable degree, stemming from his mixed racial origins, coupled with his rare "educational opportunities " Jed was readily able to pass for white, and was often confused with and treated as a white person, by both black people and white people alike. John and Jed had reasoned that if Jed could pass himself off as a white slave owner from Maryland, an easy enough disguise, he could claim that the blacks traveling with him were itinerate workers hired out on a seasonal basis by their master. Aided by a finery of clothing borrowed from the wardrobe of Dr. Wilson, and modified by Aunt Amy's master tailoring, he could pass for a white "master".

Employing Big Jake as his "black assistant", and Samuel as his trusted driver, a common enough practice, and one often resorted to by slave owners during the course of the war, especially with limited managerial manpower available, they could, if they played their roles correctly, offer a convincing front to both the curious and non-suspecting white strangers they were likely to encounter. Other light skinned, black people had passed before in a variety of guises, and so could he.

The first test of their plan came within two weeks of the escape. On their way to Hagerstown they encountered a detachment of southern infantrymen heading north to take the fight into Pennsylvania.

Incident at Hollow Creek

Travel was slow and difficult as the Scobell party journeyed north. Their progress on the back roads was treacherous, often torturous, in places, marred by fallen branches from trees downed over the winter and circuitous routes developed in piecemeal fashion over poorly treated roads. In addition, the party was required to exercise extreme caution in avoiding search parties organized by Mungo, as they anticipated, and as critically, circumventing detection by southern troops traveling toward Pennsylvania. Consequently, Scobell and his colleagues adopted a pattern of travel in which one rider on horseback, usually John, forged ahead of the wagon to scout potentially oncoming dangers, while another rider, usually, Jake or Samuel, trailed behind on horseback, on the lookout for any movement, suspicious or otherwise, following them. One potential benefit of this formula was that they frequently encountered black people that offered information and, as they anticipated, occasional food and supplies to support their efforts. Nevertheless, their movement was slow, lending a discouraging element to their desire to avoid recapture and completion of their mission. Time was running out.

Amidst their slow progress, many more soldiers were observed in route forging their passage north, and John and Jed reached the conclusion that the group would be safer if they employed the "worker rental" scheme in order to avoid what appeared to be an inevitable meeting. Agreeing to this strategy, they chanced upon a sympathetic white farmer who was willing to hire the group for a week's work in order to assist him in completing chores on his farm.

It was a fortuitous event, and one that bespoke the temper of the times in this farming community, both familiar with, as well as exhausted by the war. In conversation with their employer, farming, as customary, was discussed. But as usual, the discussion inevitably veered toward the war, its progress, and those caught up in its aftermath. The farmer they encountered was a southern sympathizer, with union affiliations. Moreover, he was a veteran of the ravages committed at Antietam less than a year earlier in September of 1862. During one of their discussions, he expressed a common theme of disillusionment, with the following statement, "I've had enough of this war. And, if I can speak for my neighbors, who have entertained similar ideas, I think that we all have.

I don't know how we got to this point. But, by God, it needs to end."

Upon hearing his comments, John, a witness and participant in both the Antietam and Fredericksburg campaigns, added his own, "Amen."

Within a week the group was well rested, having regained some strength through good, nutritious food and a sense of contentment through meaningful work activity. It was now ready to continue the journey.

At Hollow Creek, however, their luck turned. As he neared a clearing John, riding ahead of the wagon, as usual, spotted a company of Southern infantrymen heading in their direction. Quickly turning his stead, he galloped back to the wagon to inform the others of this development. After quickly conferring with Jed, they agreed to employ the disguised master-slave plan set forth previously and recently, as indicated, successfully tested. But first they hid their guns, the Kitchner grenades, the smoke bombs and other vestments of their true status.

At a junction about a mile ahead, Colonel Stephen Hooding, from North Carolina, was leading his troops across a narrow stream. One of his pickets, a Corporal Jack Gamble, riding approximately half a mile ahead of the column accompanied by two soldiers, had the wagon stopped upon the Colonel's standing orders to deter any conveyance they encountered. In response, Jed descended the wagon and ordered Mae and Lucas to start a fire in order to brew some coffee for the Colonel. After a brief series of inquiries and exchange of local gossip, they learned that the brigade of soldiers was heading for Chambersburg, whereupon Jed invited the colonel and his adjutant to share some of the good coffee they were able to obtain from their recent employer, as part payment for their services.

Gathered around a hastily drawn fire, a small group, consisting of Jed, the colonel, his captain, a James Oglethorpe Landau, and his assistant, a sergeant Oscar Prescott from Charlottesville, enjoyed the small repast. Inevitably, a discussion of the war and the new motivation for the federal cause, the end of slavery, ensued.

Sgt. Prescott initiated the conversation with the following comment, "Can you believe it? The blue bellies are actually fighting for the darkies. No wonder they are losing the war. They can't seem to get their priorities straight. And that talk of letting them join the war. Who ever heard of blacks in uniform? Or, arming them and expecting them to carry the fight to us?"

"Well, I agree with you," said Jed in a portentous voice. "It's difficult enough to get this small group to put in a full days work, without resorting to the whip. I reckon that arming them would be foolhardy and probably of little value. And dangerous, I might add. "

Obvious holding a differing opinion on the matter, Colonel Hooding coughed and interjected, "Yet, if we could get them to fight for our cause, under strict supervision, of course, they could help the war effort. I believe that General Lee proposed a "fight for freedom" plan to the government, but that it was rejected as too radical."

Upon which Sgt. Prescott added, "With all due respect Sir, it should be. I don't want armed darkies lined up behind me in a fight against the federals. What would prevent them from turning their guns on us?"

Seeking to maintain his pretense of impartiality in the face of the present company, Jed said, "Well you are certainly right about that Sargent. It wouldn't do at all. But, it would be something, wouldn't it?"

CHAPTER 14

June 1863 – A Ticking Clock

It was too late, far too late. The war had come to Pennsylvania, demanding, as all wars do, the desolation and ruin of those in its path. Both armies were on the move, marching to meet the mayhem that they would soon generate; the men on each side were armed and ready and prepared to do battle. There would be no further delays. It would only be a matter of time before the pieces were set and there would be a major conflagration, perhaps even a pivotal battle, as many hoped, between the warring parties.

Confederate veterans in the field

In truth, the two armies, after more than two years of war, sought such a confrontation. At this point in the proceedings, most participants of the oncoming battle, including Commanding General Robert E. Lee, believed that its staging offered a chance to fight a "great battle" that might decide the war. It might even, others believed, end any lagging doubt in answer to the questions of which side harbored the superior military force, as well as the "true cause/account" regarding the often-claimed, rhetorically-directed, inflamed arguments surrounding the precipitating causes and/or merits of their participation. Among the combatants on both sides it was fervently believed that this confrontation, following the major battles of the past year, including Antietam and Fredericksburg, among countless others, and which have occurred in many other places and parts of the country, would end the argument for all time.

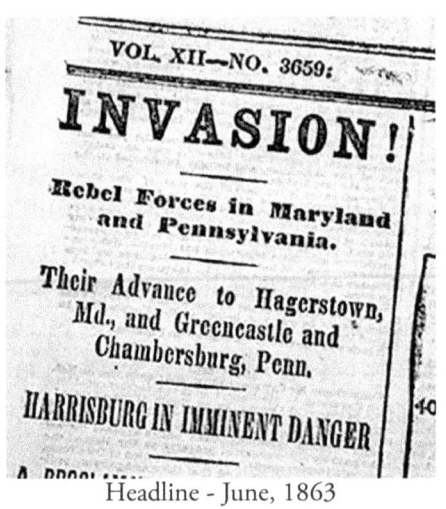
Headline - June, 1863

For our participants, trapped within a few select places, a multitude of war-related events were conspiring toward creating combustion among an increasing number of competing elements; and each of these appeared to be moving, as would inevitably be the case under such circumstances, toward an array of disparate, but tragic conclusions.

In Maryland, somewhat earlier, John was plotting for his life and pursuing an escape beyond the slave compound maintained by Mungo Monroe. There he had awaited both word and weapons to be brought by Jed Harper and Big Jake Simmons, to seize an opportunity to attack the compound and flee with Mae and her younger son within the havoc he would create in their wake. Elsewhere, Smithy Larson was on the move, as well, seeking his chance to exact revenge on John Scobell and to reclaim the human "property" he believed rightly belonged to him. Meanwhile, Mungo had hoped, initially, to break John Scobell's spirit, by obtaining information on Northern troop movement that he could sell to the Army of Northern Virginia. But that would happen only if he could move swiftly, which he hadn't, providing John and his colleagues an opportunity to escape his compound and captivity. And amidst these small machinations, vast armies were moving.

A short time earlier, with Jed and Big Jake as accomplices, John Scobell was able to rescue Mae and her son and to wreck havoc through their improbable intervention, upon Mungo's slave compound. As Mungo returned from a meeting with the Army of Northern Virginia, he arrived to witness the destruction caused by the rescuers. Upon his arrival, Mungo released his imprisoned nephew Leroy, one of the defenders of his enterprise who survived the attack, and learned of the events that transpired. He emerged with this knowledge determined at this point, to recapture "his property", and to exact revenge upon the rescuers which he is now in the process of doing. And amidst these small machinations, vast armies continue to move.

In the North, a change of command was once again taking place. Major General Joseph Hooker, whose armies were defeated by Lee and Jackson at Chancelorsville, in May of 1862 and had failed to defeat Lee with a much larger army, was being sent home; he was in the course of being replaced by Major General George Gordon Meade, who in late June of 1863 could be found in the process of leading the Army of the Potomac toward Gettysburg. The Army of Northern Virginia, meanwhile, was attempting to reorganize its high command in light of the untimely, unanticipated death of General Thomas Jonathan "Stonewall" Jackson shortly after that same battle, at the hands of his own troops; Lee had lost his strong right hand, and needed to replace his incomparable lieutenant. It would prove a hopeless task, but one that he needed to perform.

Although at different points in their respective missions, both armies were now on the move. The multitude of men, horses and supplies to assist them were on the march to confront their respective destinies, as well. And, as would prove to be the case, neither army would be quite prepared for the monumental consequences each would face in this another, pivotal meeting.

Even now, at this very moment, the preliminaries to the battle of Gettysburg were coming together. In Wrightsville, Pa., in a small town just off the leafy banks of the Susquehanna River, and within distance of the one of the battlefields surrounding Gettysburg, there was battle-related activity taking place; one of the bridges facilitating the path to Harrisburg, the Columbia-Wrightsville bridge, was being burned by Union troops.

Early on June 28, 1863, Union militia, set fire to what was then the world's longest covered bridge rather than permit the Confederate troops marching in that direction to cross the Susquehanna into Columbia and to further their advance toward the state capital, Harrisburg. The thwarted Rebels, in response formed a bucket brigade along side grateful Wrightsville residents in order to save the town from being burnt down. Despite this temporary alliance of necessity, as circumstances dictated, the male citizens of the town would, in short order, join their compatriots on the battlefield in Gettysburg three days later in opposing their southern brethren.

Burning of the bridge

THE RETURN OF SMITHY

Meanwhile, as Mungo tries to recruit slave retrievers for the recovery of his "property" a new development emerges; Smithy, his former partner and chief rival, has returned.

In the general store of the nearby town of Hagerstown, Maryland, Mungo has formed a temporary headquarters for the recruitment of slave retrievers to aid in his "recovery" mission. Notices have been tacked to the walls of the bank, the local Democrat party headquarters, the local boarding house, the regional post office and other important sites. Now Mungo awaits inquiries and applicants.

In a rare turn of events, where truth emerges from fiction, where the improbable overcomes the probable, and unforeseen events may occur, the paths of Mungo and Smithy have converged to cross once again. Learning of Mungo's predicament, and more pointedly, hoping to profit from his misfortune, Smithy has decided to reestablish their former partnership in the hopes of locating and capturing his nemesis, John Scobell, and if necessary, stealing him away from Mungo. He has learned of Mungo's plight and seeks to benefit from the unique predicament that Mungo finds himself in.

On the premise that he has fallen upon a unique opportunity, Smithy enters Mungo's temporary lair. Mungo, spotting him from the corner of his eye is overcome with suspicion at his appearance and wary of his entrance. Mungo immediately reaches for his gun and challenges Smithy.

"What are you doing here?" he inquires. "I see that the news has spread faster than I would have imagined. And to all corners. Well, get out! I don't want your help".

Disregarding Mungo's rudeness, Smithy responds, but this time without the typical rancor, "As usual, you are overplaying your hand. From where I stand, you seem short of manpower and can use the help of me and my men."

"My problem is none of your concern," spits Mungo.

"Well, it seems to me that you will never catch Scobell and his allies unless you are properly outfitted and have help", answers Smithy.

"You can't go after armed darkies with so few weapons and deputies."

"Or, without the use of a guide like my man Carter," he added, pointing to the small man standing at his side.

"I know that we have had our differences in the past", continues Smithy. "But I am willing to put them behind me for a shot at Scobell." Can you?"

Pondering for a moment, and ever on guard, Mungo, asks warily,"What do you what?"

"Well, I still want Scobell," answers Smithy. "I hold him, and that boy, responsible for the loss of my hand. And I still want my revenge."

"Now as I understand it, his two friends, Jed Harper and Big Jake Simmons destroyed your compound. So I imagine that you too have a stake in Scobell and his friends."

"I would be willing to trade Harper and Simmons, when I catch them, for Scobell, if it comes down to that. If you are agreeable," adds Smithy.

"Let me think on the matter," says Mungo as he turns and departs for a solitary moment or two to gather his thoughts. After a few minutes of contemplation, he approaches Smithy somewhat more cordially and consents to the arrangement, adding however, "Just remember I want them alive. And I will guarantee the same terms for Scobell. And I will also pay you for any other of my slaves that you recapture. Same terms as I indicated in my notice. Now, let's sit down, and seal this arrangement with a drink, while we work out a plan."

After several drinks both men appear ready to work out a mutually acceptable contract, as time and disposition permit, based on the guidelines of trade suggested. Using available maps, they then decide to get down to the hard work of sketching routes, estimating distances and allotting resources. With Smithy's guide Carter sharing his considerable knowledge of the countryside, they discern potential routes that the captives may have pursued or would be likely to pursue relative to their tracking of them. Acknowledging that there are numerous pathways leading from the compound north, they finally focus on two roads, either of which leads northeast toward Lancaster, and which appear to be the routes most suitable for Scobell and his allies to follow.

At this point, having been able to determine a possible course of action for their pursuit they decide to split into two groups, one led by Smithy and the other led by Mungo. They further agree that each team would be charged with the retrieval of any previously held escaped slaves that they would encounter in pursuit of Scobell and their subsequent return. However, when the Scobell party is located, which would occur in a matter of time, the attention of all parties would be directed towards their recapture; John and his colleagues would be the primary goal of their pursuit and all feasible efforts and resources will be placed in pursuit of that objective. Finally, before departing they agreed that each team would return to the present site, if possible, within a week of this meeting, with their hostages.

The next day, with men and provisions set in place the two teams meet up at the general store at dawn for final instructions. Mungo is anxious to start his pursuit, yet he is adamant that Smithy follow their agreement, and reminds him, "Remember, I want those prisoners captured alive. They are valuable property and are of no use to me dead."

Smithy responds to him, saying, "I'll get them. There will be no reprieve. They have a debt to be paid to me. And this time it will be paid in full." And with those words they depart in separate directions.

Meanwhile John and his colleagues continue their escape, at this point being about two to three days journey in advance of Mungo and Smithy. As they anticipated, on occasion they meet up with friendly and helpful blacks, some of which offer them food, while others contribute supplies, and still others, most importantly, information to aid them on their journey.

One unexpected source of help comes from Sidney Bousey, an escapee traveling with John. Sidney was one of the slaves that hitched a ride along with him in the wagon carrying Mae and Lucas after the prison break. Sidney, an older slave from Maryland, as John learned, has many relatives in the Virginia and Maryland countryside within which they were traveling. These people would, John hoped, prove helpful to their escape. Among them, a significant number had access to farming equipment which, within that trove of treasures, John would find implements and supplies that would prove especially helpful and of benefit as they journeyed further. He knew that in a confrontation with his adversaries, he had significantly fewer men and resources than they did which would lead to their inevitable capture. He needed to stretch and enlist additional resources, as he found them, and where he could. And, truth be told, he realized that he needed to improvise and invent implements and solutions which would not entail a direction confrontation; that approach would be disastrous.

On encountering a few of Sidney's distant cousins, the party was offered a variety of potential household aids and implements to assist them in their escape, including buckets and rope and other material. Among these offerings, in addition to some needed food and water, a few other tools and trappings were carefully selected by John and Jed to be employed in the near future. As they knew, their escape would not go unattended to. As they correctly assumed, at this point it was only a matter of time before Mungo, and unknown to them then, Smithy, as well, caught up with them. And again, Scobel knew that they would be outnumbered, and that ingenuity would have to triumph over sheer force of numbers.

Smithy in Pursuit

The spirit of the pursuers, especially with Smithy at its head, was very optimistic, perhaps, even greater than should have been. At least, that is what past experience might suggest to us. Yet, his exuberance for the chase was very high, buttressed by resources that were plentiful, as well as more than sufficient. With his expectations for success a "natural" extension of his preparations, as he would claim, Smithy rode out of town with his cadre of men. He knew that with Carter at his side, accompanied by a group of eight well-armed, seasoned men to assist him in the pursuit, and his knowledge of his foe from past encounters, that he would be able to capture Scobell. It was only a matter of time. While he would also recapture some of Mungo's slaves in the course of events, adding to the spoils for his efforts, his "business", as he saw it was to finish this affair with Scobell above all else. And he swore to himself that, as long as he was able to launch that plan, that his objective would maintain a proper place in the scheme of things.

On the afternoon of the fourth day after the escape, Smithy's opportunity presents itself. Through adept detection and arduous effort, and in spite of Smithy's continuous prodding, Carter found the embers of a small fire on a trail that he had persuaded Smithy's band to take. Although the remains of the fire itself suggested that only a few travelers were about, Carter was able to locate additional signs of activity, suggesting otherwise. These included a number of smudged footprints near and distant from the campsite, and the bones of several chickens, three or so more than would normally feed a few people. Instead, the remnants of the meal suggested that approximately 7 or 8 people feasted on this bounty. And the fact that the bones were, more or less intact, and not scattered or devored by animals, as would normally be the case, implied that the people who ate this meal had only recenty abandoned the site. He was on to something. And he knew it, as he hurried back to his group to convey the news to Smithy.

Carter choose to follow his instincts. Meanwhile, John riding at the rear of the wagon but within the vicinity of Carter, was alerted to the sounds of soft, but steady movement about a quarter of a mile behind him. As John picked up the muted distant noise of a horse moving in the silence, he sensed danger and decided to investigate. Dismounting from his stead, and carefully picking his way through some low scattered brush while holding the reins of his horse, he spotted a lone rider peering at the ground and knew by the nature of his movements that he must be a lead scout, or a tracker, in advance of a search party. The group was not only being tracked, but the trackers apparently had caught wind of them, as well.

Offering a cautious retreat, John slowly mounted his horse to avoid detection and quickly rode toward the wagon currently making its way slowly up an incline in the road. John's hurried movement alerted the others that something was afoot. As Jed spotted him racing toward the wagon, he knew that they were in danger. "What is it?" he called out.

"We are being followed," said John. "We best make haste and seek cover. They are on to us. Their scout is probably heading back right now in order to alert them. We need to be prepared as they make a run at us."

Simultaneously, Carter has ridden back to the band of pursuers and alerted Smithy to his suspicions. Hoping to seize his chance, Smithy quickly issues the following orders to his men,

"Remember, I want them all alive, if possible.

I especially want Scobell alive."

And with those words the race to recapture the escapees is on. It is a race of desperation, for the pursuers and the pursued. As Smithy and his men rush forward on galloping horses to overtake the wagon, Jed increases his demand on the horses of his unit pulling the wagon, relying on the whip in order to hurry his team at break neck speed while scrabbling both the occupants and contents contained within. Within moments of the pursuit, John issues an unusual, but loud order to Samuel and Sidney. "Now!" he shouts above the roar,

"Do it now."

"Spill those nails now."

Upon his order the two men tip a barrel of common household fasteners known as "hob nails' from the back of the wagon unto the road as Smithy and his men round a bend in the road, attempting to overtake the transport. With a whoosh and clatter, and without warning the nails scatter in all directions, as intended, spilling out onto the road as the horses behind them are driven forward at break neck speed by their riders in pursuit. As their weight and the tremendous force of their carriage land on the road, however, their driven hoofs are impaled by the spikes that have been strewn in their path.

All of a sudden the dynamics of the chase change: Smithy's lead horses in this desperate race suddenly pull up lame, some halting, other limping, in their pursuit. The shed nails have had their intended effect; they have stopped the progress of the pursuers, by disabling their horses and leaving their riders immobile.

"Stop", yells Smithy. "The horses are limping. They have been wounded They can not go any further."

The hobbled horses, moving slowly and hesitantly and each of them limping, an abrupt departure from their speedy pursuit moments ago, are of little use to Smithy and his men at this point. The injured animals will have to be carefully attended to before any further pursuit can be initiated.

As Smithy looks at the fleeing wagon containing the escaping slaves, he realizes what has happened, and he is enraged. He had Scobell in his grasp. Yet, he recognizes that he has lost his advantage; Scobell, through his use of ingenious tactics has once again snatched victory from the jaws of defeat. And more to the point, contrary to his cherished beliefs, John Scobell has achieved victory over him again, another sign of Smithy's failure as a white man to exert his superiority over the black man.

The slave pursuers will have little choice but to extract the nails from their horses hoofs and allow them a day or two of unburdened rest before they can continue their pursuit. However, by then, the Scobell party will be beyond retrieval.

Meanwhile, John and Jake, having ridden ahead of the wagon seeking a vantage point to stage a defense, now fall behind their colleagues, who continue to proceed ahead. As a precaution, John and Jake begin to backtrack upon the trail in order to observe the consequences of the actions wrought upon their trackers. Ever cautious, and suspicious of their enemy, they seek higher ground on the rising hillside in order to observe the results of this latest diversionary action.

After several moments, John, somewhat satisfied by the turn of events he witnesses, turns and glances toward Jake. He says, "By the grace of God we are rid of them. At least, for now. From the looks of it, we now know, as we suspected, that we are being tracked. They have organized their forces for this pursuit. It also appears that Smithy has rejoined Mungo in this evil play. That might have been inevitable. But Mungo is not with him on this juncture. Perhaps, they have split forces, which would have been logical, and account for his absence. Nevertheless we will have to be on the lookout for him, as well as a return of Smithy."

"I guess that we can now anticipate that we will be meeting up with Mungo and his cohorts shortly, and that he will be coming from a different direction, as well. Hopefully, we can avoid him, and we will try to do so. But, I doubt it."

A last word perhaps, since the events of this latest engagement should not be dismissed without further note. As Jake and John ride on, returning to the wagon, Jake with a bit of well-earned pride in his voice, slyly turns to John and with a barely concealed smirk on his face, he says to him, "Perhaps, Mungo will be as lucky as we have been and that his luck will continue to hold by leading him to avoid us, as well."

CHAPTER 15

BATTLE OF GETTYSBURG - DAY 1

"I always shoot at privates. It was they who did the shooting and the killing, and if I could kill or wound a private, why, my chances were so much the better. I always looked upon officers as harmless personages." Private Sam Watkins, C.S.A., July 1, 1863

On the last day of June 1863 tens of thousands of soldiers appear streaming toward Gettysburg, Pennsylvania. Among them are two Union cavalry brigades commanded by General John Buford scouting in advance of the Army of the Potomac. The Federals, at this point were streaming steadily north through Maryland in an effort to catch up with General Robert E. Lee's Confederate Army of Northern Virginia.

Meanwhile, the Army of Northern Virginia is approaching Gettysburg from the north and the west. For a week they had been rampaging through the Pennsylvania countryside seizing livestock, food, and clothes, demanding tribute from prosperous towns heretofore untouched by the ravages of war, and moving to capture the state capital of Harrisburg. A Rebel division, commanded by General Henry Heth, is now camped four miles west of Gettysburg. Heth has learned there is a hidden storage of shoes in the town and told his corps commander, General Ambrose P. Hill: "If there is no objection, General, I will take my division tomorrow and get those shoes."

At about 8:00 the next morning, Heth and his 7,461 men reach the crest of Herr Ridge, about 1.5 miles from Gettysburg, and see Buford's 2,748 dismounted cavalrymen deployed for battle along Willoughby Run below. Confederate skirmishers moved straight down the hill into a hail of lead delivered by the troopers' rapid-firing breech-loaded carbines and a battery of artillery. By their reistance, the Rebels are stalled for a short time, until Confederate reinforcements could arrive to add pressure to their assault.

On Seminary Ridge, 900 yards east of and parallel to Herr Ridge, was located a Lutheran seminary. Around 9:00 A.M. from atop one of the buildings, Buford was watching his men being pushed back from Willoughby Run when Gen. John Reynolds rode in. He announced that his corps was following him, and asked Buford to hold out until they arrived. "The devil's to pay!" exclaimed Buford. Then he said simply; "I reckon I can."

Battle Lines are Formed

"Up and down the line," wrote an artillerist on Seminary Ridge northwest of Gettysburg, Pa., on the afternoon of July 1, 1863, "men reeling and falling .. horses tearing and plunging, mad with wounds or terror' drivers yelling, shells bursting, shot shrieking overhead, howling above our ears or throwing up great clouds of dust where they struck' the musketry crashing on three sides of us' bullets hissing, humming and whistling everywhere. Smoke, dust, splinters, blood, wreck and carnage indescribable."

Meanwhile, two of Gen. Robert E. Lee's three corps had converged on Gettysburg from the west and north. At first the furiously fighting Union troops had stymied the approach of Lee's III Corps from the west. Then Lee's II Corps started arriving on the right of the Union line, and though their advance was savagely disputed, the Confederates gradually began to push the Union forces out of their position. The veteran Confederate II Corps brigade, led by General Stephen D. Ramseur, came up after the two brigades in front of them that had been pushed back and applied sufficient pressure that led to the Union soldiers' falling back from Oak Ridge. At that moment Confederate General Jubal A. Early's division of the II Corps arrived on the field, square on the Union flank, causing the Union soldiers to relinquish their line of defense and to retreat through the town of Gettysburg.

On Herr Ridge amidst his III Corps, Lee observed Early's attack and immediately sent the III Corps forward toward the Union troops still holding Seminary Ridge. Simultaneously attacked from three sides, the Union position became untenable, and the men gave way and flooded down the roads toward and through the town of Gettysburg. The victorious Confederates in vigorous pursuit, were able to take 3,500 Union prisoners in the town.

Meanwhile, privy to the battle scene, Union General Winfield S. Hancock arrived on Cemetery Hill south of Gettysburg at 4:30 P.M. that day and saw below him thousands of Federal troops stampeding out of the town and toward him. It was chaos. As one of his aides wrote, "Wreck, disaster, disorder, the panic that precedes disorganization, defeat and retreat were everywhere."

But, a fortuitous development ensued, one that favored the Army of the Potomac. Arriving at the crest of a small hill side, Hancock immediately appraised the site. He said, "I think this is the strongest position by nature on which to fight a battle that I ever saw," as he surveyed the terrain from his position atop 80-foot high Cemetery Hill on the afternoon of July 1, 1863. The town of Gettysburg, Pa., was just to the north; to the west, across a mile of fertile fields and orchards, he could see Confederate soldiers on Seminary Ridge. Culp's Hill, a 180-foot high wooded, and boulder strewn promontory, was just to his east; stretching for two miles to the south was low Cemetery Ridge. At the end of Cemetery Ridge were two more rock-strewn hills -- Little Round Top and Big Round Top. The natural advantage of the army's occupancy of the high ground was augmented by clear fields of fire. Moreover, there were a parcel of stone walls that offered protected defensive positions for the defending solders, and good roads in the rear for the movement of supplies and troops, if needed.

A furious battle had waged all day over the ridges west of Gettysburg between two corps from General Robert E. Lee's invading Confederate Army of Northern Virginia and two corps of General George Meade's Union Army of the Potomac. Late in the afternoon, the Union positions had given way under relentless attacks, and the victorious Rebels had chased the Union forces through the town and onto the high ground to the south. Hancock rallied the fleeing soldiers and set up a defensive line to try to hold his position until Union reinforcements could arrive.

Lee, despite his army's victory, was troubled. He recognized the natural strength of the high ground to which the Union army had retreated.

Consequently, he sent a message to his II Corps commander, Maj. General Richard Ewell, suggesting that it "was only necessary to press those people in order to secure possession of the heights," and urged him to do so "if practicable."

Ewell was a capable corps commander, but he was new to his position, having replaced Stonewall Jackson, who had been killed at Chancellorsville less than two months before. Noting the exhaustion of his men, Ewell did not believe the attack was "practicable." While the lines of communication between Lee and Jackson had grown somewhat legendary over time insuring a united vision across many battle fields, Ewell and Lee had not the time nor experience of command with each other to recognize the intentions of the leadership. Lee sorely missed Stonewall, a man who surely would have recognized the need to "press those people" and would have done so at once.

"Good," exclaimed General George G. Meade, commander of the Union Army of the Potomac, upon learning of General Hancock's decision to occupy Cemetery Ridge. "That is just like Reynolds, he will hold out to the bitter end." Reynolds was one of the army's ablest generals and commanded the wing of the army advancing toward Gettysburg. He had just notified Meade that he would try to hold the invading Confederate army at that town.

General John Buford

BUFORD'S CALVARY: FIRST CONTACT.

On June 30, Major General John Buford's two brigades of cavalry moved toward Gettysburg; there he met two regiments of rebel infantry supported by artillery. After some skirmishing, not wishing to use its artillery, the cavalry turned off, and reached Gettysburg in the afternoon. Buford and his troops arrived in time to meet the Confederates entering the town, where they were able to drive them back before they were able to secure a defensible position. The enemy withdrew in the direction of Cashtown, leaving a line of pickets about 4 miles from Gettysburg.

By daylight on July 1, General Buford had obtained reliable information of the enemy's position and movements, and made arrangements to hold him in check until the First Corps under Major General Reynolds, could arrive upon the field.

Between 8 and 9 o'clock in the morning, the rebels advanced with superior numbers on Buford's position. By engaging the enemy, General Buford was willing to risk deploying his outnumbered cavalry division to slow the advance of the much larger force of Southern soldiers. However, he did not make this decision lightly. Buford understood the hazards and dangers to come. Buford held a practical respect for the soldiers he knew he would soon face. In response to one of his subordinates who thought they could easily repulse any gray forces they would encounter, the cavalry commander countered, "No. You won't.

They will attack you in the morning and they will come booming, skirmishers three deep. You will have to fight like the devil until support arrives." Buford also added in further response, "The enemy knows the importance of this position and will strain every nerve to secure it, and if we are able to hold it, we will do well".

General Buford leading troops

July 1 – "We left camp at 6 A.M., passed through Heidelsburg and Middleton. At the latter place we heard firing in the direction of Gettysburg. We were pushed forward after letting the wagon trains get in our rear. We got to Gettysburg at 1 P.M., 15 miles. We were drawn up in line of battle about one mile south of town, and a little to the left of the

Lutheran Seminary. We then advanced to the enemy's line of battle in double quick time. We had not gotten more than 50 paces when Norman of our company fell dead by my side. Katz was going to pick him up. I stopped him, as it is strictly forbidden for anyone to help take the dead or wounded off the field except the ambulance corps.

The Battle - day 1

We then crossed over a rail fence, where our Lieutenant McMatthews and Lieutenant Alexander were both wounded. That left us with a captain and one lieutenant. After this we got into battle in earnest, and lost in our company very heavily, both killed and wounded. This fight lasted four hours and a half, when at last we drove them clear out of town, and took at least 3,000 prisoners. They also lost very heavily in killed and wounded, which all fell into our hands. After the fight our company was ordered to pick up all straggling Yankees in town, and bring them together to be brought to the rear as prisoners. One fellow I took up could not speak one word of English, and the first thing he asked me in German was "Will I get my pay in prison?" After we had them all put up in a pen we went to our regiment and rested. Major Iredell, of our regiment, came to me and shook my hand, and also complimented me for action in the fight. At dusk I was about going to hunt up my brother Morris, when he came to me. Thank God, we are both safe as yet. We laid all night among the dead Yankees, but they did not disturb our peaceful slumbers."
Louis Leon – Diary of a Tar Hill Confederate Soldier

Battling for Field Position

"Reverting to the story of the battle, there are one or two things I wish to mention of a personal nature. As we were on the march to the field, on July 1st, the distant booming of the cannon in our ears, one of the privates of Murray's company came up to me, during a brief halt by the roadside, and said he wanted to speak to me. It was James Iglehart, of Annapolis. We stepped aside, and I said, "What is it, Iglehart?" He answered, "Lieutenant, I want to ask your pardon." "My pardon!" said I. "Why, what on earth do you mean?" "I've done you an injustice," he said, "and before we go into this battle, I want to tell you so, and have your forgiveness." I told him I could not imagine what he meant, and he then said that he had thought from my bearing toward him that I was "proud and stuck up," because I was an officer and he only a private in the ranks, but now he saw that he was entirely mistaken and he wanted to wipe out the unspoken injustice he had done me. The next time I heard his voice was in that last terrible charge on Culp's Hill, when our column had been dashed back like a wave breaking in spray against a rock. "McKim," he cried, "McKim, for God's sake, help me!" I turned and saw him prostrate on the ground, shot through both thighs. I went back a few yards, and putting my arm round him, dragged him to the shelter of a great rock and laid him down to die. There are two things that rise in my thought when I think of this incident. One is that if he hadn't come to me two days before and relieved his mind as he did, the gallant fellow would not have asked my help. And the other is that the men in blue in that breastwork must have been touched with pity when they saw me trying to help poor Iglehart. It took some minutes to go back and get him behind that rock, and they could have shot us both down with perfect ease if they had chosen to do it.
Randolph H. McKim, A soldier's recollections: Leaves from the diary of a young confederate, 1910.

July 1, 1863 – At nine o'clock in the morning ... we began to march toward Gettysburg, our division bringing up the rear of the corps. The road was hazy with the dust of the marching column, and the farm lands, drifting by, were dry and shimmering in the sultry heat. As we neared the town from the southwest we heard away ahead to the left an unexpected warning of battle. It was cannon. We quit the road and set off through lanes and fields in the direction of the firing. Just as we left the road we met a black servant with a horse, and the servant said that the horse belonged to General Reynolds; the general was killed.

We hurried on towards a low ridge a little west of the town. Along the ridge was a scattering of trees and houses, and lording it over them was a brick building, the Lutheran seminary, which gave the ridge its name. {Seminary Ridge} Our brigade went around to the western face of the building, and there we threw up a barricade of fence rails and anything else that was handy. The barricade took the form of a crescent, bending to the west. Beyond it the ridge sloped away through the trees into fields, and beyond the fields was anther low rise of ground, topped with woods. There was fighting along that further ridge, and the action appeared to be spreading beyond our right. I recall that as I looked up at the building and saw some officers in the cupola taking a view {likely Buford and his lieutenants}, I noticed them pointing northerly…"

"As we waited by the seminary, Captain Whitehouse came to talk with me.

"Adjutant", he said, "I wish I felt as brave and cool as the colonel appears."

"Why Captain", I said "he's as scared as any of us. Cheer up! "Twill soon be over."

He tried to cheer up, and made sad work of it; his face wore a look of foreboding, and his smile was a stiff mockery. While we were talking we heard the command to fall in; and he looked me full in the face and said:

"Good-bye Adjutant. This is my last fight."

Small, Abner R. *The Road to Richmond: The Civil War* memories of Major Abner R. Small of the sixteenth Maine Volunteers.

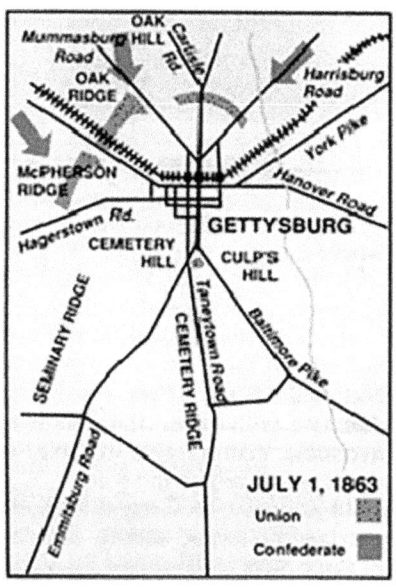

Gettysburg Map, Day 1

THE RIGHT WING OF THE FISHOOK: THE DEFENSE OF CULP'S HILL

The Battle of Gettysburg was fought on several fronts, among them Culp's Hill just south of the town.

Union Brigadier General George Sears Greene and his New Yorkers arrived with the rest of Geary's division by the Baltimore Pike shortly after 5:00 on the afternoon of July 1. Initially, he and his men were directed to the army's left, where they spent the night on Little Round Top one of the hills south of the town.

DAY 1 – INITIAL ENCOUNTERS

However, in order to anchor the line (creating an inverted fish hook in the process) they were moved to Culp's Hill (on the extreme right of Cemetery Ridge and at the end of the Army of the Potomac's right battle line) the next morning (July 2).

Upon his arrival, as General Greene soon discovered, that part of the hill was without defenses. Calling his engineering skills into play, Greene convinced his reluctant superior Brig. Gen. John Geary to permit his men to construct defensive fieldworks to strengthen their positions along the crest. It proved to be an inspired decision.

Early that evening, the rest of the Twelfth Corps had been marched away from Culp's Hill to reinforce the Union left against Longstreet's assault, and Greene's brigade was left alone to defend the hill. His preparations proved crucial when he was attacked by the entire newly formed, Stonewall Division.

When the rest of Geary's division returned after dark that night, they found the enemy in possession of their lines, and filed into positions protected by Greene's weary defenders until resumption of the battle in the morning.

At daybreak, around 4:00 A.M. on July 3, the fighting for the hill resumed, with Greene's men still on the crest where the bullets flew the thickest. However, by 11:00 that morning, after fierce fighting, the Rebels had been pushed out of the lines they had captured the night before and the Union army's right flank was restored.

Greene's men were able to hang on to their section of the line against a hillside full of surging Confederates. Greene's tenacious defense saved Culp's Hill--the key to the Army of the Potomac's right--and thereby turned back a serious threat to the entire Union position at Gettysburg. His Corps commander Maj. Gen. Henry Slocum said later of his feat, that "the failure of the enemy to gain possession of our works . . . should be credited "entirely to the skill of General Greene and the heroic valor of his troops."

Day 1 – A Final Encounter – Gettysburg's Unknown Soldier

There were numerous accounts of individual heroism, and personal sacrifice during that first day. And there were stories of special human interest, as well. The story of Sergeant Amos Humiston, a member of New York's 154th "Hardtack" regiment, a young father killed on that day, later found clutching an image of his three young children in his hands, was one of these.

Srgt. Amos Humiston was killed on the first day of fighting in Gettysburg after Confederate troops overwhelmed his company at a site known as Kuhn's Brickyard. He was one of the many Union soldiers who died in that monumental three-day conflict.

But the circumstances surrounding his death were a bit different than most. When his unidentified body was discovered, a week after the battle, lying in a secluded spot between York and Stratton streets in Gettysburg, he was holding an ambrotype, an early photographic image; it displayed the serious, round faces of his three children: 8-year-old Frank, 6-year-old Alice and 4-year-old Freddie.

Somehow during the fighting, Amos Humiston had managed to drag himself to this patch of ground after he had been wounded; Humiston, a sentimental man, who wrote poetry to his family, personified that role upon the occasion of his death - it is believed that he was probably looking at his children's faces when he died.

Amos Humiston might have faded into obscurity, as many fallen soldiers did, since there was nothing on his body to identify him; the few soldiers from his unit who survived the battle had moved on before he was found. And, of course, he didn't.

By chance, however, the photographic image of Frank, Alice and Freddie found with the body of Amos Humiston ended up in the possession of Dr. John Francis Bourns, a 49-year-old Philadelphia physician who helped care for the wounded at Gettysburg.

Several months after completing his volunteer work there, he decided to try to find out the identity of the children's father.

Dr. Bourns efforts produced a ground swell of publicity that spread throughout the North. It began on Oct. 19, 1863, several months after the battle, when the Philadelphia Inquirer published a story under the provocative headline: "Whose Father Was He?"

"After the battle of Gettysburg," the article read, "a Union soldier was found in a secluded spot on the battlefield, where, wounded, he had laid himself down to die. In his hands, tightly clasped, was an ambrotype containing the portraits of three small children ... and as he silently gazed upon them his soul passed away. How touching! How solemn! ..."

"It is earnestly desired that all papers in the country will draw attention to the discovery of this picture and its attendant circumstances, so that, if possible, the family of the dead hero may come into possession of it. Of what inestimable value will it be to these children, proving, as it does, that the last thought of their dying father was for them, and them only."

When the article on the unknown soldier appeared in print 150 years ago, newspapers did not publish photographs, so the story, subsequently reprinted in dozens of newspapers and magazines throughout the North, had to rely on a detailed description of the children portrayed in the recovered image found with the body. The eldest boy, it said, was wearing a shirt made of the same fabric as his sister's dress. The younger boy in the middle was sitting on a chair, was wearing a dark suit. It was estimated that the children's ages were 9, 7, and 5 (which was a close approximation to their actual ages).

By chance, one of the Dr. Bourn's reprints appeared in the American Presbyterian, a church magazine. That is where Philinda Humiston, living in Portville, N.Y., was first informed of the ambrotype and the dead soldier. She hadn't heard from Amos since weeks before Gettysburg, but when she saw the description of the children, she feared the worst.

But she couldn't be sure. So she contacted Dr. Bourns through a letter written by the town postmaster. Bourns had printed copy upon copy of the children's picture to respond to inquiries, but none of the people who had contacted him earlier had turned out to be the right family. He replied to Philinda's inquiry as he had to the others. It was, as she sadly discovered, Amos Humiston, her husband.

The story might have ended there. However, Dr. Bourns saw some value to posterity in Amos Humiston's sacrifice. He believed he could capitalize on the outpouring of sympathy toward the Humistons and did so, in order to raise funds for an orphanage in Gettysburg to house the children of fallen Union soldiers. Thereupon, a second publicity campaign began, one appealing for donations in order to build the orphanage.

The story touched many sympathetic strangers across all facets of Northern society. Gifts flowed from the wealthy and the humble. Many contributed to the cause and the orphanage became a reality in October

1866; it began with 22 soldiers' children ranging in age from 5 to 12. At its peak, "the Homestead", as it became known, was home to just under 100 children.

The Humiston children

A memorial to the Humiston family and the unusual circumstances surrounding the death of Amos Humiston was eventually conceived and dedicated to their collective memory at Gettysburg, where their story had begun. There, Sergeant Amos Humiston's body was also placed at rest and is interned in the Gettysburg National Cemetery.

CHAPTER 16

ON OFFENSE, SICKLE MOVES AHEAD
JULY 2, 1863 - DAY 2

Sickle Moves the Third Corps Forward

"Our division was in reserve until dark, but our regiment was supporting a battery all day. We lost several killed and wounded, although we had no chance to fire - only lay by a battery of artillery and be shot at. The caisson of the battery we were supporting was blown up and we got a big good sprinkling of the wood from it. Just at dark we were sent to the front under terrible cannonading. Still, it was certainly a beautiful sight. It being dark, we could see the cannon vomit forth fire. Our company had to cross a rail fence. It gave way and several of our boys were hurt by others walking over them. We laid down here a short time, in fact no longer than 10 minutes, when I positively fell asleep. The cannonading did not disturb me.

One of the boys shook me and told me Katz was wounded by a piece of a shell striking him on the side, and he was sent to the rear. We went on to the Baltimore Turnpike until 3 in the morning of the 3d."
Louis Leon – *Diary of a Tar Heel Confederate Soldier*

July 2, 1863

"Instead of turning to the left last night, we should have turned to the right, and by the time we were fairly started on the right road, it was daylight. At 8:30 this morning we crossed the line into Pennsylvania, and at 10 A.M. we passed through Littlestown. The civilians along the line of march could not do enough for us. Most every household standing ready with water buckets dealing out water to the boys as we marched along, and the Stars and Stripes hanging out in all directions. It made us feel as if we were home once more, and the citizens of Southern Pennsylvania, through their kindness to the soldiers have put now life into us.

Can hear heavy canonading ahead all day. At five O'clock this evening we arrived at what is called Little Round Top, a short distance from Gettysburg. Very heavy firing to our left at 5 o'clock.

At six this evening we filed left, marched some distance, when we formed a line of battle on a knoll and in some underbrush. Our troops gave way and the Rebs drove our men. The Penna. Reserves, forming on our front, counter charged the Rebs our line following up sharp. The enemy was driven back and we regained the ground lost a short time before. We halted in a hollow behind a stone fence, having marched, since last evening, thirty two miles.

At the time we formed a battle line, I threw my knapsack, being to tired to carry it into a charge, but after advancing a short distance the regiment was halted and the men unslung knapsacks and had guards placed over them.

As we were going in, General Sickles was carried past on a stretcher. Private Henry Keiser a member of Company G from Lykens, Dauphin County, PA.

The events of day 2 proved to be highly significant. It was, as many claimed afterward, one of opportunity and one of fate. And like the 3rd day, it was marked by controversy and acrimony over questionable decisions made on the part of several of its principal players. Finally, it has been argued, perhaps with some justification, that the events of that day, principally the major Southern attack on the hills off Cemetery Ridge, Little Round Top, located at the extreme left end the Federal line south of Gettysburg, and defended by the Union Army, was decisive to the outcome of the war.

Unlike the first day, in which fighting took place sporadically, almost spontaneously in places, and more or less by accident, the fighting on the second day was planned, well organized and purposeful. Both armies were in place. And they were prepared for the dramatic, as well as the grim minutiae of war.

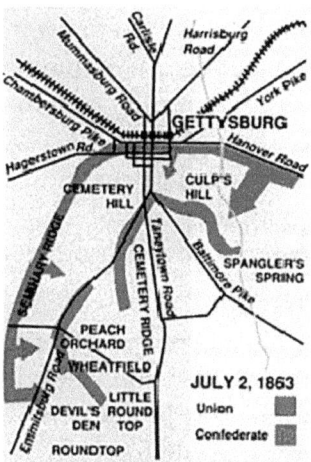

The Inverted Fishhook

The two armies, with their commanding generals, came from disparate places. They would settle across a wide wheat field previous to the battle (with the Army of Northern Virginia occupying Seminary Ridge and the Army of the Potomac, opposite it in an inverted fishhook along Cemetery Ridge.

Fighting Continues on Culp's Hill

The right flank of the Union Army situated on Culp's Hill anchored the beginning of the line. Its importance was displayed in a protracted battle that lasted over many hours in a test of the wills of both armies. The following is a report from Confederate soldier Louis Leon.

July 3, 1863

"When under a very heavy fire, we were ordered on Culps Hill, to the support of Gen. A. Johnson. Here we stayed all day - no, here, I may say, we melted away. We were on the brow of one hill, the enemy on the brow of another. We charged on them several times, but of course, running down our hill, and then to get to them was impossible, and every time we attempted it we came back leaving some of our comrades behind. Here our Lieutenant Belt lost his arm. We have now in our company a captain. All of our lieutenants are wounded. We fought here until 7 P.M., when what was left of us was withdrawn and taken to the first day's battlefield. At the commencement of this fight our Brigade was the strongest in our division, but she is not now. We lost the most men, for we were in the fight all the time, and I have it from Colonel Owens that our regiment lost the most in the Brigade. I know that our company went in the fight with 60 men.

When we left Culps Hill there were 16 of us that answered to the roll call. The balance were all killed and wounded. There were 12 sharpshooters in our company and now John Cochran and myself are the only ones that are left. This day none will forget, that participated in the fight. It was truly awful how fast, how very fast, did our poor boys fall by our sides - almost as fast as the leaves that fell as cannon and musket balls hit them, as they flew on their deadly errand. You could see one with his head shot off, others cut in two, then one with his brain oozing out, one with his leg off, others shot through the heart. Then you would hear some poor friend or foe crying for water, or for "God's sake" to kill him. You would see some of your comrades, shot through the leg, lying between the lines, asking his friends to take him out, but no one could get to his relief, and you would have to leave him there, perhaps to die, or, at best, to become a prisoner.

Our brigade was the only one that was sent to Culps Hill to support General Johnson. In our rapid firing today my gun became so hot that the ramrod would not come out, so I shot it at the Yankees, and picked up a gun from the ground, a gun that some poor comrade dropped after being shot. I wonder if it hit a Yankee; if so, I pity him. Our regiment was in a very exposed position at one time to-day, and our General Daniels ordered a courier of his to bring us from the hill. He was killed before he got to us. The General sent another. He was also killed before he reached us. Then General Daniels would not order any one, but called for volunteers. Capt. Ed. Stitt, of Charlotte, one of his aides, responded, and he took us out of the exposed position.
Louis Leon – *Diary of a Tar Heel Confederate Soldier*

THE FATE OF THE THIRD CORP

One of the most controversial and disastrous military moves rendered at Gettysburg was Major General Dan Sickle's unauthorized decision to advance his Third Corp in front of the defensive line established on Cemetery Hill by Union Commanding General George Gordon Meade.

The action was initiated without permission and without any previous communication on the part of Sickles of his intent. Perhaps naïve, certainly erroneous, and costly, Sickles behavior followed a flawed perspective. At the time, Sickles believed that his position, established on the left of the Second Corps was precarious and he sought the high ground. Some facts, however, might be in order.

Cemetery Ridge, is a low and flat section of land, rising past a small peach orchard and a section of higher ground beyond. Sickles believed that the massing confederates, already on the march, and soon to occupy the higher ground, would make his own position vulnerable. Consequently, he decided, without consultation, to move his troops forward to eliminate this possibility. He posted two divisions along the Emmitsburg road, placing one in the peach orchard and the other past a wheat field in a rocky, wooded area known as Devil's Den. By this move he separated his corps from the rest of the Army, and exposed it in the peach orchard to converging Confederate fire. In addition, he left his flanks exposed and rendered the Round Tops uncovered. When the confederates attacked, Sickle's corps would be unsupported and overwhelmed.

The fate of the Third Corp was observed and reported (shortly thereafter) by a number of fellow officers, including Lieutenant Frank A. Haskell, who faithfully recorded his observations. Previous to the fighting he notes the following:

"It was magnificent to see those ten or twelve thousand men – they were good men- with their batteries, and some squadrons of cavalry upon the left flank, all in battle order, in several lines, with flags streaming, sweep steadily down the slope, across the valley, and up the next ascent, toward their destined position! From our position we could see it all. In advance Sickles pushed forward his heavy line of skirmishers, who drove back those of the enemy, across the Emmitsburg road, thus cleared the way for the main body. The Third Corps now became the absorbing object of interest of all eyes...."

Continuing his narrative, however, Haskell begins to speak to us of the next, awful part of this story:

"Now came the dreadful battle picture, of which we for a time could be but spectators. Upon the front and right flank of Sickles came sweeping the infantry of Longstreet and Hill. Hitherto there had been skirmishing and artillery practice – now the battle began; for amid the heavier smoke and larger tongues of flame of the batteries, now began to appear the countless flashes and the long fiery sheets of the muskets, and the rattle of the volleys, mingled with the thunder of the guns. We see the long gray lines come sweeping down upon Sickles' front, and mix with the battle smoke; now the same colors emerge from the bushes and orchards upon his right, and envelope his flank in the confusion of the conflict."

And lastly, Lieutenant Haskell assesses the inevitable defeat of Sickles troops, and the powerlessness of observers like himself, to take any action in support of the Third Corps. He writes of his observations:

"These ten or twelve thousand men of the Third Corps fight well, but it soon becomes apparent that they must be swept from the field, or perish there where they are doing so well, so thick and overwhelming a storm of Rebel fire involves them. It was fearful to see, but these men, such as ever escape, must come from that conflict as best they can. To move down and support them with other troops is out of the question, for this would do as Sickles did, to relinquish a good position, and advance to a bad one.

There is no other alternative – the Third Corps must fight itself out of its position of destruction! What was it ever put there for?"
Frank Aretas Haskell – *The Battle of Gettysburg.*

Memorial to the 1st Minnesota – Gettysburg, Mathew Wilson, special dispatch to the *New York Times,* July 2, 1863

"On the afternoon of July 2, 1863 Sickles' Third Corps, having advanced from its line toward the Emmitsburg Road, eight companies of the First Minnesota Regiment, numbering 262 men were sent to this place to support a battery upon Sickles repulse. As his men were passing here in confused retreat, two Confederate brigades in pursuit were crossing the swale. To gain time to bring up the reserves and to save this position, Gen Hancock ordered the eight companies at his disposal to charge the rapidly advancing enemy.

The order was instantly repeated by Colonel William Colvill. And the charge as quickly made down the slope at full speed through the concentrated fire of the two brigades breaking with the bayonet the enemy's front line as it was crossing the small brook in the low ground. There remained the remnant of the eight companies, nearly surrounded by the enemy, holding its entire force at bay for some time and until it retired on the approach of the reserve where the charge successfully accomplished its object. It saved this position and probably the battlefield. The loss of the eight companies in the charge was 215 killed & wounded, more than 83% percent. Forty-seven men were still in line and no man was missing. In self sacrificing, desperate valor this charge has no parallel in any war. [The next day the regiment participated in repelling Pickett's charge losing 17 more men killed and wounded.]

Author's Note: Further activity involving the 1st Minnesota occurred the following day. During the chaotic fighting that took place in the repulse of Pickett's Charge, Private Marshall Sherman of Company C of the 1st Minnesota captured the colors of the 28th Virginia. After the battle, Private Sherman received the Medal of Honor for his exploit. (Sometime later, the flag was taken back to Minnesota as a prize of war and was kept, but not publicly displayed, at the Minnesota Historical Society. There is some testimony of the value and esteem of that flag even today: In the mid-1990s, several groups of Virginians unsuccessfully sued the Society for return of the 28th Virginia's battle flag to the Old Dominion.)

In further action on the part of this unit, Cpl Henry O'Brien repeatedly picked up the fallen colors of the 1st Minnesota. In addition, he hand carried a wounded comrade back to the Union lines, despite being knocked out by a bullet to the head and also being shot in the hand. In recognition of his efforts, he too was later awarded a Medal of Honor for his heroism.

CHAPTER 17

THE FIGHT FOR THE HILL
DAY 2, JULY 2, 1863 - PART II

It was a day like no other, calling forth a series of what appeared to be unremitting encounters that produced bloodshed comparable to that observed everywhere during those fateful three days. In the late afternoon of the second day of the battle, July 2, 1863, the fighting shifted to left side of the Union position on Cemetery Ridge.

As was the case of other sites, the battle was filled with intense fighting and unmatched bravery. Characteristic of its setting, this time it was a battle that occurred within a narrow segment of the landscape, set upon a local landmark known as Little Round Top, a small hillock that occupied the extreme left of the Union line.
This time the attackers were drawn from the Confederacy, July 2, 1863

"My dead and wounded were nearly as great in number as those still on duty. They literally covered the ground. The blood stood in puddles in some places on the rocks; the ground was soaked with the blood of as brave men as ever fell on the red field of battle."
Colonel William C. Oates, 15th Alabama, C.S.A.

Many years later, reflecting on the immense importance of that day of fierce fighting, Colonel Oates' Northern adversary in that encounter, Colonel Joshua Lawrence Chamberlain, of the 20th Maine wrote of those events on that fateful day, as well.

October 3, 1889

"The lesson impressed on me as I stand here and my heart and mind traverse your faces, and the years that are gone, is that in a great, momentous struggle like this commemorated here, it is character that tells. I do not mean simply nor chiefly bravery. Many a man has that, who may become surprised or disconcerted at a sudden change in the posture of affairs. What I mean by character is a firm seasoned substance of soul. I mean such qualities or acquirements as intelligence, thoughtfulness, conscientiousness, right-mindedness, patience, fortitude, long-suffering and unconquerable resolve....

We know not of the future, and cannot plan for it much. But we can hold our spirits and our bodies so pure and high, we may cherish such thoughts and such ideals, and dream such dreams of lofty purpose, that we can determine and know what manner of men we will be whenever and wherever the hour strikes, that calls to noble action."

Excerpts offered in a speech by Joshua L. Chamberlain on the occasion of the dedication of the 20th Maine Monument at Gettysburg.

Joshua Lawrence Chamberlain

CHAMBERLAIN AT GETTYSBURG

It was an unlikely position to find one's self in. He was, after all, a college professor, not a soldier. But he, and his two brothers believed in their cause, and that lead them across varied battle sites, and now to Gettysburg. So Colonel Joshua Lawrence Chamberlain found himself in command of the 20th Maine Infantry on that fateful day of July 2th 1863.

The Fifth Corps was called to the front when fighting began at 4 o'clock. Along side the remainder of Colonel Strong Vincent's brigade, Chamberlain's men rushed to the front to be placed on the southern slope of Little Round Top, at the extreme left of the Union line.

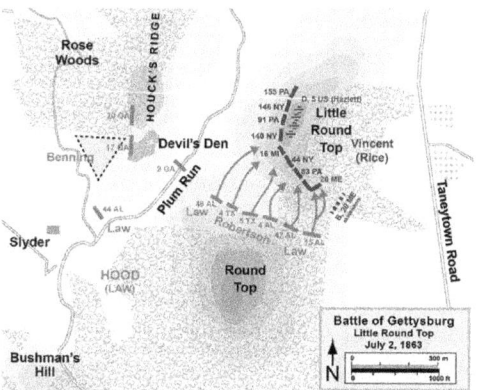

Laws Attack on Little Round Top

Within minutes they were trading volleys with Confederate skirmishers tramping down the slope of Big Round Top, soldiers assigned to General Law's Alabama Brigade. The 15th Alabama Infantry, commanded by Colonel William C. Oates, had climbed over the summit of the larger hill (Big Round Top), reorganized, and were now sweeping northward toward the Union line in the vicinity of Little Round Top, the adjacent federally occupied hill. At that point, the regiments collided on the hillside where Chamberlain's troops stood firm. It was a tumultuous scene of savagery as smoke, fire, and the groans of dying men filled the woods. Standing behind his thinning ranks, the colonel could see the effect of the Confederate charges on his position:

"The roar of all this tumult reached us on the left and heightened the intensity of our resolve. Meanwhile the flanking column worked around to our left and joined those before us in a fierce assault, which lasted with increasing fury for an intense hour. The two lines met and broke and intermingled in the shock. The crush of musketry gave way to cuts and thrusts, grapplings and wrestlings. The edge of conflict swayed to and fro, with wild pools and eddies. At times I saw around me more of the enemy than of my own men; gaps opening, swallowing, closing again with sharp, convulsive energy; squads of stalwart men who had cut their way through us, disappearing as if translated all around me, strange, mingled roar- shouts of defiance, rally and desperation; and underneath, murmured (sic) entreaty and stifled moans; gasping prayers, snatches of Sabbath song, whispers of loved names; everywhere men torn and broken, staggering, creeping, quivering on the earth, and dead faces with strangely (sic) fixed eyes staring stark into the sky.

"In the very deepest of the struggle while our shattered line had pressed the enemy well below their first point of contact... I saw through a sudden rift in the thick smoke our colors standing alone. I first thought some optical illusion imposed upon me. But as forms emerged through the drifting smoke, the truth came to view. The cross fire had cut keenly; the center had almost been shot away; only two of the color guard had been left, and they fighting to fill the whole space; and in the center, wreathed in battle smoke, stood the Color Sergeant Andrew Tozier. His color-staff planted in the ground at his side, the upper part clasped in his elbow, so holding the flag upright, with musket and cartridges seized from the fallen comrade at his side he was defending his sacred trust in the manner of the songs of chivalry. It was a stirring picture..."

The Confederate attacks came in waves, each new attack being more intense than the one that preceded it. The action on the battlefield was vigorous; the determination of the Confederate troops was only matched by the intransigence of their Union adversaries. At the height of the fighting, a Confederate bullet struck Chamberlain in his left thigh. Luckily, the metal sword scabbard hanging at his side diverted the bullet, leaving him with only a painful bruise. The colonel leapt to his feet and continued to encourage his men, directing the defense of the rocky hillside. The relentless Confederate assaults shredded Chamberlain's ranks and the situation looked grim as ammunition began to run out. Soldiers ransacked the cartridge boxes of the wounded and fallen, including the dead strewn on the hillside. But there was not enough ammunition to continue for much longer and that meager supply soon ran out. Chamberlain had not only been directing his men, but closely observing the southern attacks as well. Sensing exhaustion among the Confederates who were also probably running out of ammunition, he formulated a final plan to defend the 20th Maine's part of the shrinking Union line. There occurred a brief lull in the fighting when the colonel called all of his officers quickly to a meeting and explained his proposal: the 20th Maine was going to make a surprise bayonet charge into the ragged approaching Confederate onslaught.

As Chamberlain wrote later:

"Not a moment was about to be lost! Five minutes more of such a defensive and the last roll call would sound for us! Desperate as the chances were, there was nothing for it but to take the offensive. I stepped to the colors. The men turned towards me. One word was enough- 'BAYONETS!' It caught like fire and swept along the ranks. The men took it up with a shout, one could not say whether from the pit or the song of the morning sat, it was vain to order 'FORWARD!' No mortal could have heard it in the mighty hosanna that was winging the sky. The whole line quivered from the start; the edge of the left-wing rippled, swung, tossed among the rocks, straightened, changed curve from scimitar to sickle-shape; and the bristling archers swooped down upon the serried host- down into the face of half a thousand! Two hundred men!

"It was a great right wheel. Our left swung first, the advancing foe stopped, tried to make a stand amidst the trees and boulders, but the frenzied bayonets pressing through every space forced a constant settling to the rear. Morrill with his detached company and the remnants of our valorous sharpshooters... now fell upon the flank of the retiring crowd. At the first dash the commanding officer I happened to confront, coming on fiercely (with) sword in hand and big navy revolver (in) the other, fires one barrel almost in my face. But seeing the quick saber point at his throat, reverses arms, gives sword and pistol into my hands and yields himself prisoner.

"Ranks were broken; some retired before us somewhat hastily; some threw their muskets to the the ground - even loaded; sunk on their knees, threw up their hands calling out, 'We surrender. Don't kill us!' As if we wanted to do that! We kill only to resist killing. And these were manly men, whom we could befriend and by no means kill, if they came our way in peace and good will."

15th Alabama Attempts to Capture Little Roundtop

Report of Colonel William C. Oates, Fifteenth Alabama Infantry, August 8, 1863.

SIR: I have the honor to report, in obedience to orders from brigade headquarters, the participation of my regiment in the battle near Gettysburg on the 2nd of July.

My regiment occupied the center of the brigade when the line of battle was formed. During the advance, the two regiments enemy right were moved by the left flank across my rear, which threw me on the extreme4 right of the whole line. I encountered the enemy's sharpshooters posted behind a stone fence, and sustained some loss thereby. It was here that Lieutenant Colonel Isaac B. Feagin, a most excellent and gallant officer, received a severe wound in the right knee, which caused him to lose his leg. Privates [A.] Kennedy, of Company B, and [William] Trimner, of Company G, were killed at this point, and Private [G.E.] Spencer, Company D, severely wounded.

After crossing the fence, I received an order from Brigadier-General Law to left-wheel my regiment and move in the direction of the heights upon my left, which order I failed to obey, for the reason that when I received it I was rapidly advancing up the mountain, and in my front I discovered a heavy force of the enemy. Besides this, there was great difficulty in accomplishing the maneuver at that moment, as the regiment on my left (Forty-seventh Alabama) was crowding me on the left, and running into my regiment, which had already created considerable confusion. In the event that I had obeyed the order, I should have come in contact with the regiment on my left, and also have exposed my right flank to an enfilading fire from the enemy. I therefore continued to press forward, my right passing over the top of the mountain, on the right of the line.

On reaching the foot of the mountain below, I found the enemy in heavy force, posted in rear of large rocks upon a slight elevation beyond a depression of some 300 yards in width between the base of the mountain and the open plain beyond. I engaged them, my right meeting the left of their line exactly. Here I lost several gallant officers and men.

After firing two or three rounds, I discovered that the enemy were giving way in my front. I ordered a charge, and the enemy in my front fled, but that portion of his line confronting the two companies on my left gave ground, and continued a most galling fire upon my left.

Just at this moment, I discovered the regiment on my left (Forty-seventh Alabama) retiring. I halted my regiment as its left reached a very large rock, and ordered a left-wheel of the regiment, which was executed in good order under fire, thus taking advantage of a ledge of rocks running off in a line perpendicular to the one I had just abandoned, and affording very good protection to my men. This position enabled me to keep up a constant flank and cross fire upon the enemy, which in less than five minutes caused him to change front. Receiving reinforcements, he charged me five times, and was as often repulsed with heavy loss. Finally, I discovered that the enemy had flanked me on the right, and two regiments were moving rapidly upon my rear and not 200 yards distant, when, to save my regiment from capture or destruction, I ordered a retreat.

Having become exhausted from fatigue and the excessive heat of the day, I turned the command of the regiment over to Captain B. A. Hill, and instructed him to take the men off the field, and reform the regiment and report to the brigade.

My loss was, as near as can now be ascertained, as follows, to wit: 17 killed upon the field, 54 wounded and brought off the field, and 90 missing, most of whom are either killed or wounded. Among the killed and wounded are 8 officers, most of whom were very gallant and efficient men.

Recapitulation: - Killed, 17; wounded, 54; missing, 90; total, 161.

I am, lieutenant, most respectfully, your obedient servant, W. C. OATES, Colonel, Commanding Fifteenth Alabama Regiment.

Chamberlain and the 20th Maine

The charge of the 20th Maine Infantry was the climax of the fighting in front of Vincent's brigade and contributed to the Union victory at Little Round Top. The fighting was close, hot, and indistinguishable, at times.

There were many heroes, on both sides, at Little Round Top. Twenty-five-year-old Color Sgt. Andrew J. Tozier of the 20th Maine emerged as one of them, and was later awarded the Medal of Honor for his bravery. It had been Colonel Chamberlain's decision to promote Tozier to the post of color sergeant for the 20th Maine. {Color sergeant was a dangerous but coveted position in Civil War regiments, generally manned by the bravest soldier in the unit.} As the 20th Maine's center began to break and give ground in the face of the Alabama regiments' onslaught, Tozier stood firm, remaining upright as Southern bullets buzzed and snapped in the air around him. Tozier's personal gallantry in defending the 20th Maine's colors became the regimental rallying point for Companies D, E and F to retake the center. Were it not for Tozier's heroic stand, the 20th Maine would likely have been beaten at that decisive point in the battle and the battle of day 2 would be lost to the Confederates.

CHAPTER 18

Aftermath at Day's End
Day 2, July 2, 1863 - Part III

July 2, 1863, 11 P.M.

To: The War Department, Washington, DC

"The enemy has attacked me about 4 P.M. this day, and after one of the severest contests of the war, was repulsed at all points. We have suffered considerably in killed and wounded…We have taken a large number of prisoners. I shall remain in my present position tomorrow, but am not prepared to say, until better advised of the condition of the army, whether my operation will be of an offensive or defensive character."
George Gordon Meade, Commanding General

As customary, shortly thereafter, Colonel Joshua Chamberlain, filed his report of the day's remarkable events on Little Round Top.

Field Near Emmitsburg - July 6, 1863

Report of Col. Joshua L. Chamberlain, Twentieth Maine Infantry

Sir:

"In compliance with the request of the colonel commanding the brigade, I have the honor to submit a somewhat detailed report of the operations of the Twentieth Regiment Maine Volunteers in the battle of Gettysburg, on the 2d and 3d instant.:

Having acted as the advance guard, made necessary by the proximity of the enemy's cavalry, on the march of the clay before, my command on reaching Hanover, Pa., just before sunset on that day, were much worn, and lost no time in getting ready for an expected bivouac. Rations were scarcely issued, and the men about preparing supper, when rumors that the enemy had been encountered that day near Gettysburg absorbed every other interest, and very soon orders came to march forthwith to Gettysburg.:

My men moved out with a promptitude and spirit extraordinary, the cheers and welcome they received on the road adding to their enthusiasm. After an hour or two of sleep by the roadside just before daybreak, we reached the heights southeasterly of Gettysburg at about 7 am, July 2.

Massed at first with the rest of the division on the right of the road, we were moved several times farther toward the left. Although expecting every moment to be put into action and held strictly in line of battle, yet the men were able to take some rest and make the most of their rations.:

Somewhere near 4 p.m. a sharp cannonade, at some distance to our left and front, was the signal for a sudden and rapid movement of our whole division in the direction of this firing, which grew warmer as we approached. Passing an open field in the hollow ground in which some of our batteries were going into position, our brigade reached the skirt of a piece of woods, in the farther edge of which there was a heavy musketry fire, and when about to go forward into line we received from Colonel Vincent, commanding the brigade, orders to move to the left at the double-quick, when we took a farm road crossing Plum Run in order to gain a rugged mountain spur called Granite Spur, or Little Round Top.:

The enemy's artillery got range of our column as we were climbing the spur, and the crashing of the shells among the rocks and the tree tops made us move lively along the crest. One or two shells burst in our ranks. Passing to the southern slope of Little Round Top, Colonel Vincent indicated to me the ground my regiment was to occupy, informing me that this was the extreme left of our general line, and that a desperate attack was expected in order to turn that position, concluding by telling me I was to" hold that ground at all hazards." This was the last word I heard from him.:

In order to commence by making my right firm, I formed my regiment on the right into line, giving such direction to the line as should best secure the advantage of the rough, rocky, and straggling wooded ground.:

The line faced generally toward a more conspicuous eminence southwest of ours, which is known as Sugar Loaf, or Round Top. Between this and my position intervened a smooth and thinly wooded hollow. My line formed, I immediately detached Company B, Captain Morrill commanding, to extend from my left flank across this hollow as a line of skirmishers, with directions to act as occasion might dictate, to prevent a surprise on my exposed flank and rear.:

The artillery fire on our position had meanwhile been constant and heavy, but my formation was scarcely complete when the artillery was replaced by a vigorous infantry assault upon the center of our brigade to my right, but it very soon involved the right of my regiment and gradually extended along my entire front. The action was quite sharp and at close quarters.:

In the midst of this, an officer from my center informed me that some important movement of the enemy was going on in his front, beyond that of the line with which we were engaged. Mounting a large rock, I was able to see a considerable body of the enemy moving by the flank in rear of their line engaged, and passing from the direction of the foot of Great Round Top through the valley toward the front of my left. The close engagement not allowing any change of front, I immediately stretched my regiment to the left, by taking intervals by the left flank, and at the same time "refusing" my left wing, so that it was nearly at right angles with my right, thus occupying about twice the extent of our ordinary front, some of the companies being brought into single rank when the nature of the ground gave sufficient strength or shelter. My officers and men understood wishes so well that this movement was executed under fire, the right wing keeping up fire, without giving the enemy any occasion to seize or even to suspect their advantage. But we were not a moment too soon; the enemy's flanking column having gained their desired direction, burst upon my left, where they evidently had expected an unguarded flank, with great demonstration.:

We opened a brisk fire at close range, which was so sudden and effective that they soon fell back among the rocks and low trees in the valley, only to burst forth again with a shout, and rapidly advanced, firing as they came. They pushed up to within a dozen yards of us before the terrible effectiveness of our fire compelled them to break and take shelter.:

They renewed the assault on our whole front, and for an hour the fighting was severe. Squads of the enemy broke through our line in several places, and the fight was literally hand to hand. The edge of the fight rolled backward and forward like a wave. The dead and wounded were now in our front and then in our rear. Forced from our position, we desperately recovered it, and pushed the enemy down to the foot of the slope. The intervals of the struggle were seized to remove our wounded (and those of the enemy also), to gather ammunition from the cartridge-boxes of disabled friend or foe on the field, and even to secure better muskets than the Enfields, which we found did not stand service well. Rude shelters were thrown up of the loose rocks that covered the ground.:

Captain Woodward, commanding the Eighty-third Pennsylvania Volunteers, on my right, gallantly maintaining his fight, judiciously and with hearty co-operation made his movements conform to my necessities, so that my right was at no time exposed to a flank attack.:

The enemy seemed to have gathered all their energies for their final assault. We had gotten our thin line into as good a shape as possible, when a strong force emerged from the scrub wood in the valley, as well as I could judge, in two lines in echelon by the right, and, opening a heavy fire, the first line came on as if they meant to sweep everything before them. We opened on them as well as we could with our scanty ammunition snatched from the field.:

It did not seem possible to withstand another shock like this now coming on. Our loss had been severe. One-half of my left wing had fallen, and a third of my regiment lay just behind us, dead or badly wounded. At this moment my anxiety was increased by a great roar of musketry in my rear, on the farther or northerly slope of Little Round Top, apparently on the flank of the regular brigade, which was in support of Hazlett's battery on the crest behind us. The bullets from this attack struck into my left rear, and I feared that the enemy might have nearly surrounded the Little Round Top, and only a desperate chance was left for us. My ammunition was soon exhausted. My men were firing their last shot and getting ready to club their muskets.:

It was imperative to strike before we were struck by this overwhelming force in a hand-to-hand fight, which we could not probably have withstood or survived. At that crisis, I ordered the bayonet. The word was enough. It ran like fire along the line, from man to man, and rose into a shout, with which they sprang forward upon the enemy, now not 30 yards away. The effect was surprising; many of the enemy's first line threw down their arms and surrendered. An officer fired his pistol at my head with one hand, while he handed me his sword with the other. Holding fast by our right, and swinging forward our left, we made an extended right wheel, before which the enemy's second line broke and fell back, fighting from tree to tree, many being captured, until we had swept the valley and cleared the front of nearly our entire brigade:

Meantime Captain Morrill with his skirmishers sent out from my left flank, with some dozen or fifteen of the U.S. Sharpshooters who had put themselves under his direction, fell upon the enemy as they were breaking, and by his demonstrations, as well as his well-directed fire, added much to the effect of the charge.:

Having thus cleared the valley and driven the enemy up the western slope of the Great Round Top, not wishing to press so far out as to hazard the ground I was to hold by leaving it exposed to a sudden rush of the enemy, I succeeded (although with some effort to stop my men, who declared they were "on the road to Richmond") in getting the regiment into good order and resuming our original position.:

Four hundred prisoners, including two field and several line officers, were sent to the rear. These were mainly from the Fifteenth and Forty-seventh Alabama Regiments, with some of the Fourth and Fifth Texas. One hundred and fifty of the enemy were found killed and wounded in our front.:

At dusk, Colonel Rice informed me of the fall of Colonel Vincent, which had devolved the command of the brigade on him, and that Colonel Fisher had come up with a brigade to our support. These troops were massed in our rear. It was the understanding, as Colonel Rice informed me, that Colonel Fisher's brigade was to advance and seize the western slope of Great Round Top, where the enemy had shortly before been driven. But, after considerable delay, this intention for some reason was not carried into execution:

We were apprehensive that if the enemy were allowed to strengthen himself in that position, he would have a great advantage in renewing the attack on us at daylight or before. Colonel Rice then directed me to make the movement to seize that crest.:

It was now 9 p.m. Without waiting to get ammunition, but trusting in part to the very circumstance of not exposing our movement or our small front by firing, and with bayonets fixed, the little handful of 200 men pressed up the mountain side in very extended order, as the steep and jagged surface of the ground compelled. We heard squads of the enemy falling back before us, and, when near the crest, we met a scattering and uncertain fire, which caused us the great loss of the gallant Lieutenant Linscott, who fell, mortally wounded. In the silent advance in the darkness we laid hold of 25 prisoners, among them a staff officer of General McLaw, commanding the brigade immediately opposed to us during the fight. Reaching the crest, and reconnoitering the ground, I placed the men in a strong position among the rocks, and informed Colonel Rice, requesting also ammunition and some support to our right, which was very near the enemy, their movements and words even being now distinctly heard by us.

Some confusion soon after resulted from the attempt of some regiment of Colonel Fisher's brigade to come to our support. They had found a wood road up the mountain, which brought them on my right flank, and also in proximity to the enemy, massed a little below. Hearing their approach, and thinking a movement from that quarter could only be from the enemy, I made disposition to receive them as such. In the confusion which attended the attempt to form them in support of my right, the enemy opened a brisk fire, which disconcerted my efforts to form them and disheartened the supports themselves, so that I saw no more of them that night.

Feeling somewhat insecure in this isolated position, I sent in for the Eighty-third Pennsylvania, which came speedily, followed by the Forty-fourth New York, and, having seen these well posted, I sent a strong picket to the front, with instructions to report to me every half hour during the night, and allowed the rest of my men to sleep on their arms.:

At some time about midnight, two regiments of Colonel Fisher's brigade came up the mountain beyond my left, and took position near the summit; but as the enemy did not threaten from that direction, I made no effort to connect with them.:

We went into the fight with 386, all told 358 guns. Every pioneer and musician who could carry a musket went into the ranks. Even the sick and foot-sore, who could not keep up in the march, came up as soon as they could find their regiments, and took their places in line of battle, while it was battle, indeed. Some prisoners I had under guard, under sentence of court-martial, I was obliged to put into the fight, and they bore their part well, for which I shall recommend a commutation of their sentence.

The loss, so far as I can ascertain it, is 136-30 of whom were killed, and among the wounded are many mortally.

Captain Billings, Lieutenant Kendall, and Lieutenant Linscott are officers whose loss we deeply mourn - efficient soldiers, and pure and high-minded men.:

In such an engagement there were many incidents of heroism and noble character which should have place even in an official report; but, under present circumstances, I am unable to do justice to them. I will say of that regiment that the resolution, courage, and heroic fortitude which enabled us to withstand so formidable an attack have happily led to so conspicuous a result that they may safely trust to history to record their merits.:

About noon on the 3d of July, we were withdrawn, and formed on the right of the brigade, in the front edge of a piece of woods near the left center of our main line of battle, where we were held in readiness to support our troops, then receiving the severe attack of the afternoon of that day.:

On the 4th, we made a reconnaissance to the front, to ascertain the movements of the enemy, but finding that they had retired, at least beyond Willoughby's Run, we returned to Little Round Top, where we buried our dead in the place where we had laid them during the fight, marking each grave by a head-board made of ammunition boxes, with each dead soldiers name cut upon it. We also buried 50 of the enemy's dead in front of our position of July 2. We then looked after our wounded, whom I had taken the responsibility of putting into the houses of citizens in the vicinity of Little Round Top, and, on the morning of the 5th, took up our march on the Emmitsburg road.

I have the honor to be, your obedient servant, Joshua L. Chamberlain,

Colonel, Commanding Twentieth Maine Volunteers Southern, Assessment of Day Two.

At General Lee's headquarters in a grove of trees near the Chambersburg Pike on the outskirts of Gettysburg, the talk was confident. The assembled generals (all but Longstreet being present) spoke of a great victory to be achieved the following day.

The Army of Northern Virginia had sustained great losses but was in high spirits. Stuart's three brigades had returned, along with four additional cavalry units. And George Pickett's division was in place. "It is all well, general," Lee told A. P. Hill. "Everything is all well."

Lee's optimism was shared by the troops and his battle plan was in place. On the first day he had attacked the Army of the Potomac on the right side of their line. On the second day, he had attacked the left side of their line. Although unsuccessful, Lee knew that Meade had been forced to shift troops to the left, thereby weakening his center. That is where he would strike tomorrow, July 3rd, 1863. And Pickett's well rested division would lead the attack. If they were victorious, perhaps, the war would end on the crest of Cemetery Ridge.

CHAPTER 19

July 3, 1863 - Day 3: Part I

"A cloud possessed the hollow field,
The gathering battle's smoky shield,
Athwart the gloom the lightning flashed,
And through the cloud some horsemen dashed,
And from the heights the thunder pealed.
Then at the brief command of Lee
Moved out that matchless infantry,
With Pickett leading grandly down,
To rush against the roaring crown
Of those dread heights of destiny."

Will Henry Thompson

On the night of July 2, General Meade held a council of war with his Corps commanders. Their purpose was to decide on a course of action for the following day. Several questions were raised including whether the Army of the Potomac should remain in place or whether it should seek an alternative position. In addition, it was asked whether the army should stage an offensive attack or assume a defensive position as it had on day 2, and wait for an attack by the enemy. And Finally, they needed to decide on how long to wait for Lee to make a counter move.

The assembled generals agreed to remain in position and to await Lee's attack. However, they differed on the last issue regarding whether the army should remain idle in the face of Lee's threat. Some units, such as Sickles Third Corps were in no condition to fight. As General Birney indicated, "the Third Corps had been badly defeated, and rendered for the time comparatively useless."

In contrast, some generals, as General Slocum argued that they should "Stay and fight it out." And, in the end, that is what Meade decided to do.

As the members of the assembly filed out and left the meeting, Meade stopped General Gibbon, now commander of Hancock's Second Corp. He told him, "If Lee attacks tomorrow, it will be in your front". Gibbon's "front" was the center of the Union line along Cemetery Ridge. When Gibbon's asked Meade for clarification, Meade told him that Lee "has made attacks on both our flanks {the right on Culp's Hill and the left at Little Round Top} and failed, and if he concludes to try it again it will be on our center." Gibbon suggested that he hoped that Meade was correct, and concluded that if Lee hit the Second Corps on July 3, "we would defeat him."

THE FISHHOOK

Meade's troops were arrayed south of Gettysburg on Cemetery Ridge. There, they occupied the high ground, fronted on the north by Culp's Hill and on the south by the two hills, Big and Little Round Top. Their position resembled that of an inverted fishhook. Aside from occupying the high ground, the positioning of the line allowed Meade to shift troops from his left or right to the center. Lee's troops were aligned in front of Meade's, approximately a mile away on Seminary Ridge. They would have to cross the Peach Orchard and the Wheatfield, a distance of about one mile, in order to attack Meade's at his position on Cemetery Ridge.

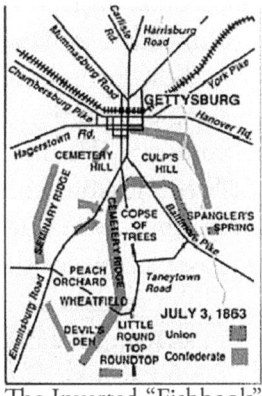

The Inverted "Fishhook"

THE ROAR OF THE CANNON

The opening of hostilities on that third day came with the most thunderous expression of cannon fire. And it came with a terrible roar that was unceasing and unearthly. No one who was witness to the events of that day could ever rid from their memory the continuous belching of smoke, the massive explosion of ash, the constant hissing of bursting shells or the cascade of agony that rained from the skies. As one witness close to the emergence of hostilities on that day noted shortly thereafter, it was a day never before seen on any battlefield.

At about one o'clock in the afternoon, in the Copse of Trees, behind the stone wall of the Union line on Cemetery Ridge (inside the fishhook) the following scene was depicted by a witness.

"Who can describe such a conflict as is raging around us? To say that it was like a summer storm, with the crash of thunder, the glare of lighting, the shrieking of the wind, and the clatter of hailstones, would be weak. The thunder and lighting of these two hundred and fifty guns and their shells, whose smoke darkens the sky, are incessant, all pervading, in the air above our heads, on the ground at out feet, remote, near, deafening, ear-piercing, astounding; and these hailstones are massy iron, charged with exploding fire. And there is little of human interest in a storm; it is an absorbing element of this. You may see flame and smoke, and hurrying men, and human passion at a great conflagration; but they are all earthly and nothing more. These guns are great infuriate demons, not of the earth, whose mouths blaze with smoking tongues of living fire, and whose murky breath, sulfur-laden, rolls around them and along the ground, the smoke of Hades. These grimy men, rushing, shouting, their souls in frenzy, plying the dusky globes and the igniting spark, are in their league, and but their willing ministers. We thought that at the second Bull Run, at the Antietam, and at Fredericksburg on the 11th of December we had heard heavy cannonading; they were but holiday salutes compared with this. Besides the great ceaseless roar of the guns, which was but the background of the others, a million various minor sounds, engaged the ear. The projectiles shriek long and sharp. They hiss, they scream, they growl, they sputter; all sounds of life and rage; and each has its different note, and all are discordant. Was ever heard such a chorus of sound before?"

As Colonel Frank Haskill relates in his continuing chronicle of events at Gettysburg, while the explosive fury of the bombardment scared the landscape and deafened the eardrums of spectators for miles around, the soldiers displayed a remarkable calmness. In the face of the confederate onslaught he writes,

"Our artillerymen upon the crest budged not an inch, nor intermitted, but, through caisson and limber were smashed, and guns dismantled, and men and horses killed, there amidst smoke and sweat, they gave back, without grudge, or loss of time in sending, in kind whatever the enemy sent, globe, and cone, and bolt, hollow or solid, an iron greeting to the rebellion, the compliments of a wrathful Republic."

❖ ❖

The General Loses his Headquarters

Hardly anyone or any one thing could escape the horrendous bombardments that befell the troops during the battle of Gettysburg. General Meade's headquarters came under attack within the first foray of cannon fire. Among the debris caused by the destruction, sixteen horses, tied in a row to a fence post now lay dead, while a near-by stationed double-hitched wagon flew apart after being hit by a missile; one of its of unfortunately hitched horses was blown away in the aftermath while its companion was left panicked standing on its three remaining legs.

The general's headquarters was also torn apart by the bombardment, a confederate shell having penetrated the walls and supporting pillars of the structure. As soldiers fled from the house during the bombardment Meade, himself, was spared injury as the draft of a errant shell speed by him.

Seeing his darting and fleeing staff, Meade (the snapping turtle, as he was nicknamed) offered a short story (and what for him was apparently an amusing incident) in an attempt at lighten the situation. Recounted later, he said:

"Gentlemen , are you trying to find a safe place? You remind me of the man who drove the ox-team that took ammunition for the heavy guns on the field of Palo Alto [A battle site of the earlier war with Mexico in which Meade, as many others, had participated.] Finding himself within range, he tilted up his cart and got behind it. Just then General Taylor came along, and seeing this attempt at shelter, shouted "You damned fool, don't you know you are no safer there than anywhere else?" Upon which, the driver replied, "I don't suppose I am, general, but it kind of feels so."

Perhaps it was simply a poor attempt at levity by the high command, one falling on deaf ears, or an ill-conceived attempt at providing relief during a heavy moment. Nevertheless, among the assembled officers who had experienced the terrific blast of the cannon, no one laughed.

THE NEXT STEP

As the Confederate artillery barrage finally ceased, the Army of Northern Virginia started to move, in mass formation, across the field. A variety of thoughts likely emerged in the minds of the Northern troops as this horde of men approached. From his vantage point among the Union troops, Lt. Haskill offers these remarks on the demeanor of the awaiting Union Army.

"All was orderly and still upon our crest; no noise and no confusion. The men had little need of commands, for the survivors of a dozen battles knew well enough what this array in front portended, and, already in their places, they would be prepared to act when the right time should come. The click of the locks as each man raised the hammer to feel with his fingers that the cap was on the nipple; the sharp jar as a musket touched

a stone upon the wall when thrust in aiming over it, and the clicking of the iron axles as the guns were rolled up by hand a little further to the front, were quite all the sound that could be heard. Cap-boxes were slid around to the front of the body; cartridge boxes opened, officers opened their pistol-holsters. Such preparations, little more was needed."
Union Staff Officer Frank A. Haskell – The Battle of Gettysburg

Pickett's division arrived at the Battle of Gettysburg on the evening of the second day, July 2, 1863. It had been delayed by its assignment to guard the Confederate lines of communication through Chambersburg, Pennsylvania. After two days of heavy fighting, Gen. Robert E. Lee's Army of Northern Virginia, which had initially driven the Union Army of the Potomac to the high ground south of Gettysburg {on day one}, had been unable to dislodge the Union soldiers from their position on day two at Culp's Hill and Little Round Top; the Federal defenses held.

Pickett's Charge

Lee's plan for July 3 (contrary to Gen. James Longstreet's oppositional council) called for {as Meade had predicted} a massive assault on the center of the Union lines on Cemetery Ridge, calculating that attacks on either flank the previous day had drawn troops from the center. He directed General Longstreet to assemble a force of three divisions for the attack—two exhausted divisions from the corps of Lt. Gen. A.P. Hill (under Brig. Gen. J. Johnston Pettigrew and Maj. Gen. Isaac R. Trimble), and Pickett's fresh division from Longstreet's own Corps. Lee referred to Pickett as leading the charge (although Longstreet was actually in command).

Aligned in solid ranks behind stone walls and fence barricades from Ziegler's Grove to the Angle, troops under the command of General Alexander Hays were more than prepared to contest the Southern attack. Hays had put two of his largest brigades on the line, stacked shoulder to shoulder. In one place the men were four ranks deep. Many of these regiments had been forced to surrender to "Stonewall" Jackson at Harpers Ferry in 1862 without firing a shot and it was a stain that unjustly had followed them since. For many this was the first opportunity to "exact retribution" for that humiliation. For others, there were other stains, most notably that of the defeat at Fredericksburg in December of 1862 under Burnside. This time they would even the score.

Through the smoke the Union soldiers watched the butternut formations approach, awed by the discipline displayed in the southern ranks. The moment was not lost on the federal troops or as the fiery General Hays observed:

"Their march was as steady as if impelled by machinery, unbroken by our artillery, which played upon them a storm of missiles. When within 100 yards of our line of infantry, the fire of our men could no longer be restrained. Four lines rose from behind our stone wall, and before the smoke of our first volley had cleared away, the enemy, in dismay and consternation, were seeking safety in flight. Every attempt by their officers to rally them was in vain."

The target of the Confederate assault was the center of the Union Army of the Potomac's II Corps, commanded by Major General Winfield Scott Hancock. Directly in the center on his line was the division of Brig. Gen. John Gibbon with the brigades of Brig. Gen. William Harrow, Col. Norman J. Hall, and Brig. Gen. Alexander S. Webb. To the north of this position were brigades from the division of Brig. Gen. Alexander Hays, and to the south was Maj. Abner Doubleday's division of the I Corps, including the 2nd Vermont Brigade of Brig. Gen. George J. Stannard and the 121st Pennsylvania under the command of Col. Chapman Biddle. General Meade's headquarters were just behind the II Corps line, in the small house owned by the widow Lydia Leister.

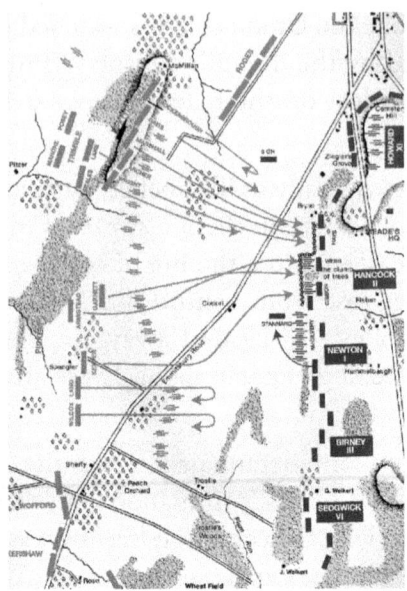
Allied Forces

From the beginning things went awry for the Confederates. While Pickett's division had not been used yet at Gettysburg, A.P. Hill's health became an issue and he did not participate in selecting which of his troops were to be used for the charge. While some of Hill's corps had fought lightly on July 1, others had not fought at all on July 2. Moreover, in the confusion, an extensive number of troops that had done heavy fighting on July 1 ended up making the charge.

Another miscalculation involved the confederate artillery. Following a massive, never before witnessed, [but largely ineffective,] two-hour artillery barrage that was meant to soften up the Union defenses, the three divisions of the Army of Northern Virginia, stepped across the open fields almost a mile from Cemetery Ridge. The attack involved approximately 12,000 to 15,000 men, and included nine brigades extended over a mile-long front. Pickett noting the brilliant display presented by his soldiers, sought to inspire them by shouting, "Up, Men, and to your posts! Don't forget today that you are from Old Virginia."

Pickett's division, with the brigades of Brig. Gens. Lewis A. Armistead, Richard B. Garnett, and James L. Kemper, was on the right flank of the assault. It received punishing Union artillery fire, and then volleys of massed musket fire as it made its way to its objective on Cemetery Ridge.

When the Army of Northern Virginia reached half the distance from Seminary Ridge to the Union line at Cemetery Ridge, which had taken eight minutes, they approached a crest in the landscape that hid them from view. There Pickett halted the line and reformed his troops so that when they emerged again into view they were once again at parade ground stature. However, their lines, it could be noted, were much shorter than before they started their initial march. General Kemper rode back behind his troop formation to see General Armistead, whose brigade was placed behind that of General Kemper. "Armistead" shouted General Kemper, "I am going to charge those heights and carry them and I want you to support me."

"I'll do it," Armistead was recalled saying, adding, "Look at my line. It never looked better on dress parade."

The first part of the Confederate advance soon approached its goal, approximately 250 yards from the Union line, and within musket range. At that point the Union Army released a barrage of fire which decimated the advancing Confederates. Half the color bearers and their banners were felled by musket power. And in the process all remnants of the parade formation had vanished.

"Their front line went down like grass before the scythe", recalled one soldier from the 1st Minnesota. And from the Confederate side of the line Lt. Tom Dooley later wrote:

"Oh, how long it seems before we reach those blazing guns. Our men are falling faster now, for the deadly musket is at work. Volley after volley of crashing musket balls sweeps through the line and mows us down."

The slaughter was awesome. After the battle, from the perspective of still another observer, a caregiver to the wounded, comes this observation:

"I was looking out of the windows facing the front yard. Near the basement door, and directly underneath the window I was at, stood one of these benches. I saw them lifting the poor men upon it, then. By this time, amputating benches had been placed about the house. I must have become inured to seeing the terrors of battle, else I could hardly have gazed upon the scenes now presented, the surgeons sawing and cutting off arms and legs, then again probing and picking bullets from the flesh. Some of the soldiers fairly begged to be taken next, so great was their suffering, and so anxious were they to obtain relief. I saw the surgeons hastily put a cattle horn over the mouths of the wounded ones, after they were placed upon the bench. At first I did not understand the meaning of this but upon inquiry, soon learned that that was their mode of administrating chloroform, in order to produce unconsciousness. But the effect in some instances were not produced; for I saw the wounded throwing themselves wildly about, and shrieking with pain while the operation was going on.

To the south of the house, and just outside of the yard, I noticed a pile of limbs higher than the fence. It was a ghastly sight! Gazing upon these, too often the trophies of the amputating bench, I could have no other feeling, than that the whole scene was one of cruel butchery."

Tillie (Pierce) Alleman, (1888) *At Gettysburg, or What a Girl Saw and Heard of the Battle.*

CHAPTER 20

Day 3 - Part II - At the Angle

Armistead's brigade made the farthest progress toward the Union lines. However, here he was stopped; his adversary, positioned at the Angle behind the stone wall, was the 71 PA Regiment with 250 men. To their left, was the 69th PA, supported by five guns of Cowan's 1st NY battery. As the Confederates pushed forward, the men and artillery at the Angle poured devastating fire into the approaching units. Still, the Confederates came, this time reaching the stone wall of the Angle. Meanwhile, General Armistead, leading the Confederate attack with a group of about 200 men overran most of the 69th and 71st PA before reaching Cowan's Battery. General Webb, who watched the attack, ordered the 72nd PA into battle. The 72nd PA halted the Confederate advance and forced many of the enemy to seek cover behind the western side of the stone wall. Fierce hand-to-hand fighting was now in order and could be observed as it raged at the Angle; meanwhile, adjacent to the proceedings Webb ordered a charge by the 72nd.

Webb Orders the 72nd Ahead

The clash of arms and ensuing violence at the Angle was horrific. It was described most vividly in Lt. Frank Haskill's acute observations in which the horror of war overshadows individual valor. He writes,

"The jostling, swaying lines on either side boil, and roar, and dash their flamy spray, two hostile billows of a fiery ocean. Thick flashes stream from the wall, thick volleys answer from the crest. No threats or expostulation now, only example and encouragement. All depths of passion are stirred, and all combatives fire, down to their deep foundations. Individuality is drowned in a sea of clamor, and timid men, breathing the breath of the multitude, are brave. The frequent dead and wounded lie where they stagger and fall – there is no humanity for them now, and none can be spared to care for them. The men do not cheer or shout; they growl, and over that uneasy sea, heard with the roar of musketry, sweeps the muttered thunder of a storm of growls."

The regiment, in the face of fierce opposition refused his order and Webb gave up the futile attempt at mobilizing his troops. By this time, Col. Devereux's 19th MA Regiment and the 42nd NY Regiment rushed into the Angle to drive the Confederates out. Within short order, among the combatants anyone left in the Angle was either captured or killed. The remaining Confederate units near the Angle slowly retreated and made their way back towards Seminary Ridge; no reserves or reinforcements were available to relieve their plight. Nor had either of the other two Confederate divisions employed in the assault on that day made comparable progress across the field. Armistead's success, remarkable as it was in reaching the angle was not duplicated, nor were his efforts supported as he and his men were quickly cut down or captured.

Armistead, himself, was mortally wounded, falling at what became known as the "High Water Mark of the Confederacy."

Pickett's charge culminated in a bloodbath. While the Federals lost about 1,500 men killed or wounded that day, Confederate casualties were many times that number; in fact, over 50% of the Confederate troops sent across the field were killed or wounded. Moreover, the officers corp was decimated. Pickett's three brigade commanders and all 13 of his regimental commanders were casualties. Kemper was wounded, and Garnett and Armistead did not survive. Trimble and Pettigrew were the most senior casualties, the former losing a leg and the latter wounded in the hand and dying during the retreat back to Virginia.

Pickett himself survived the battle personally unscathed. His position well to the rear of his troops (probably at the Codori farm on the Emmitsburg Road) was command doctrine at the time for division commanders.

As soldiers straggled back to the Confederate lines along Seminary Ridge, Lee feared a Union counteroffensive and tried to rally his center, telling returning soldiers that the failure was "all my fault." Pickett was personally inconsolable. When Lee told Pickett to rally his division for the defense, Pickett allegedly replied, "General Lee, I have no division now."

General Pickett's expressed grief and sorrow relative to the events that transpired on July 3rd resonated long after its occurrence. An expression of his thoughts is summarized in several letters sent to his fiancée shortly after Lee's retreat from the battleground.
July 6 & 12, 1863

"On the Fourth—far from a glorious Fourth to us or to any with love for his fellow men—I wrote you just a line of heartbreak. The sacrifice of life on that blood soaked field on the fatal third was too awful for the heralding of victory, even for our victorious foe, who I think, believe as we do, that it decided the fate of our cause. No words can picture the anguish of that roll-call—the breathless waits between the responses. The "Here" of those who, by God's mercy, had miraculously escaped the awful rain of shot and shell was a sob—a gasp—a knell—for the unanswered name of his comrade. There was no tone of thankfulness for having been spared to answer to their names, but rather a toll, and an unvoiced wish that they, too, had been among the missing. Even now I can hear them cheering as I gave the order, "Forward!" I can feel the thrill of their joyous voices as they called out all along the line, "We'll follow you, Marse George. We'll follow you—we'll follow you." Oh, how faithfully they kept their word—following me on—on—to their death, and I, believing in the promised support, led them on—on—on—Oh, God!

Poor old Dick Garnett did not dismount, as did the others of us, and he was killed instantly, falling from his horse. Kemper, desperately wounded, was brought from the field and subsequently, taken prisoner. Dear old Lewis Armistead, God bless him, was mortally wounded at the head of his command after planting the flag of Virginia within the enemy's lines.

Seven of my colonels were killed, and one was mortally wounded. Nine of my lieutenant colonels were wounded, and three lieutenant colonels were killed. Only one field officer of my whole command, Colonel Cabell, was unhurt, and the loss of my company officers was in proportion." Major General George E. Pickett discussing the aftermath of his assault in letters to his fiancée

A number of official and unofficial reports of the battle were compiled after the cessation of hostilities by witnesses to the events of the 3rd of July of 1863. What follows are three such accounts, an official report by a Confederate officer, the observations of a young resident living in Gettysburg at the time and a newspaper dispatch filed by Mathew Wilson, war correspondent.

The official battle report was filed by Major Charles S. Peyton, of the Nineteenth Virginia Infantry, under the command of Brigadier General Dick Garnett, of Pickett's division.

CAMP NEAR WILLIAMSPORT, MD.

July 9, 1863.

Major: In compliance with instructions from division headquarters, I have the honor to report the part taken by this brigade in the late battle near Gettysburg, Pa., July 3.

Notwithstanding the long and severe marches made by the troops of this brigade, they reached the field about 9 a. m., in high spirits and in good condition. At about 12 p. m. we were ordered to take position behind the crest of the hill on which the artillery, under Colonel Alexander, was planted, where we lay during a most terrific cannonading, which opened at 1.30 P. M., and was kept up without intermission for one hour.

During the shelling, we lost about 20 killed and wounded. Among the killed was Lieutenant-Colonel Ellis, of the Nineteenth Virginia, whose bravery as a soldier, and his innocence, purity, and integrity as a Christian, have not only elicited the admiration of his own command, but endeared him to all who knew him.

At 2.30 P. M., the artillery fire having to some extent abated, the order to advance was given, first by Major-General Pickett in person, and repeated by General Garnett with promptness, apparent cheerfulness, and alacrity. The brigade moved forward at quick time. The ground was open, but little broken, and from 800 to 1, 000 yards from the crest whence we started to the enemy's line. The brigade moved in good order, keeping up its line almost perfectly, notwithstanding it had to climb three high post and rail fences, behind the last of which the enemy's skirmishers were first met and immediately drive in. Moving on, we soon met the advance line of the enemy, lying concealed in the grass on the slope, about 100 yards in front of his second line, which consisted of a stone wall about breast high, running nearly parallel to and about 30 paces from the crest of the hill, which was lined with their artillery.

The first line referred to above, after offering some resistance, was completely routed, and driven in confusion back to the stone wall. Here we captured some prisoners, which were ordered to the rear without a guard. Having routed the enemy here, General Garnett ordered the brigade forward, which it promptly obeyed, loading and firing as it advanced.

Up to this time we had suffered but little from the enemy's batteries, which apparently had been much crippled previous to our advance, with the exception of one posted on the mountain, about 1 mile to our right, which enfiladed nearly our entire line with fearful effect, sometimes as many as 10 men being killed and wounded by the bursting of a single shell. From the point it had first routed the enemy, the brigade moved rapidly forward toward the stone wall, under a galling fire both from artillery and infantry, the artillery using grape and canister. We were now within about 75 paces of the wall, unsupported on the right and left, General Kemper being some 50 or 60 yards behind and to the right, and General Armistead coming up in our rear.

General Kemper's line was discovered to be lapping on ours, when, deeming it advisable to have the line extended on the right to prevent being flanked, a staff officer rode back to the general to request him to incline to the right. General Kemper not being present (perhaps wounded at the time), Captain Fry, of his staff, immediately began his exertions to carry out the request, but, in consequence of the eagerness of the men in pressing forward, it was impossible to have the order carried out.

Our line, much shattered, still kept up the advance until within about 20 paces of the wall, when, for a moment, it recoiled under the terrific fire that poured into our ranks both from their batteries and from their sheltered infantry. At this moment, General Kemper came up on the right and General Armistead in the rear, when the three lines, joining in concert, rushed forward with unyielding determination and an apparent spirit of laudable rivalry to plant the Southern banner on the wall of the enemy. His strongest and last line was instantly gained; the Confederate battle-flag waved over his defenses, and the fighting over the wall became hand to hand, and of the most desperate character; but more than half having already fallen, our line was found too weak to rout the enemy. We hoped for a support on the left [which had started simultaneously with ourselves], but hoped in vain. Yet a small remnant remained in desperate struggle, receiving a fire in front, on the right, and on the left, many even climbing over the wall, and fighting the enemy in his own trenches until entirely surrounded; and those who were not killed or wounded were captured, with the exception of about 300 who came off slowly, but greatly scattered, the identity of every regiment being entirely lost, and every regimental commander killed or wounded.

The brigade went into action with 1,287 men and about 140 officers, as shown by the report of the previous evening, and sustained a loss, as the list of casualties will show, of 941 killed, wounded, and missing, and it is feared, from all the information received, that the majority (those reported missing) are either killed or wounded.

It is needles, perhaps, to speak of conspicuous gallantry where all behaved so well. Each and every regimental commander displayed a cool bravery and daring that not only encouraged their own commands, but won the highest admiration from all those who saw them. They led their regiments in the fight, and showed, by their conduct, that they only desired their men to follow where they were willing to lead. But of our cool, gallant, noble brigade commander it may not be out of place to speak. Never had the brigade been better handled, and never has it done better service in the field of battle. There was scarcely an officer or man in the command whose attention was not attracted by the cool and handsome bearing of General Garnett, who, totally devoid of excitement or rashness, rode immediately in rear of his advancing line, endeavoring by his personal efforts, and by the aid of his staff, to keep his line well closed and dressed. He was shot from his horse while near the center of the brigade, within about 25 paces of the stone wall. This gallant officer was too well known to need further mention.

Captain [C. F.] Linthicum, assistant adjutant-general, Lieutenant [John S.] Jones, aide-de-camp, and Lieutenant Harrison, acting aide-de-camp, did their whole duty, and won the admiration of the entire command by their gallant bearing on the field while carrying orders from one portion of the line to the other, where it seemed almost impossible for any one to escape.

The conduct of Captain [Michael P.] Spessard, of the Twenty eighth Virginia, was particularly conspicuous. His son fell, mortally wounded, at his side; he stopped but for a moment to look on his dying son, gave him his canteen of water, and pressed on, with his company, to the wall, which he climbed, and fought the enemy with his sword in their own trenches until his sword was wrested from his hands by two Yankees; he finally made his escape in safety.

In making the above report, I have endeavored to be as accurate as possible, but have had to rely mainly for information on others, whose position gave them better opportunity for witnessing the conduct of the entire brigade than I could have, being with, and paying my attention to, my own regiment.
I am, major, with great respect, your obedient servant, Chas. S. Peyton, Major, Commanding.

And from the observations of a civilian who witnessed the events comes this report: "Upon reaching the place I fairly shrank back aghast at the awful sight presented. The approaches were crowded with wounded, dying and dead. The air was filled with moaning, and groaning. As we passed on toward the house, we were compelled to pick our steps in order that we might not tread on the prostrate bodies.
Tillie (Pierce) Alleman, (1888). At Gettysburg, or What a girl saw and heard of the battle.

A Battlefield Survivor

Special dispatch from the front by Mathew Wilson, war correspondent, *New York Times*, July 3, 1863:

They were quick and they were determined. And one of them was very lucky indeed. The 28th Virginia was one of the first of the attacking confederate regiments to reach the Angle's stone wall. From the cover of the woods, Confederate Lieutenant Thomas C. Holland of the 28th Virginia, waited with the men of his regiment alone with his thoughts. After enduring the tremendous cannonade, the stalwart Confederates bravely marched across the open fields to face their enemy. During the eventual, determined surge of Pickett's Charge and the fury of savage battle, a bullet had slammed into Lieutenant Holland's face, exiting through the back of his head.

Of the 88 men of the 28th Virginia to begin the charge, Lieutenant Holland found himself among 81of those recorded as casualties. Miraculously, despite his grave wound, he managed to survive both the battle and the war.

Author's note: Fortunately, and in a paradoxical manner, the story of Gettysburg did not end on July 3, 1863. Half a century later, during one of Gettysburg's Grand Reunions, on these same fields, Lt. Holland again stood face to face with the soldier who had shot him. It was a fortuitous occasion. This time however, these former enemies had laid down their weapons. As each beheld the other, they grasped each others extended hand in respect and friendship. To their credit, and with greater charity than many of their countrymen had shown in the times after the war, the veterans of Gettysburg and other battles fought, both won and lost, were able to lay down their arms forever, and to recognize that this war had ended for them, and for all time. They were heroes then and later, in both war and peace.

Coda from Gettysburg

Gettysburg, PA., July 5, 1863

From a quiet hillside, in a small, unlikely place, two black men gaze out to survey the most improbable of sights, an informal graveyard of more than several thousand dead men and animals; the bodies are spread out across a vast arena, arranged in an irregular, careless pattern, some mangled, others more of less intact, all contributing to a field of corpses of the recently deceased. The stench of their gaseous, blackened and bloated bodies is almost unbearable. It emanates from recent decay, including the rendering of animals but most of all, to the exposure of raw flesh to an unseasonably hot July sun. These are the victims of what happened here.

Our observers are recent witnesses to the remnants of a massive slaughter, a vicious battle fought over three days involving more than 150,000 soldiers. The final count of those killed, missing and captured from both sides will exceed 52,000 men. Gettysburg is the single most destructive military action of the war to date, and it will remain so.

Jed Harper, one of our observers, turns to face his companion, John Scobell, and says to him in a low, sad monotone, "I'm weary of this war. What I have witnessed here in the last several days should be enough to quench the appetite for war in any man."

John, in response, says, "Yes, it was wholesale murder on a massive scale. The losses for both sides were staggering and unbearable."

Jed, wearily asks, "When will it all end? Look around. There are signs of this war everywhere. Four days earlier this was a peaceful place, a farming community, unmarred by the foul odor of death. And now there is destruction all over. Everywhere that you turn there are traces of it. I saw men cut in half by cannon, others sacrificing an arm or leg by a sword-wielded by another man or as an unfortunate target accidentally positioned in the path of a Minnie ball shot by another. Clearly, God has placed a message here for us to see."

John, bewildered by the words of his companion and the sights before him, adds to his reflections, "I agree with you. It would seem so. However, we don't appear to be able to read the signs that he has left for us very well. We will continue the slaughter. Perhaps it will not be here, but elsewhere. I heard that General Meade will rest the troops for now, and then proceed to pursue the Confederates. This war is far from over in spite of what's happened here."

"Then we better keep our heads down," says Jed, "if we are to survive the next battle. And the next, after that, as well."

And from the pen of one of the survivors of the battle, a member of the Louisiana Artillery comes this memoir of the retreat:

"The day altogether was productive of different emotions from any ever experienced on any other battlefield. The sight of the dying and wounded who were lying by the thousand between the two lines, and compelled amid their sufferings to witness and be exposed to the cannonade of over 200 guns, and later in the day, the reckless charges, and the subsequent destruction or demoralization of Lee's best corps- the fury, tears or savage irony of the commanders- the patent waiting, which would occasionally break out into sardonic laughter at the ruin of our hopes seen everywhere around us, and finally, the decisive moment, when the enemy seemed to be launching his cavalry to sweep the remaining handful of men from the face of the earth. These were all incidents which settled, and will forever remain in the memory. We all remember Gettysburg, through do not remember and do not care to remember man other of the remaining incidents of the war…
Bartlett, Napier, 1874, *A Soldier's Story of the War*

Aftermath of Gettysburg

CHAPTER 21

CAUGHT IN THE DRAFT RIOTS

It was a bright sunny day when Sean O'Connor, Emma Pruitt and William Tall Tree, stepped off the train arriving in Boston on that warm July day in 1863. They were, if appearances were to be believed, seemingly, an unlikely trio, a man who walked with a slight limp, a beautiful woman of obvious social standing who walked besides him and an Indian dressed in frontier garb. Appearances aside, however, they shared a common mission.

Sean came to Boston with a special quest. He was, until recently, an Irish immigrant, one of the many who took part in the ongoing conflict, fighting on the side of the Confederacy or the Union. These "volunteers", usually newly arrived immigrants with few economic prospects or loyalties, were often posed on the battlefield in this war, by their countrymen of similar Gaelic origin; in his case he "volunteered" to fight for the South. Like others on both sides, it was a decision not rendered by choice or political belief, but as a function of time, place and social persuasion.

Most recently, Sean was a Confederate soldier who, in defending the honor of his cousin Tim, a Federal officer, who had fallen during the battle for the wall at Fredericksburg in December of 1862, less than a year earlier, was drawn into an unlikely confrontation involving a member of his own fighting unit. In defense of his cousin's body that the Confederate soldier was attempting to scavenger, a fight broke out between Sean and his Confederate counterpart in which the latter was accidentally killed. Subsequently, Sean was forced to flee the battlefield and to dessert his post, accompanied by his cousin Patrick. In abandoning the army and risking being classified as a deserter, he pledged, at the time, to go to Boston to personally convey the circumstances of his cousin's death to members of their family residing in that city. Like many men of his time, duty to family was a sacred commitment, surpassing even that of country or prior political conviction.

Following a fortuitous adventure with John Scobell and his group of fugitive blacks, a botched kidnapping attempt by the slave retrievers Smithy and Mungo and their band, he was shot and badly wounded. Subsequently, Sean was brought to Philadelphia to the home of Dr. James Wilson. There, after spending several months in the care of the good doctor and with the assistance of Ms. Emma Pruitt aiding his recovery, he began his travels to Boston, which explained his current presence there.

Emma Pruitt was a family friend of Dr. James Wilson, the brother of New York Times war correspondent Mathew Wilson. Emma's younger brother, George, another young officer in the Union army was previously wounded at 1st Manassas (Bull Run) in June of 1861. Brought to Washington, he was befriended and cared for in an army hospital by John Scobell. However, Lieutenant Pruitt did not survive his wounds; unfortunately, he died within days of the injuries he sustained in that conflict. Subsequently, John brought his body home to his family in Philadelphia for a proper burial.

Sometime later, in the spring of 1863, after Fredericksburg, John returned to Philadelphia with Sean and Patrick after escaping from the clutches of Smithy and Mungo. There, Emma and Sean became fast friends, finding themselves kindred spirits drawn together in sadness over the loss of Emma's brother George and Sean's cousin Tim.

William Tall Tree was also a friend of John Scobell. They too had shared several adventures together, including the recent interchange with Sean involving Smithy and Mungo. William was a Cherokee Indian whose father was a leader and elder member of their clan, who had suffered racial discrimination, as he with members of his nation had at the hands of the white man. Unlike many of his clan, however, William did not participate in the forced march known as the "Trail of Tears", in which many members of his clan were evacuated to Oklahoma during the administration of Andrew Jackson.

Each of these three were veterans of their times, were well-versed in the prejudices and the realities of 19th century American life, with its elitism, favoritism and discrimination of those less fortunate or less powerful. Moreover, they were touched by the violence of this latest war set forth by these practices and unfortunately, on this journey together, they would encounter more of the same.

A Family Gathering

Boston – July 8, 1863

They were gathered at the home of Sheila and Paddy O'Connor, their children and their extended family that consisted of all of the Boston members of the O'Connor clan, including our trio of travelers and some close friends. Among them was Shamus Fitzpatrick, or Fitz, as he was known in the family, a boyhood friend of Tim, Sean and Patrick. He, among the mourners, was especially grieved.

Shortly after their arrival, Sean, with Emma and William, following directions given to them at the post office, made their way to the O'Connor residence. Sean had sent a telegram to Boston a week earlier and they were expected. Once there, after brief introductions to varied members of the household were offered, they requested that they meet with the entire family that evening in order to give an account of Tim's death on the battlefield. The clan soon gathered to learn of their cousin's fate and the circumstances surrounding his death.

As Sean began his tale, he held the rapt attention of those present, including aunts and uncles, cousins, nephews and nieces and elders of the family alike. Tim was a family favorite, a kind and generous man, as well as an industrious worker, always ready with a joke and for partaking in a pint as the occasion dictated. Clearly, he was missed and mourned among his relatives and friends, alike.

"I didn't see him fall," Sean began his account. "Nor was I aware that he was on the battlefield at the time. The mist created by the enormous explosions of smoke from the muskets and cannons, aided by fog stemming from the unusual weather conditions prevailing at the time, prevented that from occurring. In addition, the mass movement of men in front of me, as they attacked our position and fell back after volley upon volley of gunfire struck them down, belied any ready identification. The battle, as it unfolded, defied description.

"It was chaos, accented in rising and falling waves of activity and the massive movement of men to and fro. Only after the fight ended... and that happened only after the federals attacked the wall again and again and finally, after they ceased coming was it safe to climb over the wall and to examine the results of the foolishness. It was a flight into madness, ill-timed and strategically foolhardy, one that I would never want to be part of or to be a witness to again.

"Many of us Irishmen, on our side of the line, probably as well as on the other, did not realize at the time that we were fighting our kin, our fellow countrymen. Only after we examined the remains of the fallen on the battlefield and saw the green clover that many of the federals wore in their caps were we certain. And that lead to many grown men on our side crying and bemoaning their actions in open displays of personal agony and grief. By God, it was an awful sight to behold!

"Patrick and I did not spot Tim immediately. It was only when I saw several of our Confederate comrades removing the clothes and shoes of the fallen Yankees that we found him. In truth, our men were desperate for the federals clothing and shoes and readily seized the opportunity to obtain them. Then I spotted Tim lying on the ground and when I asked one of our soldiers to stop removing Tim's uniform, he refused. I then tried to prevent him from stripping Tim further and he pulled a knife out on me, claiming it was his right to appropriate Tim's clothing as war spoils. Perhaps, he was right. But I could not let him continue to violate Tim's body. I dragged him off of Tim and we fought over his body. The struggle was short-lived, however. As the soldier lunged at me, I sidestepped his thrust and he fell upon his own knife. Unfortunately, he was killed instantly."

"Aware that, as immigrants, and outsiders, Patrick and I would be held accountable for the soldier's death, and granted little pardon, we fled from the scene. However, we could not leave Tim's body to the whims of fate. There was a boy, with us, whom Patrick and I had cared for, by the name of Danny. We decided to leave him with Tim's revolver, which I brought to give to you, and instructions to guard Tim's body until it was retrieved by his command. We knew then that he would be safe. We also asked Danny to accompany the body until it was buried, so that he could tell us where the body was interned and where it may be recovered at some later time. Danny was able to accomplish that task for us and I can tell you where it rests, and help you retrieve it when we can."

"From the battlefield we fled to the home of John Scobell where we told our story. John consented to bring us North and did so, but not before we encountered slave retrievers, who we fought off. In the process I was wounded and taken to Philadelphia, where I recovered from my wounds until I was able to travel here. It has been a hazardous journey, but one I owed you and needed to make. And with the assistance of these two good people, Emma and William I was able to accomplish."

Upon completing his narrative, with tears in his eyes, Sean was approached by Sheila, Paddy and Fitz. "Thank you for coming," said Paddy. "And for bringing your friends with you. We have all suffered a great loss, including you. But your return to our family, with the news of Tim," added Fitz, "gladdens our hearts, as well. And you are welcome here."

New York City - July 1863,

Civilian Riots

"Thus the days wore on, with dust and smoke, with fire and flame; with sack of private dwellings and burning of charitable institutions, armories, and draft stations; with blood and wounds, and every imaginable instance of atrocity on the part of the maddened mob, till regiments, hurriedly withdrawn from the front, came speeding back to the city, and we saw the grim batteries and weather stained and dusty soldiers tramping into our leading streets as if into a town just taken by siege. There was some terrific fighting between the regulars and the insurgents; streets were swept again and again by grape, houses were stormed at the point of the bayonet, rioters were picked off by sharpshooters as they fired on the troops from the house-tops; men were hurled, dying or dead, into the streets by the thoroughly enraged soldiery; until at last, sullen and cowed, and thoroughly whipped and beaten, the miserable wretches gave way at every point and confessed the power of the law. It has never been known how many perished in those awful days."
Episcopal minister Morgan Dix, son of the New York City's military commander

"Scenes of violence and carnage, such as I have described, prevailed in the streets of New York from Monday noon until Thursday night. The

political sentiment, which displayed itself in the original assault on the draft office, in Third avenue, disappeared after that demonstration, and thenceforward the mob was actuated solely by an instinct of rapine and plunder."
Major T.P. McElrath, U.S. Army

Draft Riots Afflict New York City

Mathew Wilson, correspondent, *New York Times*:

"The draft riots began on July 13 and continued in their madness for four days and nights. The immediate precipitant of the violence was fueled by efforts to enforce Federal conscription policies, which demanded the military service of eligible young men of age, but allowed drafted men of privilege and wealth to buy a waiver in place of such service by enlisting a substitute volunteer for $300. It was a small amount of money for men of means, but a fortune for those less fortunate.

The first draft lottery was conducted on Saturday, July 11, and a second was scheduled for two days later. On the morning of July 13, a mob gathered in the streets, attacking and beating several police officers in the process. The rioters then marched to the provost marshal's office where the draft lottery was taking place and set fire to the building. They cut the city's telegraph lines at this time and wrecked several public street cars, as well. And the mob grew eventually numbering in the thousands. As it gathered in strength it attacked both public and private property, especially businesses and homes owned by wealthy New Yorkers, as well as leading Republicans, and African Americans. Among the many sites stormed by the rioters were Horace Greeley's New York Tribune building and the Brooks Brothers clothing store. The mob burned down both the provost marshal's office and the Colored Orphan Asylum. At the latter site, at least eleven African Americans were murdered during the rampage.

After four days, the riot finally ended. At that time, the leader of the Catholic Irish community, Archbishop John Hughes made an impassioned speech to quell the mob, beseeching members of his community to return to their homes.

As a consequence of the riots, it is estimated that at least 119 people were killed, and 178 soldiers and police and 128 civilians were wounded. In addition, more than $1.5 million in property was damaged or destroyed."

Into the Maelstrom

July 13, 1863 – Somewhere between Boston and New York City

On a fast traveling train, Sean and Emma, with William and Fitz were proceeding south, back to Philadelphia. The trio had met with the O'Connor family of Boston and Sean and told them of the circumstances surrounding Tim's death. Afterward, they had spent several days in Boston at the home of Sheila and Paddy O'Connor, and now they were proceeding back to Philadelphia. One outcome of their discussion was that several of Tim's cousins had agreed to meet with Sean in Philadelphia, as the cessation of hostilities allowed, in order to retrieve Tim's remains. Meanwhile, Fitz, had agreed to travel with Sean, Emma and William, and would help in this endeavor by making preliminary arrangements to their plan when they arrived in Philadelphia. But for now Sean and William with Fitz, were in the process of escorting Emma home. As scheduled, they hoped to be off to Philadelphia after a brief layover in New York City.
New York City, July 12, 1863

It was July 12, 1863, and tension griped the city. The Battle of Gettysburg had just been fought and the federal government had instituted a draft that would compel men from New York, primarily Irish immigrants, who comprised a significant proportion of draft eligible, young men between the ages of 18-35, to serve for a three-year term in the army.

Anger was in the air and the streets of the city were filled with working men and women, reading aloud the names of those chosen for the draft. As crowds gathered the streets drew an outraged, predominantly Irish, mob into its maw. Many of them headed to Central Park while community leaders spoke out against the draft. The mob then went to the Provost Marshall's office to find out who else was drafted, while carrying "No Draft!" signs. On their way, the destruction of the city began in earnest as rioters cut telegraph wires, collected weapons, and stopped traffic. John Kennedy, the Superintendent of Police was attacked, and the homes of policemen were targeted. Rioters also laid waste to jewelry, hardware, and liquor stores, eight draft offices, and the offices of Horace Greeley's New York Tribune.

The armory was burned in route, leaving several of the same rioters that started the conflagration to perish in its flames. At 4:00 PM, protesters attacked, set fire to, and looted the Colored Orphan Asylum. Fortunately, the children were safely evacuated. However, in other parts of the city the rioters rooted out, assaulted, and lynched African-Americans. Property belonging to African-Americans, wealthy Republicans and abolitionists, and policemen was destroyed, as well.

Ostensibly, it began as a draft protest. But soon it took a different, exceedingly more ugly turn. By afternoon, it was a full-fledged race riot. William Jones, an African-American, was walking to the store to buy bread. As the crowd caught up with him, Jones was subsequently beaten and then hanged from a tree, after which his body was set on fire.

Other minority residents suffered similar fates. Peter Heuston a Mohawk Indian, residing in the city at the time, was unfortunately mistaken for an African-American and he too was beaten. Two weeks later, Peter Heuston died from his wounds in the hospital to which he had been taken to recover from his injuries.

New York City – July 14, 1863

After a lawless start on Monday, July 13, 1863, the Draft Riots continued throughout the week. Each day brought more outrages, as mobs assembled and moved throughout the city, destroying property and attacking innocent targets at random.

As was the case earlier in the week, a number of stores were looted, and public buildings burned. It was evident that amidst the escalating violence and confusion that the local authorities could not establish control. Consequently, US Army troops stationed at Gettysburg were rushed into the city to curtail the riot.

The mayhem was in full swing by the second day of rioting as protesters built barricades from debris in numerous neighborhoods to keep the police out and to be able to continue their wanton destructiveness. Rioters targeted wealthy Republican homes and businesses, and pursued African-Americans for brutal beatings and lynchings. William Williams, an African-American sailor, was walking down the street when he asked a boy where the nearest grocery store was. Edward Canfield saw this and led a group of white men to where Williams was standing. Subsequently, he was beaten, stabbed, then left to die. Rioters also attacked whites who ventured forth to help African-Americans. By now, it was no longer a protest about the draft, but was an all-out assault upon African-Americans and the Republican elite. The violence and destruction of the second day worsened as Henry O'Brien, the commander of the 11th New York volunteers, set off a cannon in the street over a mob of rioters' heads. This precipitous act was meant to scatter the mob, but instead, it ended in a possessed search for O'Brien.

Rumors ran rampant through the crowd. The cannon was said to have wounded two children and perhaps, killed up to seven people, as sources disagreed regarding its impact. Nevertheless, the crowd stirred up by the blast, went looking for O'Brien after he fled the scene; thereupon, he was quickly found and murdered. The famous Brooks Brothers clothing store was the scene of a major battle with the rioters and police, as well. The rioters looted the store, destroying it and causing more than $50,000 in damage stemming from stolen clothes and destroyed property. It was believed that the rioters targeted Brooks Brothers because of previous job losses.

At approximately noon on July 14, 1863, as their train from Boston pulled into the central station, and unbeknown to Sean, Emma, William and Fitz, the riots were in full force. Unaware of the situation, as the group descended from their train they decided to take a short stroll within the city to stretch their legs during the two-hour lay over between trains to Philadelphia. Without warning, as they left the station, they ambled into one of the neighborhoods where a mob had gathered. There they encountered an angry crowd of Irish immigrants being addressed by several inciters edging the crowd on to continue the riot.

As they edge closer to the proceedings they head one orator addressing the crowd, "They expect us to risk our lives and fight for the blacks. Well, who's going to fight for us, I ask you? Who's going to risk their lives for us? Not the politicians. Not the blacks. Not their abolitionist friends. We are alone and can only rely upon ourselves, as always.

"After this war what will we have to look forward to? Not to any help from the blacks, I can tell you. The South is being destroyed by this war. Farms and crops are being ruined and people are being forced to leave their homes with nowhere to go. And when this war is over, the blacks won't have anything, nor will the whites.

"And, I'll tell you what will happen. The blacks will have to come north or they will starve. And when they come they will look for work and settle for less wages than the white man. And the rich Republicans, who have profited from this war, will fire us and hire them. And they will seize our jobs. Then, they will seize our homes, and we will be forced out too. And, we will have nothing left after being replaced by the blacks, but to wait and watch our families starve before our very eyes.

Somewhere in the middle of the crowd another man, holding a long iron shovel, shouts to be heard: "I tell you now. I left Ireland to come here. To escape being treated like a second-class citizen by the English. But what I see happening here, in the name of the black man, is just more of the same. By damn, I won't be driven out by the black man. I will fight for my rights as a white man, before that happens."

Unable to contain himself upon hearing the outrageous claims of the speakers, Sean shouts out, "No! No! You are wrong. The black man didn't start this war. And he didn't ask to come here, even in the first place. He was a victim, just like you and me, and like many of you here are. His fight is your fight. Don't you see that?"

Unfortunately, Sean's words are ignored. The crowd is stirred up by this time, and ready to act. Neither Sean words, nor any other calming influence is likely to sooth their anger or their frustration; the propensity for destruction has been built over time and flamed by vitriolic invective that is now set to ignite. As Sean finishes speaking, a small boy throws a stone at him, simulating similar behavior by the action of a larger mob he observed earlier.

As a reflection of the growing frenzy of the crowd, racial epitaphs are now being hurled at Sean and a plethora of hard objects, including bricks and slabs of building, follow in their wake. Most of these are inaccurately thrown and miss their intended mark. Other missiles, however, narrowly miss Sean as he seeks cover. And still other missiles follow, including a barrage of nails, and other hard objects. Some strike their intended target with effect.

In response, Sean, with William, Emma and Fitz, at his side, seek shelter and protection from the onslaught of projectiles by fleeing into a nearby alley. As Emma runs to safety, seeking refuge out of harms way, she stubbles and is hit by a flying shard, a bottle in the form of a missile thrown by someone in the back of the congregated mob. As she is struck, she falls to the ground, clutching her head. Fitz immediately seeks to protect her from further injury, by dragging her into the alley. However, as he does so, members of the mob viciously attack him with sticks and poles. At that point, William rises to his defense. However, as the blows rain over his body Fitz falls unconscious before William is able to prevent the mob from committing sustained injury upon his person. The mob now turns its attention to William and Sean. But before it can vent its full fury, a troop of soldiers arrive on the scene and rush into formation, ready to act; with bayoneted muskets they drive the crowd back. However, in spite of their timely appearance, grave damage has already been done.

Fitz, unconscious, must be taken to a nearby hospital. So too, do Emma and Sean require treatment. William's injuries, fortunately, are less substantial requiring some bandaging, but less attention, and allow him to be treated on the scene.

Several hours after awaiting treatment, after being cut and bruised, and suffering soreness and fatigue, Emma and Sean are released. They are ambulatory, and will escape with physical minor scars attesting to their experience. Fitz, however, remains in critical condition. His condition, in spite of care given worsens, and within several days he too will be counted among the unfortunate fatalities, one of the many stricken, innocent victims of the draft riots.

THE RETURN TO PHILADELPHIA

It was a sad journey back to Philadelphia. Unexpectedly and without warning, Fitz had been killed in the riots trying to save Emma, who like Sean, was among the many who were wounded during those days of anger and lawlessness. Fortunately, with William's assistance, both of our travelers survived the riots and with a sadden heart they were able to bring Fitz's body back to Boston to his grief stricken and shocked family for burial. It was an unexpected and untimely development. For our travelers it would take several months for each of them, especially Emma and Sean, to recover from the physical injuries that they had sustained on this occasion.

Moreover, the suffering, as they knew, would not end there, in the tangible and the foreseeable future; likely, they would never fully recover from the mental anguish and grief they experienced. Images of the assault would follow them in their thoughts, and private moments in the days, weeks and months ahead, sometimes to the exclusion of all else, both in terms of attending to the tasks of daily living and in their ability to augur for the future, constantly drawing them back to the question of why?

William too questioned what had happened to his friends, for he too, shared some, but not all of their pain. He pondered whether they would be able to sustain the spiritual optimism they birthed together and that they had kindled over the last several months of their relationship and were able to sustain in spite of the harsh times and the hardships accompanying them. He knew, that above all, that they needed him now, even in helping them sort out the most minute events of their lives, and they needed him now more than ever. And he was determined, in good fellowship, to assist them, as warranted.

CHAPTER 22

THE RETURN

They were going home. For Emma Pruitt, she would complete the disrupted journey initiated in Boston, and return to Philadelphia, where she and her family resided. For Sean O'Connor and William Tall Tree, Philadelphia was not home, for in truth, they had no home, either there or elsewhere. It was a condition that plagued their thoughts, which was especially so, at this terrible time. Philadelphia would serve as their temporary residence, at least for now, and perhaps, beyond.

As they sat together on the train heading south the prevailing mood, shared by Emma, Sean and William alike, as they hid behind the confines of their private thoughts, was one of gloom and depression. Their apparent sadness was palpable and the numbness associated with their thoughts of recent days was overwhelming, invading all facets of their being, including those moments evident in their infrequent, sparse attempts at communication.

Numerous difficult questions were posed by the recent events associated with the riots in New York City. The recent, senseless death of Fitz raised numerous queries. It also rekindled the thoughts of other deaths, those anonymous, and those near. The fates of Emma's brother Lt. George Pruitt and Sean's cousin, Captain Tim O'Connor continued to overwhelm and permeate their recollections and memories, ever present, and now underscored by a newly formed grief.

"I don't understand what has happened", voiced Emma. "We experienced a tragedy, but why? Why were we attacked? Why was Fitz murdered? He was a kind and good friend who was on a mission of mercy, to bring Tim home. And he was a hero. With disregard for his own self, he sacrificed his life for mine. That shouldn't have happened, least of all, to him."

"George too, was a good man, and a good son and a good brother too. And as Tim, he too was killed, each a victim of an unwarranted fate. How can we continue living our lives, when such events befoul the fortunes of those we love and cherish?"

"Our lives seem to have become contaminated by events and circumstances that are beyond our control," she continued. "Are we simply victims of a blind fate in the midst of a never ending catastrophe?"

"I don't know the reasons for our plight. I can't explain these things," ventured Sean. "But, there must be some explanation. Or else, everything we believe in and strive for is for naught, both the good and the evil. And what befalls us cannot be predicted or controlled. But that cannot be."

"How can God let these things happen?" responds Emma. "That's not the God that I knew as a child and that I was led to believe in. He is just and fair. What has happened here is neither. It was random and capricious."

"Justice and fairness may not be the issues that are raised here. Nor, are they likely applicable. Perhaps, we should not look to God for an answer to things that we cannot explain, or as a recipient to attach blame," says William. "Perhaps, the answer lies in ourselves not in him... in our own worthiness and in our own willingness to solve our own dilemmas without resorting to violence. God does not cause our problems, why should we expect him to solve them for us?"

"Both sides claim that the current conflict was preordained. And that God is on their side. But why would he be? He did not cause this war, nor can we claim, like some, that he blesses one side over the over. We cannot use God as an excuse for our own shortcomings" notes William.

"Each man and woman must be accountable for their own behavior. Perhaps, when we are willing to take that approach, to accept the fate that we experience as a function of our own choosing, can we then begin to understand how evil happens. And then, maybe, we can find more effective ways to combat its destructiveness."

"Well, we know that violence is not the answer," suggests Sean. "Clearly, our experiences demonstrate that. Even a blind man can see that."

"Maybe, part of the answer is to help those that are not blind to see the truth. Perhaps, we need to put down our guns and seek other solutions. We have become a violent society, a nation of people likely to pick up a stick and strike down someone who disagrees with us. We need to offer a helping hand to others, to present a vision of a just society to someone who has gone astray, and not to use a person's wantonness as an excuse to strike him down", he continues.

"While we cannot prevent the manufacture of weapons, or even shutter their limited use, we need not support their use. Perhaps we can also close or restrict academies of death and their advocacy of war as a first step to resolving conflict. The men who are directing this war all come from the same mold, the military academies whose sole purpose is to train other men to kill each other. If these men were better trained to use their talents for loftier goals, perhaps to teach or care for others, the likelihood of the present course of events occurring would be restricted, as well. We could prevent war by not fueling its embers."

"We must maintain our hopes for a better future and for a more just society. It is only hope that will assuage the stings of the cruelty and brutality we see around us, or he adds,…help us sustain our best impulses for a more just tomorrow."

Postscript

November 1864

One year later we find our principals, once again, in Philadelphia. They have gathered together, joined by the O'Connor's from Boston in the living room of Dr. Wilson's home for a special event, the christening of a newly born set of twins. As we join them and listen in, the minister continues his recital, "and may these new members of our community offer us a hope for the future, where men of good will sit down and negotiate their differences at a table of equals, in lieu of a battlefield marked by cannon and guns… and graves".

In the period between the draft riots of New York City, and the present, a series of interrelated events have transpired among our players. John and his rescuers have returned safely to Lancaster having outwitted their pursuers and with Mae and her sons Noah and Lucas as they had hoped. Their mission accomplished, they were accompanied there by a number of other former prisoners, several who were part of the successful escape from the slave compound of Mungo and the clutches of Smithy and Mungo in their pursuit. As others before them, several have joined the ranks of those serving in the Underground Railroad. And several would join the Army of the Potomac.

Subsequent to our last account, John and Jed, with William as a new recruit, returned to their posts as Union agents under the guidance of Major General Winfield Scott Hancock. For the present they had been given a new assignment, to assist the efforts of Commanding General U. S. Grant in the eastern theatre. Their temporary presence in Philadelphia on this occasion would be followed by their assignment to their new chief.

Big Jake, to the joy of his family, returned to Lancaster to rejoin his wife and children there. He would resume his former life as a farmer, at least, until he was called upon to serve his people and his country in the future. Aunt Amy decided to remain in that community, as well. Patrick and Danny recognized that they had other work to do; based on their experiences as teacher and pupil in Lancaster, they chose to journey east at the suggestion of Representative Stevens. With the help of Mrs. Smith, Congressman Stevens associate and Mae, they hoped to establish a school for former slaves in Philadelphia.

Many of the group had now gathered in Philadelphia to celebrate their hopes for the future with Emma and Sean. Their story, like those of the others described here, continued, as well. Shortly after returning to Philadelphia Sean accepted a post with Emma's father, a well-known journalist and publisher in the city, to learn the newspaper trade. Within a short period of time, and with applied diligence and commitment, his former education had proved useful in preparing him for an unanticipated occupational vocation; he had risen to the post of city editor on the Pruitt newspaper, having shown a keen talent for writing.

On another level, unsurprisingly, and somewhat predictable to the observant bystander, Sean and Emma grew closer during the interim between the riots and their return. Over time, recognizing their deep affection for each other, perhaps somewhat kindled in their shared grief, they decided to marry in that fall of 1863. The marriage had gone well and both Emma and Sean had achieved happiness in these times. That was especially true in the place where they first met, the home of Dr. Wilson where they were gathered. Now, with family and friends, they were celebrating the first fruits of their union, in a formal welcoming into their community the arrival of their newly-born sons George Pruitt O'Connor and Timothy Fitzgerald ("Fitz") O'Connor.

ABOUT THE AUTHOR

Stewart Cohen, PhD., taught for 36 years, in the Department of Human Development and Family Studies at the University of Rhode Island.

During his teaching career, he developed a special interest in the American Civil War, especially the men and women who lived during that turbulent era in our nation's history. Cohen's research and travels to American battle grounds helped him understand the crucial contributions of black people who had contributed to the war effort. Cohen found that often the involvement of black Americans in the Civil Was had only been footnoted by historians, many barely acknowledged, who had contributed to the war effort.

The stories in this book capture the contributions of those Black Americans as they lived, how their varied roles lead to greater freedom for all people, and the special facets and accomplishments that were characterized by the spirit of their lives. Stewart Cohen lives in Rhode Island with his wife Joan and her two cats, "Bonita" the Inquisitor and "Timi 2" the Bold.

E-BOOKS BY STEWART COHEN

Antietam: Autumn Blight: Slaughter at the River

Fredericksburg: Massacre at the Wall

Gettysburg: Death at the Angle

Shiloh: Battle to Save the West

Petersburg: The Last Siege (*coming soon*)

Charlie Wright: The Spy that Saved Gettysburg (*coming soon*)

www.ingramcontent.com/pod-product-compliance
Lightning Source LLC
Chambersburg PA
CBHW061634040426
42446CB00010B/1413